On Foot to Canterbury

KEN HAIGH

On Foot
to Canterbury
A Son's Pilgrimage

UNIVERSITY *of* ALBERTA PRESS

Published by

University of Alberta Press
1–16 Rutherford Library South
11204 89 Avenue NW
Edmonton, Alberta, Canada T6G 2J4
Amiskwacîwâskahican | Treaty 6 |
Métis Territory
uap.ualberta.ca

LIBRARY AND ARCHIVES CANADA
CATALOGUING IN PUBLICATION

Title: On foot to Canterbury : a son's
    pilgrimage / Ken Haigh.
Names: Haigh, Ken, 1962– author.
Series: Wayfarer (Edmonton, Alta.)
Description: Series statement: Wayfarer |
    Includes bibliographical references.
Identifiers: Canadiana (print) 20210188952 |
    Canadiana (ebook) 20210189371 |
    ISBN 9781772125450 (softcover) |
    ISBN 9781772125900 (EPUB) |
    ISBN 9781772125917 (PDF)
Subjects: LCSH: Haigh, Ken, 1962––Travel—
    England—Pilgrims Way. | LCSH: Hiking—
    England—Pilgrims Way. | LCSH: Christian
    pilgrims and pilgrimages—England—
    Canterbury. | LCSH: Christian pilgrims and
    pilgrimages—England—Winchester. |
    LCSH: English literature—History and
    criticism. | LCSH: Pilgrims Way
    (England)—Description and travel.
Classification: LCC DA670.S63 H35 2021 |
    DDC 914.2204/86—dc23

First edition, first printing, 2021.
First printed and bound in Canada by
Houghton Boston Printers, Saskatoon,
Saskatchewan.
Copyediting and proofreading by
Maya Fowler Sutherland.
Map by Wendy Johnson.

University of Alberta Press is committed to
protecting our natural environment. As part
of our efforts, this book is printed on Enviro
Paper: it contains 100% post-consumer
recycled fibres and is acid- and chlorine-free.

University of Alberta Press gratefully
acknowledges the support received for its
publishing program from the Government of
Canada, the Canada Council for the Arts, and
the Government of Alberta through the Alberta
Media Fund.

For my father
Walter Malcolm Haigh
1937–2005

Contents

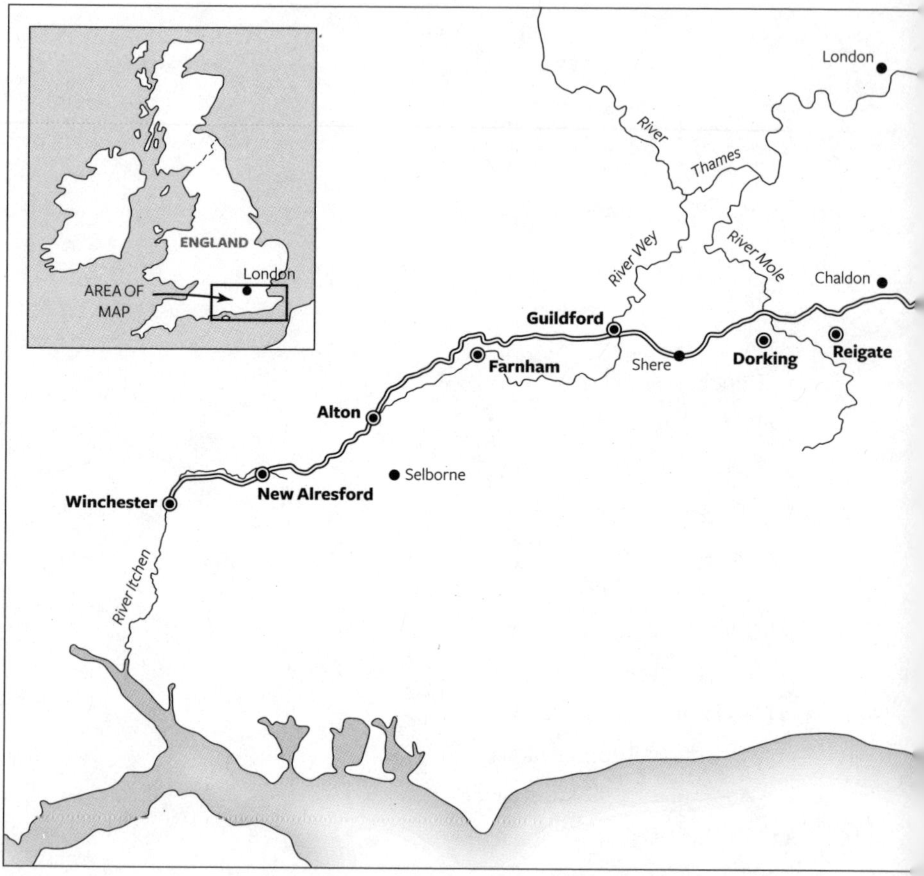
ENGLAND
London
AREA OF
MAP
London
River
Thames
River Wey
River Mole
Chaldon
Guildford
Shere
Dorking
Reigate
Farnham
Alton
Selborne
New Alresford
Winchester
River Itchen

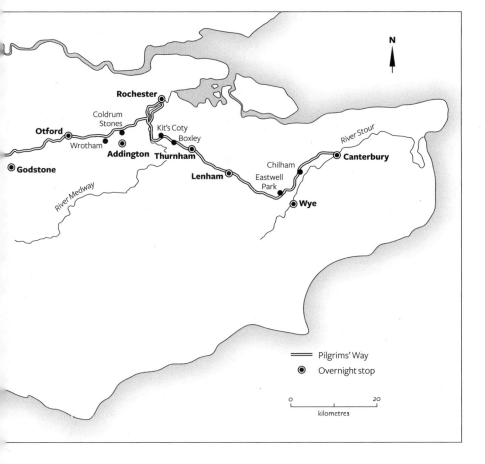

Prelude

When that April with its sweet showers
The drought of March hath pierced to the root,...
Then people long to go on pilgrimages
And palmers seek on foreign strands
The distant saints, hallowed in sundry lands,
And specially, from every shire's end
Of England, to Canterbury they wend
The holy blissful martyr there to seek,
To give them help when they are sick.

—GEOFFREY CHAUCER,
"The Prologue" from *The Canterbury Tales*

FOR THREE NIGHTS AFTER MY RETURN I was troubled with the
same dream. In this dream, I was entering the outskirts of Canterbury
on foot. The towers of the cathedral stood proudly over the crooked
roofs and chimney pots of the city. The cathedral, my destination
and the end point of my pilgrimage, seemed tantalizingly close; but
as I penetrated the warren of streets, I became confused and could
find no way forward. Dark alleys and cramped staircases led to dead

ends or locked doors. Ancient cobbled lanes looped back upon themselves and returned me to the place from where I'd begun. Each night, I would awaken, troubled and frustrated, but no closer to the cathedral. I wondered what it meant. My wife explained the dreams as muscle memory.

"Your body has become used to walking every day," she reasoned. "And now that you are back at your desk, it's protesting."

And it was true that when I awoke each morning, my legs, particularly my calf muscles, were stiff and sore, as if I had been walking all night. But I suspected something else was at work here. I had walked the old pilgrims' trail from Winchester to Canterbury, that was certain, but had I truly arrived? Perhaps my pilgrimage to Canterbury was still incomplete.

The pilgrimage from Winchester to Canterbury along the old Pilgrims' Way had been my idea, something to do with my father to mark his retirement. This was the traditional route followed by medieval pilgrims to the shrine of the murdered archbishop Saint Thomas Becket in Canterbury Cathedral. I knew the idea would appeal to him. He was an active member of his local Anglican church, and Canterbury Cathedral, our destination, was the mother ship of the global Anglican Communion. My father was also a keen outdoorsman. He loved to walk. It was from him that I learned to pitch a tent, build a fire, clean a fish, and paddle a canoe.

My own reasons for going were a bit more tenuous. Unlike my father, I had drifted away from the church. Growing up, I had been an altar boy, a choir member, a youth group leader and a Sunday school teacher. When I entered university, it was with the intention of enrolling in theology and becoming an ordained minister. But when push came to shove, I couldn't follow through, for I was beginning to have serious doubts about the things professed in the Apostles' Creed. Did I believe in the bodily resurrection of the dead? No. Did I believe in the virgin birth or the doctrine of the Trinity? Not really. Did I even believe in God anymore? I wasn't sure. This knowledge didn't make me a happier person, and it certainly didn't make me feel intellectually superior to those who did believe. It made me sad. When Julian Barnes wrote "I don't believe in God, but I miss him," I knew exactly what he meant.[1]

But I had another motive for walking the Pilgrims' Way: I wanted to spend more time with my father. We had seen very little of each other since I had left home following my parents' divorce. It was not that I loved him less. It was just that I had been busy with my own life. I'd finished university with degrees in English literature, education, and library science. I had been a teacher in Bhutan, China and the Canadian Arctic. But now that I had settled down and was married with three children of my own, I felt there was more my father and I had in common. Perhaps I could benefit from his experience. So I raised the idea of a pilgrimage to Canterbury, and to my delight he accepted.

But fate intervened. Within weeks of my broaching the subject, my father was dead of a massive heart attack. He died on a Sunday morning, while assisting a disabled parishioner with the elevator in the parish hall. One moment he was laughing and closing the elevator door behind him; the next moment he was dead. His heart had simply exploded.

So the idea of walking to Canterbury was put on a shelf, but never quite forgotten. Many years passed, and then in the spring of 2014 I began to reconsider the notion. Perhaps it was because I was finding life a bit overwhelming. I missed my old man, and I could have used his advice. I also sensed that I was approaching a mid-life crisis, with all of the clichéd existential anguish it implied. I felt trapped in a job I did not enjoy, and my life lacked any meaningful purpose. I knew I had to do something or spontaneously combust.

"Go," my wife said. "You've been thinking about doing this for ten years."

"But my father is dead. What would be the point now?"

"Then do it *for* your father," she said gently. "Go. The kids and I will be fine."

But I wondered if I had left it too late. Søren Kierkegaard, the Danish philosopher who gave us the phrase "leap of faith," suggested that our inner spiritual life needed constant attention, and if we let it lapse, if we let the flame of faith burn out—as did the foolish virgins in the parable—then we may not be able to revive the religious impulse. Faith, it seemed, or the possibility of faith, had a "best before" date, and I worried I might have left mine too long on the shelf. My faith, at this point, felt like a much-loved sweater, a garment I continued to wear even though it became more threadbare and full of holes with each passing day.

I decided to go anyway.

I think this is the place to admit that I've suffered from depression for much of my life. There are days when I feel I will drown in despair, when the simple act of getting out of bed in the morning requires an almost impossible effort of will. But whenever things get really dark, I always hear my father's voice in my ear saying, "Stop feeling sorry for yourself. There are plenty of people in this world worse off than you. And there are people who depend on you. Dust yourself off and get back to work." And I do. But the depression never really goes away. Winston Churchill, a lifelong sufferer, referred to his ailment as the "black dog." I can relate. Depression feels like a large sinister hound that follows me all the days of my life. The hound is threatening, yet familiar. I can't shake him, but perhaps he can be tamed.

I don't think this was a conundrum my father ever faced. For the most part, I think he was happy. He loved his family, his friends, and his coworkers, and that love was returned. (I don't think he ever loved his job, though, and in that we are alike). He also had his faith, which is something I envied. Perhaps a pilgrimage would help me find happiness. Perhaps I could walk my way into a better frame of mind, and somewhere along the road to Canterbury I would find a new purpose for my life. It was worth a shot.

1

Winchester

Life is either a daring adventure or nothing.
—HELEN KELLER, *Let Us Have Faith*

AS THE BIG BOEING 777 DESCENDS and begins its approach to Heathrow, the clouds disperse. We are soon gliding over irregularly shaped fields, fields so green that green-ness seems the dominant note in the landscape, except that, here and there, I can see a splash of bright yellow where the canola is in bloom. There are wiggling rivers and small ponds picked out in silver. In North America, all the lines in the landscape would have been straight and crossed at right angles, but here the field patterns are uneven, Hobbit-sized and bounded by the contours of the land and by the vicissitudes of history. As I fly over the suburbs of London, the field patterns persist, but the field boundaries turn inward with spirals of row housing. The streets and closely packed houses start to resemble computer circuit boards.

Heathrow Airport is better organized than Toronto's Pearson International, and I am soon on a direct bus to Winchester. The bus is cleaner, roomier, and more civilized than the plane. Beyond the sealed windows, the fields are incredibly verdant and lush. Back in Canada there are still patches of dirty snow in the woods, but here the ditches and hedgerows are starred with blossoms. The knot in my stomach begins to loosen. Maybe a solo pilgrimage across southern England is not such a bad idea after all.

An hour and a half later and I am standing on a cobbled street in the centre of Winchester, gazing up at an idealized bronze statue of Alfred the Great. The king stands atop a granite pedestal, shield grounded and sword held aloft, staring fiercely off into the distance. The sword is reversed, so that the hilt forms a cross, signalling that Alfred, perhaps the first truly English king, was also a pious Christian. I'm reminded of just how old Winchester is. Winchester was Alfred's city, the first capital of a united "Angle-land," but before that it was a Roman city. In fact, the cobbled street up which I am bouncing my wheeled suitcase was once the Roman road.

It's Sunday and High Street is crowded with the stalls of the weekly antiques market. I pass under bowed windows and bracketed shop signs, beneath roofs of pitched red tile supported by leaning walls of red brick and flint, with the occasional oak-framed and whitewashed shop front breaking the uniformity. I pass market stalls selling LP records, old postcards, dented Bovril tins, faded daguerreotypes of solemn gentlemen in bushy side whiskers, trays of heavy Victorian mourning jewellery in black jet, distressed Rupert the Bear annuals, much-loved Ladybird books in plastic sleeves, wonky Sheraton-style rectilinear chairs with worn seat cushions, cracked kitchen crockery, and polished copperware of dubious authenticity. My destination is at the top of the street—the Westgate, a Victorian railway inn perched kitty-corner to the city's old medieval west gate, the last of the battlemented gates that had once protected the old city.

I wrestle my luggage under the gate arch, cross the busy traffic circle, and shoulder my way through the double doors of the inn. As I am negotiating the awkward door, a large grey Weimaraner with a very stoic expression sticks his schnozz in my face, silently blocking the entrance.

"Out of the way, you," growls a man behind the bar. When he sees the startled look on my face, he smiles and adds, "Not you, the dog. Thinks he owns the place." The dog promptly decamps to a battered sofa beside the bar and curls up with a disgruntled "hrumpf."

"You must be Ken. I'm Guy." He holds out his hand. "We've been expecting you. Derek should be along in just a bit. Take that bag?" He gestures to the suitcase, which I gladly relinquish, and he stuffs it beside the sofa. "Room's not quite ready, but I'll carry it up for you soon as it is."

"Derek" is Derek Bright, owner of Walk Awhile Holidays. We've never met, just corresponded though email, but Derek has promised to be my personal Sherpa, organizing each night's lodgings and making sure my luggage precedes me along the route each day. Derek is also the author of *The Pilgrims' Way: Fact and Fiction of an Ancient Trackway*, a history of the route I will be walking for the next two weeks, so I am anxious to meet him. But I am early. No matter. There is somewhere special I want to see, and it is very close by.

Just across the street and up a short, cobbled lane are the ruins of Winchester Castle. During the English Civil War, Winchester had backed the Royalist cause. The old Norman castle was besieged and taken, and Cromwell ordered it dismantled so that it could no longer offer shelter to his enemies. But the Parliamentarians left one building standing: the Great Hall. I would like to think that some Parliamentary general had a soft spot for architecture and recognized its beauty, but it was more likely that the hall was seen as too useful to tear down. For the next three hundred years it was the setting for important public meetings and for the courts of assize. It was here in 1685, at what became known as "the Bloody Assizes," that Judge Jeffreys condemned the rebels of the Monmouth Rebellion to death and exile. And it was here in 1603 that another important trial took place.

I walk to the large open door and enter the vast empty hall. A plump young man in a dark suit catches my eye and nods as I step over the threshold.

"May I come in?"

He shrugs. "If you like." I wait for him to say something else. The occasion seems to warrant it, but instead he casts his eyes up to the open timber roof trusses and purses his lips in a silent whistle. The hall is brighter than I expected, with a wealth of rich stained glass. The walls are flint with limestone facings around the windows and doors, and, inside, twin rows of polished Purbeck marble columns support the vaulted ceiling. All the tourist websites, including the official Visit Winchester website, call it "one of the finest surviving aisled halls of the 13th century" (in quotes), though no one ever mentions who decided this. This is the problem with the Internet: good quotations are constantly copied from one site to another, until the original source is lost, misquoted or misattributed. At any rate, it *is* impressive. I turn to the young man again.

"May I take a picture?"

Again, he shrugs. "Suit yourself."

As I am framing my shot, a stout middle-aged couple enter the hall. They look around in stunned silence. "Whoi, it's jest a big empty room," whispers the woman. She turns to the young man. "Do you work here?"

"Mmm," he acknowledges grudgingly.

"So what's so special about this place?"

"Round Table, I suppose." He gestures to an enormous oak tabletop hanging high on the west wall, minus its legs. Around the rim, in gothic letters of red and black, are painted the names of all of King Arthur's knights. The woman looks momentarily excited. "Laaa," she trills.

"But it's a fake," the young man adds with a smirk.

"Nois stenned glass," ventures the man.

"Fake," counters the guide.

"What aboot that air family tree?" asks the man pointing to an elaborate genealogical table stencilled high on the east wall.

The guide sighs wearily. "Fake."

Worst. Tour guide. Ever.

It's now the woman's turn to sigh. "Well, come on, dear. Let's go see summin else." And they leave.

I want to call them back, tell them that history has been made in this room. Sure, the Round Table is a fake, but it's a very old fake. The table has been dated using dendrochronology to 1275, which means it was probably made for King Edward I for one of the Round Table tournaments he sponsored. The current paint job dates from a visit by Henry VIII in the sixteenth century, when he entertained the Holy Roman Emperor, Charles V, during a state visit in 1522. This would explain why a Tudor rose was painted in the centre of the table, like the high-scoring target on a dart board. Henry was scoring a political point here, one his visitors couldn't fail to note. Look at me, he was saying, I am the heir to Arthur.

But I have not come to the Great Hall to see a phony bit of Arthuriana. My interest lies in another direction. For it was here, on a cold November day in 1603, that Sir Walter Raleigh stood before of a hostile jury of his peers to defend himself against a charge of treason.

Raleigh is one of those larger-than-life figures who leap from the pages of the history books. A soldier, explorer, pirate, politician, courtier, historian, scientist, and poet, he was a walking illustration of the term Renaissance man. Seventeenth-century English writer and natural philosopher John Aubrey described him as "tall, handsome, bold...and damnable proud"—just the sort of young buck Queen Elizabeth I liked to surround herself with at court.[1] Raleigh's Achilles heel was his conceit, and he made a number of highly placed enemies. As long as Elizabeth was alive to protect him, he was safe, but Elizabeth's successor, James I, did not take to the dashing cavalier, and Raleigh's enemies were quick to poison the king's mind against Elizabeth's knight. In 1603, a plot was uncovered to depose the king and to replace him with his cousin, Lady Arabella Stuart, who was the granddaughter of Henry VIII. Raleigh was accused of being the brains behind the conspiracy, and his enemies said it was Raleigh's idea to approach Lord Aremburg, the Spanish ambassador to the Netherlands, and to seek Spanish financial backing for the coup d'état.

Normally, a trial like this would have been held in Westminster, but plague was sweeping through the dirty lanes of London in the winter of 1603, so it was decided to hold the trial in Winchester instead. As Raleigh progressed across the country under guard, large angry crowds gathered to watch him pass. His guards were hard-pressed to keep him alive long enough to stand trial.

In the Great Hall, Raleigh faced a hostile room. The prosecution was directed by Sir Edward Coke, the Attorney General, whose rather simple legal strategy consisted of shouting abuse at Raleigh, hoping to browbeat him into a confession. "I will prove all," shouted Coke. "Thou art a monster! Thou hast an English face, but a Spanish heart."[2]

The familiar "thou" was designed to be insulting and accusing Raleigh of possessing a "Spanish heart" was a somewhat ludicrous accusation, given that Raleigh had spent most of his adult life fighting Spain on land and sea. He also accused Raleigh of being an atheist, then a capital offence. All that was done, Coke insisted, "was by thy instigation, thou viper, for I *thou* thee, thou traitor! I will prove thee the rankest traitor in all England."[3]

He continued to hurl insults and abuse at Raleigh, but Raleigh kept his cool and answered each point logically. The charge was based on hearsay, he argued. Why not bring his accuser, Lord Cobham, to the court to challenge him directly? Unbeknownst to the Attorney General, Raleigh had an ace up his sleeve, a letter from Cobham recanting his accusation. But unbeknownst to

Raleigh, Coke also had a letter from Cobham, reiterating the accusation, a letter written later than Raleigh's own. When the letters were produced and compared, the jury had no choice but to find Raleigh guilty as charged.

However, the trial had gone awry. Raleigh had entered the Great Hall a rank villain but left a hero. His eloquence had won the crowd, and the verdict was an unpopular one. King James had no choice but to suspend Raleigh's sentence of execution and imprison Raleigh in the Tower of London for an indefinite period. Raleigh was to spend the next thirteen years of his life locked in the Tower, and it was while he was in prison that he wrote many of the works for which he is remembered, including his ambitious *History of the World*. Finally, in 1616, he convinced the king to release him from the Tower to outfit another expedition to the New World to seek El Dorado, the lost city of gold.

The expedition was a disaster from beginning to end. While Raleigh was laid low by fever, his party was attacked by the Spanish on the Orinoco River. His lieutenant, Lawrence Keymis, retaliated by sacking the Spanish settlement of San Thomé. Raleigh's son was killed in the attack. The expedition failed to find El Dorado, and sailed home in disgrace. Raleigh knew he was sailing to his doom—the charge of treason still hung over his head, having never been reversed, only suspended—but he seemed strangely resigned. Even though both France and Venice offered him asylum, he journeyed home to face the music. With the Spanish calling for Raleigh's head, the king, who did not want renewed hostilities with Spain, felt he had no choice but to order Raleigh put to death. When Raleigh walked into Palace Yard in Westminster in the early morning of October 29, 1618, the crowd was unusually subdued. This was not a popular execution. Raleigh stood calmly on the scaffold and said in a clear voice, "So I take my leave of you all, making my peace with God. I have a long journey to take, and must bid the company farewell."[4]

He refused a blindfold and knelt at the block. The executioner hesitated. "What dost thou fear?" asked an exasperated Raleigh. "Strike, man, strike!"[5] The axe fell twice, and when it was over, a deep groan burst from the crowd. After the execution, the following poem was discovered in Raleigh's Bible:

Even such is time, which takes in trust
Our youth, our joys, and all we have,
And pays us but with age and dust,
Who in the dark and silent grave
When we have wandered all our ways
Shuts up the story of our days,
And from which earth, and grave, and dust
The Lord will raise me up, I trust.[6]

Raleigh's head was preserved and given to his widow, who kept it by her side in a velvet bag to the end of her life. Odd keepsake, that. I can't see my wife doing the same should I predecease her. ("What's that you got there, Nancy?" "Oh, just Ken's head. Would you like to see?")

But it was another of Raleigh's poems, "His Pilgrimage," that I had in mind as I stood in the Great Hall, one more appropriate to my own journey:

Give me my scallop-shell of quiet,
My staff of faith to walk upon,
My scrip of joy, immortal diet,
My bottle of salvation,
My gown of glory, hope's true gage;
And thus I'll take my pilgrimage.[7]

I take a last look around the large empty hall before I turn to go. An empty room is a good metaphor for where I am right now in my life, for I feel like an empty room, a shell. I know what my father would say: "If life is an empty room, fill it." He was not a man for introspection, but for compassion. He would fill his life by thinking of others, not looking inward. His large and cluttered home was always full of guests, people in need of a bed for the night or a refuge: those who had lost their jobs or had nowhere else to live, those whose spouses had thrown them out or who were going through a messy divorce and had lost everything. Everyone was welcome. No one was turned away. I have many photographs of my father, and in every one he is smiling. And here's the thing: it isn't a smile put on for the camera. It's a smile of welcome.

When I return to the Westgate, Derek Bright is waiting for me. We sit down in the bar and order cups of coffee. Derek is a little shorter than my six feet, stockier too, and definitely more upbeat. His enthusiasm is infectious. From a shopping bag he pulls ten folded maps. He opens the first to show me the start of my journey, which he has outlined with a yellow highlighter. We get right down to business.

"As you may know, we've had a lot of flooding this spring, and there are two bridges, here and here, that have been removed. So, I've outlined a detour for you. After that you should be fine."

"Have you had many walkers this year?"

"No, to be honest, not too many walk the whole route, as you'll be doing; most just walk the last stretch, from Rochester to Canterbury. In many ways, it's the most scenic and the trail is well marked and easy to follow. By contrast, on your first three days— St. Swithun's Way, it's called here in Hampshire—the way-marking is pretty poor, so you'll need to follow your map quite closely. Have you had much experience with a map and compass?" I nod. "You should be fine then. But just in case," he reaches into his jacket pocket and produces a cellphone, "it's just a cheap burner phone, but I've programmed my number into the directory, and you can reach me in an emergency. I'll call you tomorrow night to see how the first day went."

His hand plunges deep into the grocery bag, and he withdraws three books, which he places on the table in front of me. "I brought you these as well—background for the walk." He taps the covers of each in turn as he introduces the titles: Julia Cartwright's *The Pilgrims' Way from Winchester to Canterbury* (1895), Hilaire Belloc's *The Old Road* (1904), and the most recent edition of the North Downs Way guide. I've read the first two before and doubt I'll have room in my luggage to carry them, but I gladly accept the latter. He then extracts a fourth book, his own guide to the history of the road I will be following, but I surprise him by pulling my own copy from my rucksack and asking him to sign it.

"You've read it?" he asks. He seems genuinely surprised and pleased.

"Twice," I tell him. "Once at Christmas—it was a present from my wife—and again last night on the flight here."

He signs the title page and hands it back.

"Look, Derek, I have to ask you: Do you really think medieval pilgrims followed this route?"

It's a valid question and the one Derek's book seeks to answer, but having read it twice now, I sense that he is still sitting on the fence. During the golden age of pilgrimage, roughly 1100 to 1500 CE, the shrine of the murdered archbishop of Canterbury was the third most popular pilgrimage destination in Europe after Rome and Santiago de Compostela. Thousands of pilgrims travelled to Canterbury. But what route did they follow?

Julia Cartwright believed there were three principal routes to Canterbury. Travellers coming from London and the north, like Chaucer's pilgrims in *The Canterbury Tales* and those Europeans who, like Erasmus, entered England from the port of London, would have followed the old Roman road south, then known as Watling Street. Today it is the busy A2 highway. Those coming from the Continent landed most likely at Dover or Sandwich Haven and approached Canterbury from the south—while those coming from the west (and this would include those coming from Brittany who had sailed into the port of Southampton, just south of Winchester) would follow the Pilgrims' Way. Cartwright believed that thousands of pilgrims followed this third route, for "there can be little doubt that in the twelfth and thirteenth centuries this road was, if not the only means of communication between West and East, at least the principal thoroughfare across this part of England, and as such the route naturally chosen by pilgrims to Canterbury."[8] This is the route I will be following.

Hilaire Belloc's book, published a few years after Cartwright's, was the first to systematically trace the entire route of this "old road," for, over the centuries, certain sections had fallen out of use. The pilgrims' road followed a chalk escarpment called the North Downs, which ran east-west across southern England from Dover to the Salisbury Plain. Some parts had naturally become paved highways, while others were now little more than scratches on a hillside. Belloc also stressed the road's antiquity, positing that it may, in fact, be the oldest road in Britain, dating back to Neolithic times. Belloc noted that where the road crossed the Medway Valley it was lined with the greatest concentration of Neolithic ruins in Britain, monuments like Kit's Coty House and the Coldrum Stones, which actually predate Stonehenge. Later scholars disagreed. They argued that the label "Pilgrims' Way" had only been applied to the route in the eighteenth century—the earliest reference to the "Pilgrim Road" appeared on a map of Kent published in 1769.[9] They also argued that the small towns along the route could not possibly have accommodated the thousands of pilgrims travelling to Canterbury. To this second objection, Derek found his own answer. Re-examining the records of donations to the shrine at Canterbury, and factoring in the estimated population of England at the time and the limited number of people who would have had the freedom to make a pilgrimage, Derek concluded that earlier scholars exaggerated the numbers of pilgrims travelling to Canterbury from the west. On any given day, he wrote, as few as five pilgrims began a journey using the North Downs track way.[10]

"Do you think it was *the* pilgrims' route to Canterbury?" I ask.

He looks briefly uncomfortable. "The more I examine it, the less sure I become, but I will say this. In the Middle Ages, the lowlands between the North and South Downs were still heavily forested and in places quite boggy. The soil is a kind of claggy clay, and the Roman roads, by that time, were in ruins. After a rainstorm, any road could become quite impassable. The advantage of the Pilgrims' Way, as Belloc points out, is that it is above this heavy soil, on well-drained chalk and on a south-facing slope (which would be quickly dried by the sun) and yet below the crest of the ridge, so that it would be sheltered from the wind. It would be an ideal route for those travelling on foot or by horseback. Some people certainly followed it. Did most? He shrugs. "I don't think we'll ever know for sure." Then he smiles. "It's a pilgrimage, after all. Some things you just have to take on faith."

My room is on the third floor at the back, up a wobbly narrow staircase. As I pass each door, I notice the rooms are named after famous people with Winchester associations: Walter Raleigh, for one, but also Christopher Wren, John Keats, Sir John Moore, and Nell Gywn. The white placard on my own door reads: "Trollope." I'm pleased. I recently reread the six novels that formed Anthony Trollope's *Chronicles of Barsetshire*, and I notice that someone has thoughtfully left the Everyman edition of *Barchester Towers* on my bedside table. I set my rucksack on the bed and quickly thumb through the pages. Then I catch sight of the bedside alarm clock and whistle. I don't have time to read; I'm late for church.

Now, I don't wear a watch. I don't wear jewellery of any kind, actually. It irritates me. And I find that, in my normal life, I am surrounded by clocks, so I don't need one. But on this trip, I'm carrying a cheap pocket watch that I picked up many years before in a Chinese street market. It keeps decent time, if you remember to wind it...and I haven't.

Thus, I'm late for evensong—just fifteen minutes late—but too late to join the worshippers in the embrace of the wooden choir stalls, so I have to sit in the echoing nave along with about a dozen other latecomers. The service is amplified, so we can hear the lessons and the responses, but we don't really feel included, sitting as we are at the bottom of a set of broad stone steps that separate us from the choir. I'm disappointed and feel a bit like Lazarus outside the gates of Dives being licked by the dogs. It seems important to me that I begin my pilgrimage by attending a service in the cathedral and by receiving the priest's blessing, but today I feel more like an onlooker than a participant.

The cathedral is supposed to be closed once the service begins, but someone has forgotten to secure the doors. Tourists continue to drift in, chatting loudly and snapping photos. A well-dressed woman and her young daughter pause in the aisle beside my pew.

"Mum-mee, what are those people doing?"

"They are worshipping God, dear."

"What is god?" The little tyke speaks with the plummy accent of a British public school education, an accent which is so charming in a little girl, but which begins to seem contrived as she grows older.

The mother pauses. "Well, dear. Some people believe in a supreme being who created the universe."

"Do we believe that, mummy?"

"No, dear."

This little interchange occurs as the voices of the choir swell and fill the stone vault of Winchester Cathedral with the opening lines of the Magnificat: "My soul doth magnify the Lord, and my spirit hath rejoiced in God my Saviour." In front of me, a teen stands up holding an iPad at arm's length above her head, trying to film the church service as if it were a rock concert.

"Oh my God!" squeals a girlish voice over to my left. "She's right here! I'm standing right on top of her!" I watch as three young women crouch together, brush their hair back from their foreheads, pout their lips and take selfies over what I know must be Jane Austen's grave. I wonder if she is rolling over.

I suppose I should not have been surprised. In the most recent British census, only 6.3% of the population admitted to being regular churchgoers. These people clearly viewed the cathedral as some kind of museum and the service as a cultural show put on for their amusement. They show no shame in photographing the worshippers as they kneel in the pews, and some of those worshippers are starting to grow annoyed at being treated like zoo animals. Strange country, I think, to be starting a pilgrimage in, and, once again, I miss my father's company. He might have made sense of this. He certainly wouldn't have been bothered by the tourists. He would have felt they were showing healthy curiosity and that a visit to the cathedral might even do them some good. I can almost hear his voice in my head: "Don't worry about what other people think. This is your pilgrimage, no one else's. What they say or do shouldn't change the way you feel."

I leave the cathedral and drift south under the impressive flying buttresses and through the picturesque cathedral close, past the old pilgrims' hospital (now a music school), past the lovely Bishop's Court House (now called Cheyney Court), probably the most photographed building in Winchester, all lemon plaster and draped wisteria, and out the castellated Priory Gate and the subsequent and tunnel-like Kingsgate to College Street. I turn right past a yellow townhouse where a plaque affixed to the wall informs me that Jane Austen lingered here for the last eight months of her life, before death carried her off to be buried beneath a marble slab in the cathedral. I head down College Street, outside the high brick walls of Winchester College.

The college is one of England's oldest public schools. Among its famous alumni are numbered a Rajah of Sarawak (Sir Vyner Brooke), a climber of Everest (George Mallory), an Antarctic explorer (Apsley Cherry-Garrard), an opera impresario (Rupert D'Oyly Carte), a British fascist (Sir Oswald Mosley), an art historian (Kenneth Clark), a Viceroy of India (Archibald Wavell), a poet (Matthew Arnold), a dodgy travel writer and court jester to

James I (Thomas Coryat), a popular film director (Joss Whedon), and a seemingly endless list of cricketers, scholars, politicians, soldiers, and churchmen. But the pupil who interests me most is the novelist Anthony Trollope, for I believe it was while he was a ten-year-old student at Winchester that he discovered the setting for the first of his Barchester novels, *The Warden*, in the Hospital of Saint Cross, my final destination for the evening.

When I reach Saint Cross (called Hiram's Hospital in the novel), the porter is just getting ready to lock the gate for the night.

"May I have a quick look around?" I plead.

The porter, a good-natured soul, says "yes," providing I don't go into any of the buildings or disturb any of the inmates.

Saint Cross is the oldest charitable institution in the country, an almshouse established by Bishop Henry de Blois in 1133 to shelter thirteen poor men and to provide food for an additional hundred. A fifteenth-century expansion would increase the number of permanent residents to twenty-five. The chapel, the great hall, the kitchens, and the apartments form a lovely honey-coloured quadrilateral, reminiscent of a monastic close or an Oxford college. In the Victorian era, Holy Cross was the centre of a scandal, when it was discovered that the warden of the day was embezzling funds intended for the inmates of the institution. Trollope, who would have heard all the sordid details when the story broke in 1851, used it as the central plot device in *The Warden*.

Trollope's novel is a touch more sophisticated than the story that inspired it, for his warden is a saintly man, much loved by his charges, who has no idea that he has done anything wrong until it is pointed out to him by a crusading journalist who hopes to marry the warden's daughter. All comes right in the end. The warden is exonerated, and the lovers are reunited, and Trollope paints a fascinating picture of the lives of those who depend upon the church for both their living and their support.

Holy Cross is peaceful and beautifully situated in a meadow by the banks of the river Itchen, and I can't help but think that, despite the scandal, it is quite a successful institution. I wouldn't mind ending up in a place like this at the end of my life. Sure, there are hordes of tourists, and I would have to dress up in an official gown for meals and chapel—black for the original thirteen brothers of the Foundation of the Hospital of St. Cross and red for the twelve additional brothers of the Order of Noble Poverty, but the apartments look snug and I know that I would spend my final years in dignity, surrounded by great beauty. Much scorn is thrown on the notion of Christian charity, but here it seems to work. The problem is that institutions like this, however well-intentioned, can never keep up with the numbers of elderly poor who will need them. But that fact doesn't invalidate the intention.

Holy Cross also has another lovely institution that better fits my immediate situation. Each day, from the porter's lodge, they distribute the "wayfarer's dole," a hank of bread and a horn of ale for the poor weary traveller. I inquire but am not surprised to learn that I am too late. The day's dole has been exhausted.

I choose to walk back to town along the banks of the river, following a path the tourist bureau has dubbed Keats's Walk. I push through a kissing gate and cross the meadows. It is that golden time of the day, beloved of photographers, where the setting sun gilds the feathered grass and paints the brick garden walls with a rosy hue. A pair of swans glides in stately fashion down the stream, while groups of people stroll along the bank, chatting and taking their ease. Birdsong fills the air. Amongst the reeds, blue flag iris and marsh marigolds bloom. Grazing cattle lend an air of John Constable to the scene.

The poet John Keats loved this walk and he described it in a letter to his brother and sister. And it was here in the fall of 1819 that he was inspired to write his ode "To Autumn," perhaps his most perfect poem. It is a poem about growth, maturation and the approach of death. It was also his last, since money troubles and declining health had forced him to abandon poetry for more potentially lucrative ventures. A little over a year later, Keats would lie dead of tuberculosis, in a small *pensione* just off the Spanish Steps in Rome at the young age of twenty-six. I know something of the vicissitudes of a writer's financial life, so I am sympathetic. I tried for several years to make a living as a freelance writer before giving it up for a regular salary.

In "To Autumn," Keats was trying something new. He called it negative capability. He was trying to remove his own ego from the poem and any tendency of the poet to express philosophical certainty. Instead, he tried to see the world from other points of view, even from the point of view of an inanimate creature or, in this case, an abstraction, like "autumn." He once wrote to a friend that he could imagine a billiard ball's delight in "its own roundness, smoothness, volubility and the rapidity of its motion." He was striving for universal empathy, and in "To Autumn" he perhaps came as close to this ideal as is possible.

But of course, it wasn't autumn today—it was spring—and the world wasn't dying; it was being reborn.

The meadow walk ends under the crumbling walls of the old Bishop's palace and continues along a paved path by the banks of the river. Here the Itchen is walled and channelled and continues at a crisp pace through the town. The water is like champagne, and I rest on a bench under the walls of another old almshouse, listening to the birds in the willows and watching as two kids zip back and forth on their scooters, laughing and shrieking with delight, while their mother, who sits on another bench, calls, "Not so far, dears. Stay where mummy can see you."

And just as I'm thinking that these are the very waters Izaak Walton fished, I see a fisherman walking toward me along the path. He is wearing green chest waders and carrying a bowed fly rod with the hook clipped to a wire guide—Walton's Piscator in the flesh. He pauses and leans on the railing just in front of me, looking down into the river. This is too good an opportunity to miss.

I sidle up to him, lean on the rail by his side, and pretend to consider the water as well. Sensing my presence, he turns to me and smiles.

"Any luck?" I venture.

"Five, so far."

"Trout?"

"Aye, brown trout."

I notice that he isn't carrying a creel.

"Oh, I let them go," he says. "But they were a nice size." He holds up his hands, fingers measuring empty space. "Maybe ten, twelve inches on average."

"Is the Itchen a good trout stream?" I ask.

"Good! Why it's one of the best! I'd say the second-best chalk stream in England after the Test." I express my ignorance, and he explains that streams that are born in chalk run clear and cool. Trout love them.

I am under the impression that all water in England is private, so I ask if he needs special permission to fish here.

"Not here. This bit, in Winchester, is public. All you need is a rod licence. But elsewhere, yes. You can pay up to £200 for one day of fishing on some of the more famous reaches of the Test. That's why I work part-time as a ghillie. Do they use that word where you're from? Ghillie?"

"No, I guess we'd say a fishing guide."

"Ah, well, if I work as a guide then I fish for free."

We contemplate the water, scanning for fish. "It's remarkably clear," I say.

He ponders me for a moment, frown creasing his brow. "Clear, you say? Why, it's terribly murky. Did you not hear of the flooding we had earlier this year? See, across there?" He points across the stream to a brick garden wall. "See the high-water mark? That's how high the water rose. It's still recovering. Clear," he snorts. "And the mayflies are late, too.

"Normally, I like to fish a dry fly," he continues, "but you can see what I'm using today?" He unclips the hook. It's a small caddis fly pattern with gold bead for a head. "The bead keeps the fly deep in the water, so the fish can see it. Otherwise," he laughs, "you're not fishing. You're just waving your arms around."

We stare at the water some more, and I try to think of something to say.

"Winchester is a lovely city," I remark.

He looks surprised and then glances around. "I suppose it is," he admits, as if seeing everything for the first time, "but I love the river. I live just above the old mill." He points upstream. "This morning, I took my coffee into the garden, and there were two otters playing right there. You can't beat that."

We shake hands and part—he, to his home, and I, to climb High Street once more to my bed at the Westgate.

When I return to the Westgate, I have a quick shower to wash away the travel grime, and crawl into bed. I've been up for almost twenty-four hours, with only an hour's rest on the plane. I'm exhausted, but I am determined not to fall asleep too early. The longer I can stay awake, I reason, the sooner I will conquer jetlag. So I turn on the TV and flip through the channels until I find an animated Japanese film, *From Up on Poppy Hill*; but even my love for all things Miyazaki can't keep my eyes open for long, and at about seven o'clock, I give in, turn out the lights, and fall asleep. Later I awake, and checking my unreliable pocket watch on the bedside table, see that it is nine o'clock. Cursing the lateness of the hour, I struggle out of bed and begin to dress. Then I pause. The world outside my door seems curiously quiet, and it is dark beyond the window blind. Remembering my lateness at the cathedral the day before, I pick up my watch and hold it to my ear. It's ticking steadily. I turn on the TV to a community news channel and see by the clock in a corner of the screen that it is indeed nine o'clock— nine o'clock at night. I have been asleep for only an hour and a half and am now fully awake. I turn off the lights and try to go back to sleep, but it's hopeless. I turn on the TV again, but then think better of it. The hotel is old and the walls are pitiably thin, and I do not want to disturb the other guests, so I decide to read instead. I reach into my suitcase, extract John Bunyan's *Pilgrim's Progress*, and crack open the cover.

Phil Cousineau, in *The Art of Pilgrimage*, writes that there are seven stages in the sacred journey, stages he claims to have discovered while reading Bunyan's allegory. The first stage is "The Longing," followed by "The Call." (Incidentally, the other stages are "Departure," "The Pilgrim's Way," "The Labyrinth" [a moment of doubt or confusion], "Arrival," and "Bringing Back the Boon"—a structure I found helpful when writing this narrative). In Bunyan's story, his pilgrim, called Christian, is so overburdened by the weight of his sin, which he carries about on his back like the burden of Sisyphus, that he is paralyzed. He is so anxious about his impending doom that it even destroys his relations with his wife and children. Then he meets Evangelist who points him in the direction of the wicket gate, and Christian begins his allegorical journey along the straight and narrow path to the Heavenly City. Along the way, Christian must overcome many obstacles. The first is the slough of Despond, where he threatens to drown under the burden of his sin, until he is rescued by a passerby and set on his feet again. From the time it was first published in 1678, until the late nineteenth century, *Pilgrim's Progress* was a bestseller. The full title is *The Pilgrim's Progress from This World to That Which Is to Come; Delivered under the Similitude of a Dream*. For many pious households in the seventeenth, eighteenth, and nineteenth centuries there would have been this book, their Bible, and possibly Foxe's *Book of Martyrs* on their bookshelf—that was all. Puritans could read *Pilgrim's Progress* in good conscience, for it was a long allegorical sermon disguised as an adventure novel. It had been on my to-read list for a very long time, and so I thought, *What better time to read it than now?*

As a pilgrim, I always expected to identify with Christian, but I find, as I read, that I actually have more in common with the next person Christian encounters, Mr. Worldly Wiseman. Worldly Wiseman counsels Christian to give up his foolish quest, to collect his family, whom he had abandoned in an act of great selfishness, and to live in the village of Morality, where he could be guided by two gentlemen called Legality and Civility. This seems like perfectly reasonable advice to me, what one might call the secular version of the good and just life, and Christian is persuaded to take a different road. But on the road to Morality he encounters pesky Evangelist again, who makes him feel guilty for having given up his quest so easily and bids him take up his burden and turn back to the narrow path.

Cousineau explains that part of *The Call* is "the dedication." This often involves dressing up in a special costume as an outward sign of your intention. Muslims on the haj to Mecca dress in white. So do Japanese Buddhist pilgrims, who add a conical hat and a staff to the ensemble. Christian pilgrims once did the same. Sir Walter Raleigh gives us the picture of a medieval pilgrim in his poem "His Pilgrimage" (already quoted): the scallop shell (which is often fastened to the pilgrim's broad-brimmed hat as a symbol of his pilgrimage), the staff, the scrip (a small satchel), the bottle, and the gown. The serious pilgrim sets out with next to nothing, putting his trust in God and in the kindness of strangers to provide succour and sustenance along the way. The medieval pilgrim often travelled a dangerous road and, like Christian in Bunyan's story, had many trials to overcome before he reached his destination. Many fell ill or were set upon by thieves. Some were sold into slavery or were turned back by hostile armies. Many died upon the way.

Musing on these thoughts, I finally fall asleep just as Christian is knocking at the wicket gate and awaiting permission to begin the next stage of his journey.

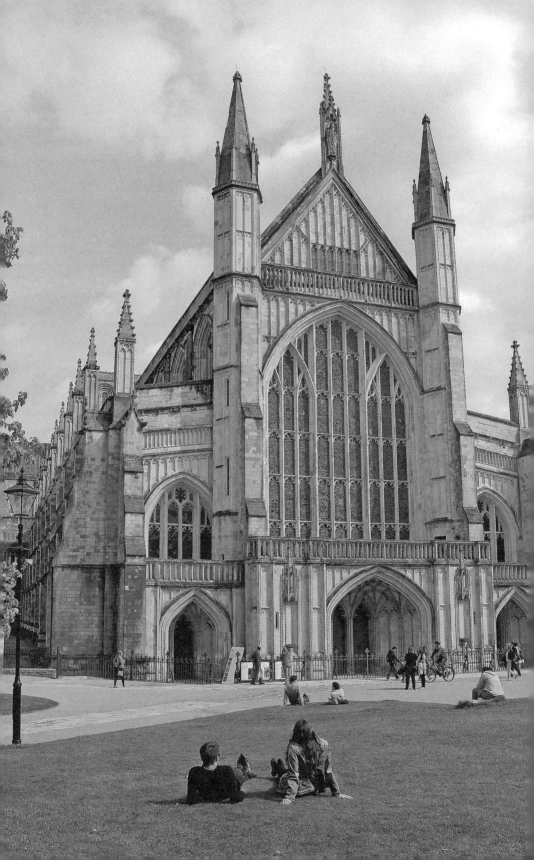

2

Winchester to New Alresford

Make it your ambition to lead a quiet life.
—ST. PAUL, First Epistle to the Thessalonians 4:11

DESPITE MY FRAGMENTED SLEEP, I rise early and carry my small suitcase downstairs to be stashed behind the bar. After finishing a heavy English breakfast, I wave goodbye to Guy and his wife in the kitchen, pat the sombre Weimaraner on the head, hoist my rucksack to my shoulder, and set off. This will become my pattern for the next two weeks. As I walk down the cobbles of High Street, it's almost deserted. I pass just two others, who stroll briskly in the other direction, cardboard cups of take-out coffee in their hands. It's Monday morning. Where is everybody? The streets should be full of shop clerks and office workers on their way to work. Then I remember. It's a bank holiday. Everyone who doesn't have to be at work is still in bed. In a few minutes, I'm back at the cathedral.

In spite of my disappointment the day before, I am determined to give Winchester Cathedral another chance. I am the only person at the door that morning when the security guard unlocks the new glass entrance door. I enter the vast and subdued cathedral, and for the first hour or so, I have the whole place to myself—just me and the few cathedral employees who have drawn the short straw, and they are too busy about their own business to pay much attention to me.

Of all the periods in architecture, the Gothic is my favourite, and Winchester is certainly a beautiful example. For one thing, it has the longest nave of any church in Europe, which makes it the longest medieval church in the world at 169 metres (554 feet). As you stand in front of the west doors, looking down the long nave under the sweep of the soaring roof, with the twin rows of giant pillars flanking you on either side, and the stone arches pushing up into the shadows, you feel you have entered the forest primeval cast in stone. I am not the only one to feel this way. Goethe, writing of Strasbourg Cathedral, noted that the columns rose "like a most sublime, wide-arching Tree of God,...with a thousand of boughs, a million of twigs, and leafage like the sands of the sea."[1] The art critic John Ruskin, also enamoured of the Gothic, drew a similar parallel, though he denied that the architects of the Gothic were inspired by nature, rather they "developed into" natural forms because of their familiarity with these forms and their love of the natural world—a rather fine distinction, I think—but he, too, saw the naves of the great High Gothic cathedrals as "summer woods at their fairest."[2] Some people find Gothic architecture overpowering, and resent feeling so small and insignificant in its presence, but I don't think that is the intention. Abbot Suger, who built the first true Gothic church, the abbey church of St. Denis, believed that "the dull mind rises to truth through that which is material."[3] That is to say, beautiful things can aid our understanding of the divine.

There are, of course, styles of architecture that celebrate human achievement—the Classical, Neo-Classical, and Modern spring to mind. These are the architectures of the classical world, the great nineteenth-century republics, and the skyscrapers of modern cities like New York. They are humanistic. The Gothic, on the other hand, humbles us. When we walk into a place like the nave of Winchester Cathedral, we are reminded of how small we are in the universe. And somehow this is not depressing. It is uplifting. The ego is crushed, so the spirit may soar. I truly feel that the Gothic uplifts my spirits in the same way that mountains do, or giant sequoias, or sunsets. It takes me out of myself, and, for a moment, I am relieved of the burden of being myself.

One of my aims in returning to Winchester Cathedral is to find the grave of Izaak Walton, author of *The Compleat Angler,* one of my favourite books. I locate Walton's tomb in a tiny side chapel in the south transept known as Prior Silkstead's Chapel, where the writer lies pressed beneath a thick slab of black marble before the altar. Walton died on December 15, 1683, aged ninety, and there is a pious, rather conventional poem etched on the stone, ending with this Latin tag: *votis modestis sic flerunt liberi.* I stand there a long time trying to puzzle that one out. The best I can figure is, "This modest prayer his weeping children lament." The chapel has been recently restored, and I take a seat on the rustic pew before the altar. The morning's sun casts a beam of harlequined light across the tomb from the window above the altar. This window is relatively new, installed in 1914 in Walton's memory by admiring fisherman from Britain and America.

I raise my eyes and spend some time contemplating the stained glass. My gaze comes to rest in the bottom right hand corner where I can see an illustration of Walton, dressed in plain, almost puritanical, garb, quietly reading on the bank of the river Itchen with St. Catherine's Hill rising in the background. He sits beneath the shade of a modest tree, his rod, net, and creel resting by his side. The scene is captioned with Walton's favourite quotation, "Study to be quiet," which is taken from St. Paul's first epistle to the Thessalonians, and which is also the last line of Walton's famous book. Walton seems perfectly composed, and I wonder what he is reading. I clear my throat, and he looks up from his book with a smile of patient expectancy.

"Any luck?" I enquire, indicating the creel.

"No, not yet. But no day is spoiled that is spent fishing. For if I have not as yet caught a trout, my morning has not been wasted, for have I not had ample time for contemplation?"

"I suppose. Any profound thoughts to share?"

"I was thinking that the world is full of wonders and how it is man's lot to know so little of God's creation. For example, Pliny," he points to the book in his hand, "is of the opinion that many of the flies with which we tempt the trout have their birth from a kind of dew that falls in the spring. The dew that falls on the leaves of trees breeds one kind of fly, that which falls upon flowers and herbs another, that on cabbages, yet another. In the same way, Gesner, who has written much on fishing, states that the pike, who is the tyrant of these waters, is bred by generation, as other fishes are, but may also spring spontaneously from the pickerel weed with the help of the sun's heat. Though men of science ponder these mysteries and others like them, I feel that we shall never plumb their bottom."

"Indeed." I don't know quite what to say to this, so I change the subject. "I saw some very nice trout in the Itchen yesterday. I'm surprised there aren't more fishermen about." I point to the meandering river winding out of sight beyond the frame of the stained glass.

"Oh, this is private water. It belongs to the Bishop of Winchester, who is an old friend of mine. He is jealous of his privileges and does not give permission easily."

"Must be nice to be rich."

"Nay, for the rich are always worried for coming of the next day. I would much rather be an angler, for do we not sit on cowslip banks, enjoy the cuckoo's song, and possess ourselves in as much quietness as this silver stream? I envy no man who eats better meat than I do, or who wears better clothes than I do, only him who catches more fish than I do." He laughs. "God never did make a more quiet, calm, innocent recreation than angling."

"So I've read."

He raises his eyes to the heavens and snaps his book shut. "The noonday sun is passed. You will forgive me, but there are reaches of this river I wish to tempt before the afternoon is spent and I must return to my daughter's fireside for the evening repast." He slips the book into his pocket and gathers up his fishing materials. "Remember, he that hopes to be a good angler, must not only bring an inquiring, searching and observing wit, but he must bring a large measure of hope and patience to the art. Adieu."

And with that he walks out of the frame.

Izaak Walton lived as an ironmonger in London until the time of the English Civil War, when he chose to wrap up his business, take an early retirement, and move to a small farm in the country near Shallowford, there to begin the book that would make him famous. *The Compleat Angler* is a scrapbook of everything that Walton gleaned from the sources available to him about the pursuit of angling. The first edition was published in 1653, two years after the war ended, but he never really stopped working on it. New editions would continue to be published until Walton's death. The final edition of 1676 was greatly expanded, and included an additional book written by his good friend Charles Cotton about the art of fishing with a dry fly.

But the book is not just a how-to manual for fishermen. If that's all there were to it, it would not have stayed in print all these years, for *The Compleat Angler* is the most frequently reprinted book in English after the Bible. Walton equates angling with an approach to life that is at once gentle, pious and reflective. When fishermen are accused of being simple, Walton's narrator, Piscator, replies: "if by that you mean a harmlessness, or that simplicity which was usually found in the primitive Christians, who were, as most Anglers are, quiet men, and followers of peace; men that are simply wise, as not to sell their consciences to buy riches, and with them vexation and a fear to die; if you mean such simple men as lived in those times when there were fewer lawyers...then myself and those of my profession will be glad to be so understood."[4]

Some readers have detected a hidden code in the book as well, where "Angler" may be read as "Anglican," where the virtues celebrated in fishermen are really the virtues Walton championed in Englishmen of a certain stripe. For at least one cause of the English Civil War was the desire of some sects, like the Scottish Covenanters and the English Puritans, to break free of the English Church, to abolish bishoprics and replace church hierarchy with a looser Presbyterian-style organization. Walton was an Anglican and a Royalist. He stood for tradition and received wisdom. But he was not a violent man. In fact, there is only one story that portrays him as an active participant in the conflict, and it may be apocryphal. He is said to have once helped smuggle an important royal jewel, called the lesser George, out of England to Charles II. Otherwise, Walton led a retiring life during that period of upheaval, choosing to sit out the war in a quiet country backwater, spending his time writing and fishing. It is this gentle, good-natured man who comes across in the pages of *The Compleat Angler*, full of friendly advice, not all of it wise, and it is his lyrical celebration of pastoral life, with its cowslip banks and birdsong, its musical milkmaids and quiet country inns with their lavender-scented sheets that we remember with such fondness.

Leaving Walton behind for the moment, I decide to take a stroll around the cathedral while I still have it more or less to myself. I climb the weathered stone steps, past the presbytery, to the retrochoir. A brass canopy marks the place where St. Swithun's shrine once stood, before it was dismantled in 1538 by the agents of King Henry VIII. Before the creation of the retrochoir, however, Swithun's bones had resided in a gilded and bejewelled reliquary that was placed behind the high altar. You can still see a tiny doorway at ground level against the back wall of the choir, much like the one Alice had to pass through at the bottom of the rabbit hole.

At one time, this door would have been outside the cathedral, and poor pilgrims crawled through it and beneath the saint's shrine to be closer to his bones, praying for the saint's intervention, and hoping that their proximity to the saint would aid their plea. Barren women might pray for a child, the ill for a cure, and the troubled in spirit for peace. Swithun had been the bishop of Winchester in the mid-ninth century and had been renowned for both his humility and his compassion for the poor. Indeed, he was so humble that he asked to be buried outside of the earlier Anglo-Saxon minster, so that the rain would fall on his grave. Legend has it that, nine years after his death, the monks tried to move his body inside the church, and the saint was so annoyed that the heavens exploded with a clap of thunder and the clouds burst, drenching Winchester in a deluge that lasted forty days and forty nights. July 15 has become known as Saint Swithun's day, and as the rhyme says:

St Swithun's day if thou dost rain
For forty days it will remain
St Swithun's day if thou be fair
For forty days 'twill rain nae mare[5]

It is worth noting that Winchester was the second most popular place of pilgrimage in medieval England, after Canterbury. And before Becket's death, most pilgrims would have followed the Pilgrims' Way in the opposite direction, walking to Winchester to pray at the shrine of St. Swithun.

Not far from Swithun's shrine is the brass statue of a deep-sea diver. This is a monument to William Walker, the man who single-handedly saved Winchester Cathedral from collapse. In the early part of the twentieth century, it was discovered that the foundations of the cathedral were flooded and slowly subsiding. Without intervention, the Cathedral would eventually topple. For six years, starting in 1906, and for six hours each day, Walker worked underwater, in darkness, shifting heavy bags of concrete to shore up the foundation. This small statue is Winchester's way of saying thanks.

The retrochoir also has several other interesting monuments. There is the tomb of Bishop Fox, who is represented as an emaciated cadaver, perhaps to remind us that we are mortal and that death comes to us all. There is also an interesting crusader tomb of a knight in chainmail twisting at the hip, frozen in the moment of drawing his sword from its scabbard. The sculpture is so old and so weathered most of the details are worn away. The tomb wasn't labelled, and I wonder for whom it was created—some local knight, perhaps, who had ventured to the Holy Land and who had returned years later only to find the world he'd left behind had changed out of all recognition. I wonder if he felt it had been worthwhile, if following his own personal path to salvation had, in the end, only made him a stranger to his wife and children.

As you come down the aisle on the other side of the presbytery, there are six large chests resting on the top of the wall. These are mortuary chests and contain the bones of the early rulers and bishops of Winchester, including the remains of the legendary King Canute who tried to command the tide, and when he failed said to his followers: "Let all the world know that the power of kings is empty and worthless."[6] In the English Civil War, these chests were emptied by roundhead soldiers who used the bones as projectiles to smash the stained-glass windows. After their departure, the bones were gathered up and returned to the chests. There was, however, no way for the caretakers to determine which bones belonged in which casket. To this day, they remain all jumbled up, the bones of kings, one queen and several bishops all muddled together.

I admit that I also visit the grave of Jane Austen and take a picture of her tombstone. I'm a fan, and Miss Austen will be dogging my footsteps all the way to Canterbury, so I feel obliged.

My last stop is a lovely chapel in the north transept, which is deserted at this hour. I sit in an empty pew and admire the rich stained glass with designs by Edward Burne-Jones. After Gothic, I love the Pre-Raphaelite period best, perhaps because it *is* re-imagined, romanticized Gothic. I kneel on the hassock and try to say my first prayer in many years, a prayer for my father, but it feels forced. It reminds me of the time when I was about twelve years old, and the teacher in choral music class asked me not to sing at our recital, but simply to open and close my mouth *as if I were singing*, so as not to ruin the performance for everyone else. Prayer pantomimed, I gather my things, and leave the cathedral.

I exit by the west front, cross the park under a shady avenue of lime trees, turn down a narrow close past St. Lawrence Church, and enter High Street by the ancient butter cross. I cross to St. Peter Street, leaving the medieval and Roman city for the Victorian one, until I come to Hyde Street and the modern suburbs. I am struck by how many churches I pass. Every block has one. I realize that, at one time, the heart of every parish was its church, and the local parish church would have been a busy place seven days a week, not just on Sunday morning. But today many of these small parish churches have been decommissioned and serve other functions, such as community centres, office spaces, or apartment blocks.

I wonder if this is how people coped in the Middle Ages. They must have been depressed, though they would have given it another name like melancholia or an excess of black bile, but they had the church for therapy. We don't. Today, we live in a vast mechanical universe without a beating heart at its centre. We lack their reassurance.

At Hyde Street, I pause to photograph the massive medieval gateway—all that remains of Hyde Abbey, which once held the bones of Alfred the Great. The church that stood outside the Abbey, St. Bartholomew's, still functions as a parish church. From St. Bartholomew's, my path follows a raised causeway beside the river, heading upstream. I wonder once more about my walk and what I hope to achieve.

When I decided to take this journey, I wondered how best to proceed. I was of two minds: Does a true pilgrim trust to fate and let the journey chart its own course, or does he plan for every eventuality? I suspect the former is more in the spirit of true pilgrimage, but I only had two weeks. It was all my work allowed and all I could afford, so I resolved to seek help planning my itinerary. I couldn't trust in serendipity, so instead I trusted Derek, and asked him to handle the logistics. This was less stressful, but also potentially less rewarding, especially for a writer, where disaster often makes for good copy.

The other question was whether to walk alone or to invite a friend. After all, I had originally planned this pilgrimage as a journey with my father. Did I want a companion? In some ways, a companion would make the walk more pleasurable. I am an introvert. I don't do well in social situations. I can't make small talk. A gregarious companion might help smooth the way. But my purpose in taking the walk was to use the time to think, and a companion, even the closest friend, requires you to be companionable. I wanted to set my own pace, stop and see the things that interested me, spend as much, or as little, time examining them as I pleased. A companion meant negotiation and compromise, so I decided to walk alone. I am a solitary person, not a lonely one. I am rarely lonely. I have my wife, my children, and my friends to fend off loneliness, and for that I am grateful. What I don't often have is privacy. "The soul of a journey is liberty, perfect liberty, to think, feel, do, just as one pleases," wrote William Hazlitt in "On Going a Journey." "Give me the clear blue sky over my head, and the green turf beneath my feet, a winding road before me, and a three hours' march to dinner—and then to thinking!"[7]

A jogger bobs by. I nod. A woman approaches holding the bejewelled leash of a Pekingese, staggering along on impossibly high cork-heeled sandals.

"Nice day,' I venture.

"Ooh, it's lovely," she gushes.

And it *is* lovely—a warm and sunny May morning, with moor-hens gliding past in the quiet reaches of the river and hawthorn blooming whitely overhead. The path is flanked with yellow flag iris, red campion, and cow parsnip. Chestnut candles tip at the sun. I soon shed my jacket and walk in shirtsleeves. In places, the cindered path along the river meadows follows an older road, which links the ruins of Hyde Abbey with a series of small villages, Headbourne Worthy, Kings Worthy, Martyr Worthy—"worthy" being the Anglo-Saxon word for an enclosure—Easton, Itchen Abbas, Ovington, and leading all the way to my bed at the Swan Hotel in New Alresford at the end of that first day. As I walk, the knots of anxiety loosen. I start to enjoy myself. My father would have enjoyed this too, and despite my observations to the contrary above, I would have enjoyed walking it with him. Perhaps there is something to this pilgrimage idea after all.

I mentioned Izaak Walton earlier, but another famous fisherman also plied these waters: Charles Kingsley, the Victorian clergyman and author best remembered for his children's story *The Water-Babies*. Many claim that Kingsley was inspired to write the novel by a stay at the Trout Inn, in Itchen Abbas, during a fishing holiday in 1862. However, I suspect that, like much local folklore, the story has changed in the telling. The truth is that when he arrived at the Trout in the spring of 1862 (then called the Plough), the book was already well underway, but Kingsley did work on parts of chapter six during his stay. Kingsley's widow, in a biography of her husband published shortly after his death, remembered how the book came to be:

> *Sitting at breakfast at the rectory one spring morning, [Kingsley] was reminded of an old promise, "Rose, Maurice, Mary have got their book and baby must have his." He made no answer, but got up at once and went into his study, locking the door. In half an hour he returned with the story of little Tom. This was the first chapter of "The Waterbabies," written off without a correction.*

*The rest of the book, which appeared monthly in "Macmillan's
Magazine," was composed with the same rapidity and ease as
the first chapter—if indeed what was so purely an inspiration
could be called composing, for the whole thing seemed to flow
naturally out of his brain and heart, lightening both of a burden
without exhausting either; and the copy went up to the printer's
with scarcely a flaw. He was quite unprepared for the sensation it
would make."*[8]

I only wish writing were that easy for me. Imagine, a whole
chapter in half an hour. I struggle for weeks to get the first draft
down, then revise again and again, draft after draft, endlessly.
Perhaps, for Kingsley, the setting and the subject matter helped
speed things along.

The Water-Babies is a curious book, not much read today because
of some of its prejudices, but tremendously popular during the author's
lifetime and for several decades following his death. It is the story
of an abused chimney sweep named Tom who, wrongly accused of
theft, runs away and falls into a river where he is transformed into
a "water baby," a tiny human-like creature with gills. Tom has many
adventures until he is finally redeemed by helping the very master
who had mistreated him and is restored to human form.

Kingsley clearly loved the natural world of a trout stream,
which he observed closely. When Tom falls into the water, Kingsley
compares his transformation to that of a caddis fly:

*The fairies had washed him, you see, in the swift river, so
thoroughly, that not only his dirt, but his whole husk and shell
had been washed quite off him, and the pretty little real Tom was
washed out of the inside of it, and swam away, as a caddis does
when its case of stones and silk is bored through, and away it goes
on its back, paddling to the shore, there to split its skin, and fly
away as a caperer, on four fawn-coloured wings, with long legs
and horns.*[9]

Standing on the bridge over the Itchen, looking down into the clean water and seeing the tresses of weed waving in the current, I begin to understand just how much of the story came from Kingsley's experience of standing thigh deep in the cool water, waving a bamboo rod in pursuit of a fish.

Not far from Itchen Abbas I pass a pub called the Bush Inn, which is doing a roaring business on the bank holiday with families picnicking on the lawn and children wading on the banks of the Itchen holding dip nets. I see dozens of small trout in the streams hereabout, confirming the river as a mecca for fishermen. Narrow East Lane is cool and lined with tall ivy-clad beeches, but treacherous for the pilgrim, for the single lane is bounded by water-filled ditches and busy with traffic. I cross a hectic traffic circle and enter the outer reaches of New Alresford, past stinking watercress beds and industrial building lots to modern stuccoed suburbs.

In a scraggy copse on the edge of town I spy two buck rabbits in a fierce dust-up. They leap at each other again and again, landing belly to belly, kicking out with their powerful hind legs. It's a savage spectacle. Their back claws rip out so much fur that the air is thick with it, like exploding dandelion seed pods. The fur is, quite literally and idiomatically, flying.

I trudge up a steep hill and pass over a railway bridge, pausing to peer down on the terminus of the Watercress Line, a heritage railway restored by local steam rail enthusiasts. The name reflects a time when this railway was used to transport fresh watercress from the ponds of Alresford to the markets of London to feed the growing metropolis. The restored station looks like a film set for railway's golden age, a reminder of a how much the railroad must have changed the Victorian countryside, when journeys that used to take weeks could now be accomplished in hours. A quiet path takes me through the old churchyard and down a narrow lane to the centre of New Alresford and the Swan.

The Swan has been around for quite a long time. The first reference to it is in 1552, where it is listed in the census along with a court, garden and barn, located on Sheepcote Street (now West Street), a reference to Alresford's importance in the medieval cloth trade. An interesting feature of the hotel is the massive brick undercroft, then used for storage, but now converted to a banqueting hall for weddings. During the Napoleonic wars, the undercroft served briefly as a prison for French officers.

I enter the lobby of the hotel, passing through the lounge, which is full of whiskered men in tweed, nursing pints and holding tiny dogs in their laps. I look briefly at the menu and decide I can't afford to eat in the hotel. Once I check in and dump my backpack, I set off to explore the town, following the bucolic Riverwalk to see the ancient fulling mill. Coming back up Broad Street, I stop to browse a second-hand book shop, one of the few businesses open on the bank holiday, and pick up a copy of Julia Cartwright's *The Pilgrims' Way* for just £3. Even though I'd told Derek I had no room in my luggage for extra books, it seems too good a deal to pass up.

New Alresford suffered during the Civil War. After the battle of Cheriton, retreating Royalists tried to raze the town and many houses were burned to the ground. As a result, the main street is very uniform architecturally, with beautiful Georgian-style homes lining both sides painted in pastel colours. I pick up a sandwich and some apples at the local grocery coop to eat in my room.

It has taken me just four and a half hours to walk from Winchester to New Alresford, but I estimated it would take me half that time, since it is only nine miles, my shortest day of walking on the trip. What I hadn't calculated on were the dozens of little stops I would make along the way to take photos or to explore village churches. I may have to set a better pace in the coming days. I'm not really worried about the distances I will be covering—the Pilgrims' Way is, after all, a relatively easy trail—but I am worried about my feet, for I'm committing the cardinal sin of long-distance walkers, I'm starting a journey in a new pair of boots.

To be fair, I hadn't intended to. I meant to have my new boots broken in long before I arrived in Winchester, but I just hadn't had the opportunity. My old boots, which I had loved and which had served me faithfully for many years, had blown apart the previous summer, so I had purchased a new pair over the winter, confident I would have plenty of time to break them in before I travelled to England. But the winter of 2013–2014 was one of the longest in living memory. The snow came early, and it stayed. The trails I normally walked were buried thigh deep in snow well into April, so I never got much of a chance to try out my new boots except around the house and when running errands in town. Indeed, there were still patches of snow in the woods behind my house when I left for England on May 3.

Worse still, my new boots are an unfamiliar brand. Try as I might, I couldn't locate another pair of my comfortable old favourites, so I had travelled to the Mountain Equipment Coop store in Toronto and tried on about twenty pairs of new boots, walking up and down on wooden ramps under the careful scrutiny of a youthful sales clerk, before I found a pair that felt reasonably comfortable when worn with my orthotic inserts.

Today has been the first real test. It was a short day, but it should indicate if I am going to have any problems. I had briefly debated walking the trail in running shoes, but at the last minute decided to risk my new boots. Now I will find out if that has been a wise decision.

When I reach the privacy of my room, I sit on the edge of the bed and carefully unlace my boots. My feet are sore, but that is to be expected. I peel off my socks and carefully inspect my feet, looking for abrasions or the hot spots that predict the formation of a blister. But they are fine. My feet look great—much better than I have any right to expect. I breathe a sigh of relief. But as I will find in the coming days, my relief is premature.

Nevertheless, I go to bed reassured. Day one has been pleasant, if unenlightening. And I still have two weeks of walking before me in which to meditate on my spiritual health.

Before I fall asleep, I dip back into *Pilgrim's Progress*. When I last left Christian, he had passed his first tests and had entered the wicket gate. Now he finds himself at the house of the Interpreter, Bunyan's stand-in for the Holy Spirit, who takes him on a tour of the house, where each room is arranged in an instructive tableau. I skim these pages. There is too much expostulating for my liking, but things begin to pick up again once he continues his journey. Beyond the Interpreter's house, Christian comes to the foot of a cross on a small hill, and suddenly the burden of sin slips from his shoulder and rolls down the hill into an open sepulcher. Three angels appear and tell him that all his sins are now forgiven. They clothe him in a pilgrim's garb, set a mark upon his forehead, and give him a "Roll with a Seal upon it" to comfort him on the road ahead and to serve as a kind of passport into the Celestial City.

Not for the first time, I wonder if I too shouldn't have adopted some badge of intent to mark me out as a pilgrim, a scallop shell, perhaps, sewn to the brim of my hat or a pilgrim's staff.

"Who are you kidding?" I hear my father say. "You were painfully shy as a child. You never wanted to stand out. You hated it when your mother signed you up for art classes or tennis lessons. Just enjoy the journey."

Good night, Dad, I whisper, marking the page in the book and reaching for the bedside lamp.

3

New Alresford
to Alton

—————

Ah! There is nothing like staying home for real comfort.
—JANE AUSTEN, *Emma.*

I RISE AT ABOUT SIX O'CLOCK after sleeping fretfully. The Swan
has character, but bad plumbing. The pipes groan and rattle each
time a toilet is flushed, and the noise from the pub and beer garden
in the courtyard below carries into my room all evening. Even with
the windows closed, it takes me quite some time to settle down and
fall asleep. After breakfast, I walk past the church in the centre of
Alresford again and pause to read the tombstones along the wall
opposite the west door. The memorials are written in French, and
the headstones mark the graves of four French officers and one offi-
cer's wife who died in Alresford as prisoners during the Napoleonic
war. I wonder if they were held in the undercroft of the Swan. Their

headstones do not mention the cause of their deaths. Did they die of jail fever? Heartbreak? Wounds received in battle? Or were they executed for breaking their parole?

I retrace my steps of the day before, passing over the picturesque railway depot, past the busy local school with Range Rovers and BMWs pulled out all along the verge, dropping off neatly uniformed children. At the bottom of the hill I turn left on Whitehill Lane. This bit is not much fun, since I am sharing the road with the morning commuter traffic, but I soon leave the road at Bishop's Sutton. I stop for a break and a drink of water at St. Nicholas Church. The original Norman doorway is fascinating. A row of weird bird-faced creatures, straight out of a Pieter Bruegel nightmare landscape, rest their beaks on the arch above the door, scrutinizing those who pass beneath.

The path leading out of Bishop's Sutton, a flooded lane contained between two dense hedges, is a disaster, and later I will wish I had stuck to the road. My new hiking boots have been advertised as waterproof, so I plunge in. As it happens, they are not, and I walk the rest of the day in squelching socks. By evening, I will have a large blister on my left heel and smaller blisters on the small toes of each foot. These will need continual draining and taping for the rest of the trip.

A pair of pied wagtails harasses me as I cross a ploughed field. I must have been treading close to their nest, for they buzz and dive-bomb me in squeaky desperation, with angry cries that remind me of a busy fox terrier chomping on a rubber chew toy. I dash across the busy A31 at a roundabout and set out on a quiet country lane. The A31 would have been the old pilgrims' road at one time but is no longer feasible as a safe route for pedestrians. But my lane runs parallel to the highway, so I don't feel I am cheating too much, and I head cross-country through a series of rolling pastures and woodlots to the little village of Ropley. Just as I climb the hill into Ropley, school lets out for recess, and the sound of children's voices fills the air. At the top of the hill sits an ancient church with an apron of old graves, and across the road, a post office, several plump thatched cottages, the Church of England primary school, and stunning views in all directions. (Alas, the pretty church in Ropley was lost in a fire not long after I walked past it). Lambs and their dams fill the surrounding fields. In fact, the bleating of hundreds of newborn lambs threatens to drown out the children's cheerful schoolyard shouts. The lambs' tails have yet to drop off, and they wag them like happy puppies as they suckle at their mothers' teats. The ewes are branded with multiple layers of coloured spray paint, which soak into their shaggy coats in inscrutable palimpsest with a meaning known only to their owners. It is as if a mad posse of vandals invaded the fields during the night and tagged the sheep like railway boxcars. Descending from Ropley and crossing a broad valley, I briefly lose my way in Old Down Wood, where recent logging has obscured the trail, but carpets of bluebells are my reward. Exiting the wood, I flush a family of Hungarian pheasants and, later, a pair of grey partridge from a hawthorn hedge.

The path underfoot is earth packed with sharp flints. They stud the chalky soil like raisins in a pudding. I am reminded of one of my favourite passages in Robert Louis Stevenson's *Travels with a Donkey in the Cevennes*, one of the best justifications for walking I have ever read:

> *For my part, I travel not to go anywhere, but to go. I travel for travel's sake. The great affair is to move; to feel the needs and hitches of our life more clearly; to come down off this feather-bed of civilization, and find the globe granite underfoot and strewn with cutting flints.*[1]

I have never understood the reference to "cutting flints" before. Now I do. Even with the best boots in the world, the flints bruise the soles of my feet. I hope Stevenson is right about the other thing as well—that a long walk will cut through the distractions and help me to see my life more clearly.

From Ropley, it's a short easy walk to Chawton. Chawton is famous as the home of the novelist Jane Austen. She lived in a two-storey brick house that stands in the centre of town, and which had once served as the bailiff's house for the local estate of Chawton Manor. A childless couple named Knight, who owned the estate, had adopted Jane's elder brother Edward as their heir. The Austens and Knights were cousins, so it wasn't such an unusual thing to do at the time. When Edward inherited, the house was standing empty, so he established his widowed mother and his two unmarried sisters here along with their servants. It is a comfortable house, if a bit cramped, and I imagine Jane was quite happy here. She was certainly very productive. While she lived in Chawton, she revised *Sense and Sensibility* (published in 1811) and *Pride and Prejudice* (1813), and wrote *Mansfield Park* (1814), *Emma* (1815), *Northanger Abbey* (1818), and *Persuasion* (1818). I thought it curious that the memorial stone I had seen in Winchester Cathedral did not mention her writing, but simply referenced her virtues. The stone had been erected in her memory by her other brothers, who were both naval officers. Visiting the museum helped to explain this. There is a great deal of information about these brothers, who visited their sisters and mother at Chawton whenever possible. No doubt their feelings on the stone slab were sincere. Jane looked after their mother while they were off sinking French ships and winning glory for England. She kept the family together. She was the dutiful daughter. I never really thought of Jane Austen like that before. There is a story, often told about Jane Austen, that she kept her writing secret. And this story is reinforced in the museum. Her writing table and chair are preserved in the dining room of the house. They sit right in front of a large mullioned window that overlooks the street—a quiet place to reflect and watch the world go by. The story goes that the door into the dining room had a loud squeak, and that Jane never had it fixed, for it served as a warning should someone, a visitor perhaps, enter the room unannounced. When she heard the squeak, she could quickly slip her writing under a blotter or her sewing before the visitor entered the room. But I wonder if this story stands up. It is true that her stories were published anonymously "by a lady," but that was the convention at the time, since a true lady of standing would never tarnish her reputation by doing something as vulgar as penning a romantic novel, then considered a rather low form of entertainment. But I can't imagine she kept her writing a secret from anyone she knew, and certain passages in her letters indicate she took a keen interest in the fate of her books and that they were discussed with friends and family. Her royalties were mentioned in her will. The truth is that walking through her home doesn't really give me any better sense of Jane Austen as a person than reading her books did. She is still a bit of a cipher.

However, I do come away with a greater admiration for Austen's achievement. It can't have been easy to write and run a busy household. How *do* you live a contemplative or artistic life when daily responsibilities interfere? How *do* you devote time to yourself and to your art, when society expects you to do something else? Has there ever been an artist who hasn't been at least a little bit selfish? How do you balance your needs against the needs of others? I am aware that going on a pilgrimage is considered a privilege in my culture, even considered self-indulgent. At my age, my father could not have afforded the time or the expense of doing what I am doing now. It had to wait until his retirement (and he didn't retire until age 68). Even in the golden age of pilgrimage only a privileged few could afford to go. I must admit, this troubles me.

Would my father have even gone on a pilgrimage if I hadn't suggested it? Honestly, I don't think he would have. Canterbury Cathedral, though the heart of Anglicanism, would not have held much meaning for him. It was just a big church. His heart was in the simple red brick church where he taught Sunday school, led songs with his guitar and even, on occasion, dressed up as a clown to entertain the kids. My father didn't need this walk, not the way I do. For him it would have been a fun way to spend some time with his son. He had, I begin to realize, a talent for living in the moment. Something I have yet to learn.

The path from Chawton to Alton, where I will be spending the night, is fairly short, and there is still one more place I hope to visit today, but it is a bit off the beaten track. However, the volunteer in the gift shop assures me I can reach it by bus, and that the bus will collect me right outside Jane Austen's door, and, if I hurry, the next bus will leave in five minutes. Thus, I am able to step directly from one adventure into another.

The bus is a long double-decker, and the road a rolling and twisting country lane bounded by high hedges. I climb to the second deck to enjoy a sweeping view of the surrounding countryside. For the driver, however, it must be very much like driving down a long, green tunnel. I think this is the place to record my admiration for British bus drivers. Along much of the route there seems barely enough room for the bus itself to squeeze through, let alone allow oncoming traffic to pass, and in places the hawthorn hedge brushes the window as we swoop by, and yet the driver never reduces speed, nor is there even a hint of concern, not so much as a scraped side mirror. I wonder if it was while riding on a bus such as this that J.K. Rowling dreamed up the Knight Bus of the Harry Potter novels.

My destination is the tiny village of Selborne, a place made famous by a retiring country curate named Gilbert White in a book called *The Natural History and Antiquities of Selborne*. The book has charmed generations of readers for over two hundred years in more than one hundred editions and has never been out of print. White was completely fascinated by the natural world. He had a comfortable home in Selborne, called the Wakes, which he had inherited from his grandfather. It had extensive gardens that he designed, and, thanks to a secure income, White was left with a lot of free time to pursue his vocation as an amateur naturalist. For close to forty years, he filled his notebooks with observations of the natural world—observations he later shared in letters to fellow naturalists. This correspondence formed the germ of his famous book.

It is useful to compare White's *Natural History*, published in 1789, with Izaak Walton's *Compleat Angler*, published 130 years earlier. Walton's *Compleat Angler*, delightful as it is, is a scrapbook of received knowledge on the subject of fish and fishing techniques. Walton, a high church Anglican, believed in the power of a higher authority, so he quoted liberally from classical authors to explain the goings-on in the natural world. This sometimes led to risible results, such as the ones alluded to in my earlier "conversation" with the Walton in the stained-glass window. These ideas include the suggestions (inspired by Conrad Gesner, sixteenth century Swiss physician) that pike are generated from pickerel weed left out in the hot sun or that certain tiny flies are born out of the dew which gathered on certain flowers.

White, on the other hand, relied on his own observations to explain the natural world. He was a scientist, a contemporary of Rousseau and Diderot, a product of the Enlightenment, and so, a man of his time. He kept careful records of the birds he observed and recorded their habits. He wrote about the insects in his garden and took particular note of the earthworms. He recorded when each of the plants in his neighbourhood sprouted, when they burst into bloom, and when they went to seed. He kept detailed records of his own garden experiments, listing how much he had planted in each bed and how much each bed had yielded. One sometimes wonders what he, a single gentleman living on his own with only a few servants, meant to do with six hundred-plus heads of cabbage? He talked to his rural neighbours, recorded their anecdotes and observations, and included these in his book. Many of his observations have been superseded by more recent discoveries, and some of his conclusions have proven erroneous, but I do not read White to gain scientific knowledge. I read him for the sheer pleasure of his prose and for a glimpse of English village life in the eighteenth century, a time when most Englishmen rarely left the boundaries of their parish and when travel meant a long and uncomfortable coach ride, bouncing over rutted roads in poorly sprung wooden boxes. I read him, too, because I like White. His personality, his gentleness and humanity, shine through on every page, especially when he is observing his pet tortoise, Timothy, gambolling about the garden. White might also be called an early conservationist, for he did his best to preserve the countryside as he found it. The Hanger, the oak-draped scarp that leans out over the village, is still there largely because he celebrated it in prose.

The village of Selborne is strung along a narrow road with the Hanger to the west and steep hills and valleys to the east. It is picture postcard perfect, and it still resembles the etched illustrations found in my edition of *The Natural History*. It has its share of timber-framed thatched cottages, brick villas draped in wisteria, two ancient pubs, and an attractive village green called the Plestor, with a seat circling the trunk of a large plane tree. (White explained the name by saying that "plestor" came from the Anglo-Saxon word "play-stow" meaning a playground). It has an impressive rectory beside an ancient parish church, and a large humped graveyard full of gnarled yews. And, of course, it also contains the Wakes, Gilbert White's old house, which is now a museum. The only thing that spoils Selborne is the traffic, for the single lane running through the village is choked with cars. When I step off the bus, a brewery van has stopped to unload outside one of the pubs and it blocks half the street, forcing traffic to take turns squeezing past. It's a hot day and the noise of the traffic, its proximity, and the choking exhaust make the street stressful to walk along.

Once you're in the museum, though, the traffic is forgotten. White's comfortable home turns its back on the high road, facing instead the meadows below the Hanger. The view through the large windows of the hall and library are much as they would have been in White's day. There is a waxwork statue of White in the study, dressed in black clerical garb, and I am surprised to see how short and slight he was. Somehow, reading his prose, I had pictured him as a large bluff roast-pudding of a man, a typical country squire, but he was quite the opposite: tiny, gentle, almost mousy.

When the White house was in danger of being lost, a book collector named Robert Washington Oates bought the house in 1954 to preserve it on the understanding that it would also serve as a memorial to two famous members of his family. It's an odd association. White was a retiring man who spent most of his life writing about the village where he was born, whereas the Oates boys, an uncle and nephew, were world travellers and adventurers in the heroic mould of the British Empire. Captain Lawrence Oates, a veteran of the Boer War, is best remembered as a member of Robert Scott's ill-fated Antarctic Expedition of 1911–12. He was one of the small party, led by Scott, who made the dash to the South Pole using Shetland ponies and sleds, hoping to be the first men to stand on the southernmost point of the globe. As they were returning from the Pole, exhausted (having lost all of their ponies to the bitter cold), frostbitten, starving, savaged and delayed by ferocious blizzards, and disheartened because they had lost the race to the Norwegian Amundsen (who had used sled dogs and was better prepared) Oates valiantly sacrificed his own life in hopes that the others might survive. His last words, as he left Scott and his companions in the storm-battered tent, were, "I am just going outside and I may be some time." His body was never found.[2]

His uncle, Frank Oates, was a naturalist-explorer who travelled across Central and North America and later Africa. A stunning display of his Central American bird specimens is found on the second floor. Frank Oates also lost his life far from home, having contracted a fever in Africa while returning from an expedition to Victoria Falls. His brother later edited and published Oates's African journals and sketches as *Matabele Land and Victoria Falls: A Naturalist's Wanderings in the Interior of South Africa* (1881), giving him posthumous fame. While I find the Oates displays interesting,

I also find the experience of descending the stairs and returning to the less bumptious eighteenth-century world of Gilbert White rather jarring.

After a stroll through the carefully restored gardens, I head to the village church. White's grave is tucked away behind the church and is marked with a simple headstone, engraved with his initials, "G.W.," and the dates of his birth and death. A humble grave for an unassuming man. There is a more grandiose memorial in the church itself, but that is actually for White's grandfather, also named Gilbert, a clergyman and founder of the village school, who is frequently confused with his more famous grandson.

I sit on a lichen-encrusted bench overlooking the steep valley behind the churchyard. The air is full of birdsong. The sun shines brightly. Fleecy clouds meander across the sky. I munch an apple from my pack and take a long swig of water from my Nalgene bottle, musing on the life of Gilbert White. He never married, his career in the church was marginal, and he never really did anything but take careful and affectionate note of everything around him and share these observations with a few likeminded correspondents. In its quiet way, his was a useful life. He followed the tenets of Voltaire's *Candide*—that true happiness lies, not in great deeds or great wealth, but in cultivating one's garden—and two hundred years later we are still reading about his enthusiasms. I wonder, too, if a place doesn't really come into its own until it has its chronicler. If White had not written of these hills and trees, their denizens and feathered inhabitants, would they still contain the same glow of recognition that makes us value them today?

I catch the last bus of the day, and within fifteen minutes I am in Alton.

| Derek had suggested we get together that evening in Alton for dinner. I think he wanted to reassure himself that I am making out okay on my own. But my side trip to Selborne has put me behind schedule, and by the time I check into my hotel, have a

quick shower and put on a fresh T-shirt, I am running late. Derek is staying in a pub several blocks away. It's definitely not in the same tax bracket as the room he's booked for me. Outside Derek's pub, on the sidewalk, a burly young man with a shaved head and a spider web tattooed on his neck is screaming into a cellphone. He is decked out in shiny new orange high-top sneakers, a fluorescent green tracksuit, and a spotless New York Yankees baseball cap twisted sideways on his polished head. Between the fingers of his left hand, a cigarette hangs neglected, dripping ash as he waves it about. In his right hand, the cellphone is held, not to his ear, but to his face, as he screams abuse into the screen, bending at the waist as he does so, as if to drive his message home. I can't understand a word coming out of his mouth, because it's all slang, delivered in a dialect so thick it might as well have been a foreign language. I slip into the pub and leave him to it.

Inside, things are not much better. I have already discovered in my short time in England that there are pubs, and then there are pubs. Some are congenial communal living spaces where you can safely bring the kids and grandparents, and some, like this one, are hardcore drinking establishments. Behind the bar, a stone-faced barmaid is looking at her fingernails, as a sloppy drunk alternately pleads and cajoles, weeps and threatens.

"Time to go, Sylvia," says the barmaid in an even tone, not meeting the now weeping woman's eyes. "You've been asked politely."

The other customers, I note, are looking away and quietly nursing their pints.

The weeping drunk suddenly turns vicious. "Bitch!" she spits.

Good time for me to step in.

"Excuse me. Sorry to interrupt. I was supposed to meet a friend here, Derek Bright, but I was held up. Do you know if he's been in?"

The barmaid turns to me and smiles. Her eyes are saying, "Thank you, thank you, thank you."

"I believe he's staying here," I add.

Her eyes go out of focus for a moment, as if she is consulting some internal filing system behind her eyelids, then she smiles again. "Yes. If you would like to follow me, I can show you to his room." As we leave the bar, I notice an older woman approach the weeping drunk and guide her by the elbow toward the door, muttering, "I know, love, I know..."

I find Derek in a corner room at the back overlooking the parking lot, a room that is actually taller than it is wide and where the bed occupies most of the floor space. The coverlet is strewn with crisp sheets of paper. They are, he explains, the galley proofs for his new book.

"More English history?"

"Actually, no. It's about my other passion, the blues. I've always loved blues music, even taught myself guitar, so I could play. A few years ago, I went to America and travelled the blues highway—Highway 61—from Chicago to the Mississippi Delta. My pilgrimage, I suppose. The book's about that journey."

"How does it look?"

"The pictures turned out okay, better than expected actually, and I haven't found any typos. The layout is okay, too. I don't know. I can still see things I would like to change, but there comes a point when you just have to say, 'I've done the best I can,' and let it go."

We head back out into the street and he asks me how the day's walk has gone. "Terrific," I say and tell him of my side trip to Selborne, but I can see it draws a blank. He has never heard of Gilbert White or his book, but he is interested and asks for details. I suspect Selborne might find itself on the itinerary of future walkers.

"You're not in any hurry to eat, are you?" he asks. I assure him I am not. "Then let's walk to the church. I always like to show walkers the church, if I get a chance. It should still be open." As we walk, Derek continues. "There was a large battle outside of Alton during the Civil War, which the Royalists lost. As the Royalist Army retreated through Alton on their way to Winchester, they left behind a small force commanded by Sir Richard Boles to cover their retreat. It was a fighting retreat, bitter fighting, and the survivors fell back on the churchyard. Eventually, Boles and the surviving rear guard barricaded themselves in the church."

We cross the street and follow a diagonal path through the churchyard to the south porch of the Church of St. Lawrence. We pass beneath the Norman arch into the cool shade of the porch and pause before a massive oak door tarred black.

"I'm glad they never replaced this door," he continues. "You can see where the musket balls have struck it, here and here, and," he points to a star-shaped hole that went right through the planks, "you can see where someone jabbed a halberd, trying to force the door. The Royalists barred the door behind them and built crude scaffolding so that they could shoot down on the surrounding parliamentary troops from the church windows. But it was hopeless. They had nowhere to go."

"How many were left?"

"Contemporary accounts say 'four score.'"

"Did they surrender?"

"No. They were defiant to the end. The parliamentarians lobbed grenades through the windows and broke down the doors with axes." He points to the damage around the lock where gaping holes had been mended with thinner planking. "Let's go inside."

St. Lawrence is a curious old church. Constructed shortly after the Norman Conquest, it has been modified so many times over the intervening years that the current structure is a mongrel blend of periods and styles—though not unattractive. When it was decided to enlarge the church in the fifteenth century, they removed the northern wall of the nave, replaced it with seven arches supported by stout pillars and then created a mirror church beside the first, so that the resulting structure had two naves, two choirs and two chancels in tandem, constructed side-by-side-by-side, like twin lanes in a bowling alley.

Derek carries on with his story. "As the parliamentarians forced the door, the royalists fell back toward the chancel in the northeast corner." He points to pock marks in the heavy pillars where musket balls have chipped the stone. We pause before a glass display case, which holds some relics of the battle: a clay pipe, some musket balls and a uniform button. We walk up the north aisle toward the altar. They must have been standing almost muzzle to muzzle in the end, nearly invisible in the musket smoke. And the sound would have been deafening. The church would have been full of screaming men and with the clash of pikes and swords. Derek directs my attention to a raised hexagonal pulpit on a stone base, which stands free above the level of the pews like a tiny tower. "They say Colonel Boles made his last stand there and died on those stone steps."

"My God," I remark. "It was brave, I suppose, but insane. Why didn't he negotiate a surrender?"

"Civil wars are vicious affairs. Boles threatened to kill any man who asked for quarter. Perhaps some were spared." He shrugs. "There's a memorial to Sir Richard around here somewhere." We find it, a brass placard set into one of the pillars. It reads in part:

> Alton will tell you of that famous Fight
> Which ye man made & bade this world good night
> His verteous Life fear'd not Mortalyty
> His Body must, his Vertues cannot Die
> Because his Bloud was there so nobly spent
> This is his Tombe that Church his Monument

The final line makes no sense at first, until we realize that we are reading an exact copy of the memorial brass found in Winchester Cathedral above Sir Richard's tomb.

I find it reassuring that this history is preserved, even though it is rather ugly. In Tiananmen Square, the bullet holes in the Monument to the Heroes of the Revolution have been filled in. The massacre of just thirty years before is largely forgotten. But here, people talk about history as if it happened yesterday. Derek made Sir Richard Boles feel very much alive to me. If we are to understand how we got to where we are now, we need the past. After all, walking a pilgrimage is really just walking in the footsteps of those who have gone before, and there is some comfort in knowing that.

As we leave the church and close the scarred door behind us, Derek points to the towering evergreens flanking the walk. "Did you notice those on the way in?" I hadn't. "I've always found them curious. They aren't native to Britain and yet they are obviously hundreds of years old. Do you know what they are?"

I look closely. They are enormous and remind me of the temple trees near the monastery where I had lived for two years in eastern Bhutan. "Cypress?"

Derek seems impressed but shakes his head. "They are actually cedars of Lebanon," and then forestalling any questions, continues, "I actually have no idea how they got here. Some tourist in the eighteenth century perhaps, returning from the Holy Land? Hungry? Let's get something to eat."

And we do. I have a delicious stone-baked pizza with spinach, sundried tomato and goat's cheese, and he a plate of spaghetti Bolognese, and we talk long of family and careers. We wander back to our lodgings in the warm spring night and promise to meet up again in two days. I go straight to bed, for Derek has warned me that the following day will be my longest, and I want to be well rested.

4

Alton to Farnham

Those who make pilgrimages do so for many reasons, very seldom for legitimate ones.

—MARTIN LUTHER, *Works*

I SLEEP BETTER ON MY THIRD NIGHT. Rising early, I am out the door of the Alton House Hotel in good time. I dodge through sleepy suburban streets, passing children on their way to school. High school kids in their uniforms slouch past, shoulders hunched, heads down, earbuds in. A pair of stout girls in matching kilts walks silently in tandem, texting on their cellphones, lost in digital space. I seem to be the only one paying attention to my surroundings, and this saddens me. But, to be fair, I am the one with the day off, and everything in this dreary suburban landscape is new to me. They have seen it a hundred times before. I follow a bike path to the edge of town, cross a football field, and then loop around the playing fields of a high school and a local college on an overgrown bridle path. I stop at Holybourne Church, set in a pretty green bower next to a duck pond, and admire its witch's hat steeple. There is a fading garland of roses over the door, suggesting that there might have been a wedding in the church over the weekend. Beyond Holybourne, my map indicates a Roman settlement with a Roman road, but it's well-hidden beneath a blanket of canola in brilliant yellow. I look in vain for the point where the Roman road, marked on my map, crosses my path, but can't find it, which somewhat dampens my fantasy of being a field archaeologist on BBC's *Time Team*.

By this time, the skies are growing grey and overcast, and a light rain is beginning to fall. My next landmark, the village of Upper Froyle, is the first non-pretty village I encounter on my walk. The large Jacobean manor in the centre of the village is now a hotel specializing in weddings and business conferences, but had been, until quite recently, a charitable school for boys and girls with disabilities.

The grounds around the manor are being torn up by back-hoes and bulldozers, and a billboard promises "luxury estates." But it seems sad. My trail winds around the wall of the manor and proceeds down a long tree-lined avenue, hinting at an elegant history. The view over my shoulder is still impressive, very Downton Abbeyesque, but I wonder how long it will last. Curious too are the trees themselves. Each one has been clumsily pollarded at some date in the distant past, and the resulting silhouette is spoiled by a rookery of new growth at the top of each tree, like twin rows of giant toilet brushes pointing at the sky. Why?

Over the next dozen miles or so, I pass many such estates. Some are still working farms, and one, Pax Hill, which had once been the home of Lord Baden-Powell, the founder of the Boy Scouts movement, is now a nursing home for the elderly. Others are obviously the retreats of the wealthy, guarded by high brick walls and hedges of hazel and holly, through which I catch glimpses of azalea and rhododendron in bloom, and ranks of candy-striped terracotta chimney pots arranged like banks of grouped artillery pieces aimed at the sky. One, called Jenkyn Place, even has its own cast iron footbridge spanning the public road.

Bentley Church is interesting, chiefly for the walkway leading up to it, which tunnels beneath a copse of ancient yews. Some of these trees are so old and decrepit that their branches are propped up with crutches. In the tiny village of East Green, I pass a working man's cottage, a small timber-framed hut with a crooked tile roof. It's the sort of thing that would have housed a poor day labourer a century ago, but now sports a Jaguar in the driveway. Beyond East Green, I enter a forest called Wallfield Copse with a signpost that reads: "Dogs must be on leash. Game birds." And I do, in fact, flush two grouse. I also see a small deer with a rusty red coat and creep right up upon her before she bounds off into the trees. The woods are full of gnarled grandfather oaks, and I draw an imaginary bow as I follow the deer's progress, feeling like Robin Hood.

From here to Farnham the land is pitched with rolling hills, and I pass green fields dotted with sheep and horses, with the ratio of sheep to horse growing more horsey the closer I draw to Farnham. The woodlands are carpeted with bluebells, and individual hills crowned with more lovely mansions, each with a commanding view of the surrounding countryside. On one particularly muddy track between Old Middle Park and Park Farm, I have to cling to a hedge as a rider, an elderly woman, tries to coax her horse through a deep mud puddle.

"Come on, old girl," she soothes. "Don't like to get your feet wet, do you, pet?"

The horse hesitates. It examines the pool, turns a white-rimmed eye toward me, as if asking my opinion, before finally plunging in. I don't blame it. The horse is wearing fetching blue stockings, and the mud comes up to its knees. A little further on, I walk past a man in faded blue coveralls shearing a sheep on a concrete platform outside a brick barn. I nod good morning, but both man and sheep ignore me.

I enter Farnham from the north, descending to the town on the shoulder of a curving highway that winds its way around the moat of Farnham Castle. It's a steep narrow defile and the traffic is backed up all the way to the top of the hill. Diesel exhaust from idling trucks makes it hard to breathe. I dodge across traffic and climb to the top of the castle, which has lain in ruins ever since the Civil War, when—since it guarded an important crossroads—it was fought over and defended by both Royalists and Parliamentarians. The Parliamentarians eventually dismantled it, so that it would no longer be a source of contention. The more modern Bishop's Palace, which is attached to the castle, was once the home of the Bishops of Winchester, and, for a while, housed the writer Izaak Walton when his friend Bishop Morley was resident bishop. As I descend the hill, past stalled traffic, it starts to rain in earnest. Buckets of rain, cauldrons of the stuff, a Biblical deluge. I take shelter in old St. Andrew's Church, which is hidden in the heart of Farnham in a green and tumbled churchyard surrounded and overshadowed by commercial buildings that have turned their backs on it. It's cool and dim in the echoing church, and I leave puddles of water wherever I stop on the uneven flags. I find a memorial to Augustus Toplady, the composer who wrote the hymn "Rock of Ages," but my goal is to find the memorial to Farnham's most famous son, the political pamphleteer and member of parliament William Cobbett. I locate it high on the wall near the bell tower. It has a nice marbled profile of the old curmudgeon and was placed there by a fellow MP, John Fielden. (Cobbett is buried in a prominent altar tomb in the churchyard behind a green iron fence, but I don't linger in the rain to read the inscription).

Son of a local publican and farmer, William Cobbett became England's most famous radical journalist. Born in a pub called the Jolly Farmer in 1763, Cobbett's first job was as a gardener's assistant in the Bishop's Palace up the hill. He later ran away from home, went to London and became a lawyer's clerk. Then he joined the army and quickly rose to the rank of regimental sergeant major. His attempt to expose some senior officers who were fiddling the books became his first brush with prosecution and forced him to move to France and later to America, where his pugnacious sense of right and wrong involved him in more lawsuits. While in America, he wrote an attack on Thomas Paine that he would later regret, and he would try to make amends by repatriating Paine's bones to England for reburial. Throughout his career as a journalist, Cobbett was a defender of the rights of the common man, particularly the farm labourer, and he was fiercely devoted to the English rural way of life, calling London "the Wen" (or "the boil"). Today, he is best remembered for a series of columns, explorations of the English countryside on horseback, which he wrote for his own radical newspaper, the *Political Register*, and which were later collected and published as *Rural Rides* in 1830. *Rural Rides* has had its share of admirers over the years, from Ruskin to Dickens to Marx, but it is also valued by historians for the picture it captures of England just as it underwent great change: Cobbett commented on the depopulation of the countryside and the death of rural traditions, the enclosure of the commons, the rise of the industrial revolution, and the growth of capitalism and international trade. He would have hated the car traffic in Farnham and the growth of the commuter belt in today's England, just as he hated seeing poor people kicked off their land to create larger estates for absentee landlords in his own.

Cobbett is also of interest to me because his *Rural Rides* carried him all over southern England, particularly around the counties through which I am walking. We are covering the same ground, though two hundred years separates us. Cobbett loved this countryside. Curiously, he visited Selborne for much the same reason as I did: "I was desirous of seeing this village, about which I have read in the book of Mr. White, and which a reader [of the *Political*

Register] has been so good as to send me." Sitting upon his horse and looking down on Selborne from the hill above, he remarked:

> The village of Selborne is precisely what it is described by Mr.
> White. A straggling irregular street, bearing all the marks of great
> antiquity, and showing, from its lanes and its vicinage generally,
> that it was once a very considerable place. I went to look at the
> spot where Mr. White supposes the convent formerly stood. It is
> very beautiful. Nothing can surpass in beauty these dells and hill-
> ocks and hangers, which last are so steep that it is impossible to
> ascend them, except by means of a serpentine path....The church-
> yard of Selborne is most beautifully situated. The land is good, all
> about it. The trees are luxuriant and prone to be lofty and large.
> I measured the yew-tree in the churchyard, and found the trunk to
> be, according to my measurement, twenty-three feet, eight inches,
> in circumference. The trunk is very short, as is generally the case
> with yew-trees; but the head spreads to a very great extent, and
> the whole tree, though probably several centuries old, appears to
> be in perfect health.[1]

Alas, the famous yew celebrated by both White and Cobbett is no more. A fierce winter gale in 1990 knocked it down, though the stump remains to astound travellers by its great girth. Nevertheless, this gives you some sense of the countryside cele-brated by Cobbett. He also notes that the grape vines in Selborne, though badly pruned, were yielding vast quantities of delicious fruit (which he sampled), when he visited in 1823, but he observes that the hops, an important local crop, were failing and "full as black as a sooty bag or dingy coal-sack, and covered with lice," which he notes disparagingly, will please "the over-production men."[2] In this remark we see some of his irascibility, but we can also see some of his humour in another passing observation. Seeing such a beautiful valley, he remarks to a farmer that everyone who lives here must be happy. The scowling farmer says, nay, "he did not believe there was a more unhappy place in England: for that there were always quarrels of some sort going on," which, I suppose, just goes to prove that people are people wherever you go.

When I leave the church, the rain has tapered to a steady drizzle. Farnham has the reputation of being the best-preserved Georgian town in England, but somehow, I am no longer in the mood for sightseeing. Perhaps it's the rain, perhaps it's my sore feet, but I keep my tour of Farnham short. I walk to the pub of Cobbett's birth, now called the Cobbett, but I can't drum up the enthusiasm to go inside and order a drink. I snap a photo of the outside and decide to carry on, as I still have a mort of walking to do before I reach my destination for the night.

When Daniel Boone, the famous frontiersman, was once asked if he ever got lost in the woods, he was said to have answered, "I can't say I was ever lost, but I was bewildered once for three days." After bragging to Derek about my skill with a map and compass, I must confess that I become bewildered for a spell too. It happens like this.

Perhaps because I am in a low mood, or perhaps because of the rain and the fact that I have had my head down much of the time, I misread the map and take a wrong turn. I find myself walking down the wrong side of the river Wey through industrial estates along a path littered with chip wrappers, plastic bottles and other trash. I walk for perhaps a mile before I begin to suspect I have made an error and consult my map again. Once I realize what I've done, I must backtrack and cross the river on a bridge near the train station, where I regain the trail and head out of town. I have lost about half an hour through this foolishness. The only bright spot of this detour is that, amid the old tires and floating bits of Styrofoam on the Wey, I see a type of heron I've never encountered before (the little egret, I later learn). It's small and white with bright yellow feet that make it appear as if the bird is wearing tiny rubber galoshes. I also spy a grey heron and a kind of jay with red stripes. My inability to put names to many of the things I see on my walk bothers me, and I realize that, here in England, I am distinctly flora-and-faunally challenged.

Just past the train station, the trail enters the woods and I come to a curiously carved wooden bench that is meant to resemble a giant bee orchid. This marks the start of the North Downs Way. I am now, according to the note carved on the bench, 153 miles from my goal. From here on, the signposting will be clear, and I am unlikely to get lost again. Not that I was ever really lost, you understand, just briefly bewildered.

The next stretch, as if to make up for my earlier disappointment, is quite lovely—a clearly marked trail through a broad water meadow past elegant old farmhouses and through the yard of an old mill, now converted to apartments. My accommodation for the night is the Princess Royal, an old pub wedged into a strip of land between an old country road and a major highway. I picked up some sandwiches in Farnham, so, after checking in, I retreat to my room, take off my wet clothing and have a hot bath. I rinse out my wool socks, then drape my jacket, trousers and socks over the shower rail to dry. I pull the liners out of my hiking boots and stick the hotel's courtesy hair dryer in each in turn, set on "low." Removing the hair dryer, I stuff balls of newspaper in the toes of each boot to try and draw out as much moisture as possible overnight. I drain a new blister, rub some Polysporin on the old ones, and apply new Band-Aids to the lot. I sit on the bed and flip through the television channels, settling on an old movie, *The Gentle Gunman*, an English film noir starring Dirk Bogarde and John Mills, and eat my sandwiches.

Today is my longest day of hiking so far, and, despite the blisters and the extra miles in Farnham, I have done fine. I should feel chuffed, but I don't. I can't help wondering what I am doing this for. I feel guilty about abandoning my family and about the selfish expense I am incurring. My mind is so wracked with worry that I'm not really enjoying the experience at all. Walking should lead to self-reflection, but my brain is like a hamster wheel, and I can't slow my thoughts enough to think deeply about anything. Have I found myself more contemplative? No. Do I feel any sign of a spiritual awakening? Not at all. On the contrary, I feel like I am heading for a nervous breakdown. I miss my father more than ever. My happiest moment so far has been in Selborne, and perhaps that in itself is a lesson: Don't be afraid of side trips or detours. Now that I know I am physically capable of doing this walk, I should be able to relax, slow down. Lying on my bed and looking at my map, I realize with a start that, for the first time, I am actually on the Pilgrims' Way. The road in front of the Princess Royal is the same Old Road documented by Hilaire Belloc in his book. That thought comforts me somewhat as I turn off the light and go to sleep.

5

Farnham to Newlands Corner

This world is but a thoroughfare full of woe
And we are pilgrims, passing to and fro.
    —CHAUCER, "The Knight's Tale"

IT'S STILL RAINING WHEN I LEAVE the Princess Royal the next morning. I had purchased a nylon pack cover before I left home, and today I break it out for the first time. I am soon glad that I have. I backtrack a little on the first part of walk, because I want to find a mansion called Moor Park—though when I find it, I have to be content with viewing it over a distance, from across a brook and a vast expanse of carefully cropped lawn, under a grey and lowering sky.

In 1689, a young and ambitious Jonathan Swift came to Moor Park to become the secretary to Sir William Temple. It was there that Swift would write _A Tale of a Tub_ and _The Battle of the Books_, satires of, respectively, fundamentalist religion and literary reputation. The job turned out to be a disappointment and not quite the step-up in life he had hoped for; but while at Moor Park, Swift met a young girl, Esther Johnson, the daughter of Lady Temple's companion. Over the years, as Swift left, returned, and left Moor Park again, his regard and affection for Esther blossomed. During his initial time there, Swift acted as Esther's tutor as well as Temple's secretary, but his subsequent relationship with a grown Esther has always been subject to speculation. It was rumoured that they were secretly married, though this was never proven.

Why they never openly declared their love, we can't be sure. His witty and entertaining letters to Esther would later be collected and published as *The Journal to Stella*. Reading between the lines of the correspondence with "Stella," you realize that Swift must have been captivated by her intellect as much as her beauty. You didn't write letters like this to a dullard. On January 28, 1728, Esther died after a lengthy illness. Swift was completely distraught and wrote *On the Death of Mrs. Johnson*, in which he praised her intelligence and grace, and lamented that he had lost, "the truest, most virtuous and valuable friend that I, or perhaps any other person, was ever blessed with."[1] In later years, a lock of hair was discovered in his desk drawer, believed to be Johnson's, labelled, "Only a woman's hair."

With that gloomy thought, I turn and plunge once more into the rain. I follow bridleways for a good part of the morning, through dripping forests on sandy sunken trails, through some quite pretty and ancient woodlands, but it all remains a bit of a blur because of the constant rain. I remember some beautiful views of a high ridge to the north called the Hogsback. Somewhere on the Hogsback, Cobbett bought a farm in later life. There, he was happy working the land, running his seed-selling business, raising his four boys, publishing the *Political Register*, and riding over the countryside, collecting the material that would become the *Rural Rides*. It was at this point in his life that he was most content, but Cobbett was never one to just let things be. As an old man, he successfully ran for parliament and the stress of keeping on top of all of his projects and of dividing his time between his farm and his duties in London drove a wedge between him and his long-suffering wife. He died an exhausted man, but in character.

As I muse on Cobbett's life, head down in the rain, I drift into reverie and the miles pass by unremarked.

I imagine I am walking along a cart track with a tall hedge on one side and a page wire fence on the other. I look up and squint into the sun as a man approaches on horseback. My attention is drawn first to the horse. It's large and chestnut-coloured with hoofs as big as pie plates. An enormous horse. But then I look at the man on its back and realize that such a man requires an enormous horse. He's tall and portly, dressed in brown riding boots, corduroy breeches, and a navy-blue smock coat with brass buttons. His thighs and chest are massive, but not fat, if you know what I mean, just solid. He wears a broad-brimmed hat, and his plump but decisive face is ruddy under a broad forehead and a thatch of grey hair. But it is his eyes that catch your attention. They are very dark—grey, I think—small and set perhaps a little too close together. When his face is turned to me (which it wasn't at first), I feel uncomfortably aware of his intense scrutiny. You suspect not much escapes this man's observation.

He is so much the picture of a country squire that I at first assume he is out riding and examining his own land, but after our initial greeting he sets me straight.

"No," he says, this is not his land, but he knows it very well, for he grew up in this neighbourhood. "It grieves me though to see it like this."

I'm surprised, for the land looks quite fertile and prosperous, so I ask him what he means.

"There was a time when these fields supported four farmers and their families, but now they are all owned by one landlord, who lives in London and farms them as if they were a factory

floor. No hedges, no ditches, no commons, no grassy lanes, just
a countryside divided into a few great fields. Worse still, all of
the produce is trucked to Southampton, where it is shipped to
the Continent for sale. England's strength should be in her countryside. She is blessed with some of the most fertile land in the
world, and though I dislike Shakespeare as a rule, he was in the
right of it when he called her a 'green and pleasant land.' My ideal
is the English village, and a local economy based on agriculture.
A strong yeomanry should be England's treasure, not her foreign
investments."

I ask him if he has read Wendell Berry.

He seems interested, takes a notebook from his pocket and jots
down the name. "An American, you say?"

He turns those piercing grey eyes upon me. "When you first
spoke I thought you were an American, but now I detect something
in your accent that leads me to believe that you were born a bit
further north. Am I correct?"

I admit I am Canadian.

"I knew it! Though I must sympathize. I spent six years in
Nova Scotia and New Brunswick, and did not like it. Not a land for
farmers. Nothing but black, ragged, hideous rocks."

I explain that I am from southern Ontario, and that it is quite
different there. In fact, where I live, it is quite a lush farming country.

"What sort of soil have you there?" he enquires.

"Sand and clay, mostly, I think, but I'm not an expert. But the
land is moderated by a large body of water nearby, and the climate
is such that apples grow quite well."

"Ah, apples," he exclaims. "Did you know that I was responsible
for introducing Newtown Pippins to this country from America?
They are uncommonly large and hardy and bear well. I had hopes
that they would add to the income of rural cottagers. Mr. Waller
near Faversham in Kent has had good success, but I can't say it has
been as widely adopted as I'd hoped. Farmers have small capital for
investment in these troubled times."

I have to admit to him that apple growing in Canada is much the
same as in Surrey: "We used to have a saying that if a man tended
ten acres for ten years, then his apples would look after him for
the rest of his life. Now it's more like a hundred acres, and even
then, it's a dicey proposition. We have to compete with juice from
China and apples flown in from South America. No one wants to
buy a local apple in February, soft from cold storage, when they can
have a fresh crisp one from Chile for the same price. Most of the
smaller farms are being bought up by international corporations
and turned into large factory farms employing foreign labourers."
I explain that even the farming practices are changing, as the new
owners rip up the old trees and replace them with dwarf varieties
espaliered along wires, grown more like grapes than apples. "They
are easier to prune and tend, become mature sooner, and they yield
more fruit per acre, or so I'm told."

He is curious and asks me to draw him a mental picture. He
seems impressed and says that he has planted orchards of his own
and might try something like this on an acreage that has yet to
be planted. You get the impression that he is keen on agricultural
innovation. He asks me the purpose of my walk. I explain that I am
on a pilgrimage to Canterbury.

Well, if that doesn't start him on about religion. I get the
impression that he has very low opinions of clergymen in general—
"magpies," he calls them—and Christian charity in particular. "I
hate it when the Church uses charity to hold a man down. Hand
him a morsel with one hand and beat him with the Bible in the
other, just to keep him in his place. Organized religion, as far as I
can see, has always been a tool of the rich for oppressing the poor.
That idiot Wilberforce! Bleating about the condition of the Negro
slave, and yet telling the poor English working man to meekly
accept his lot in life as God-given. The utter hypocrisy of it! If you
want to help a man, then help him. Help him to stand up. Don't
push him to his knees, and then comfort him with stories of a
better life in the hereafter."

We part, and he recommends a pub in the next village. "It's a hot day," he says. "Nothing better than a pot of light beer on a hot day. Don't let them serve you tea. Worst thing you could do. There is no useful strength in it, nothing nutritious; it weakens your nerves, and keeps you from sleep, thereby robbing the body of much needed rest. On top of that, think of the cost involved in brewing a pot of tea! The time wasted! The precious fuel spent in boiling the water! If every honest housewife in England were to foreswear tea, think of the increase in daily productivity and of the energy saved for more useful purposes. Wholesome beer—that is what's wanted. Good day to you, sir."

Of course, I don't meet William Cobbett on my way to Canterbury, but my fertile imagination helps fill a comfortable half hour, and for a time I even manage to ignore how thoroughly soaked my clothing has become. But reality has a way of reasserting itself—in this case as an icy trickle of rain working its way down the back of my collar. Daydreaming can only carry you so far.

The trail leaves the dripping forest and I find myself walking down a twisting narrow road between mossy dry-stone walls. Before I know it, I am walking down the main street of the village of Puttenham. There really is only one road, known as "The Street," in Puttenham, at the bottom of a rather deep and narrow valley with pretty cottages squeezed in tight on both sides. I pass a village pub called the Good Intent. The pub sign, swinging on a bracket above the door, pictures a pious parliamentary soldier, wearing his breastplate and round helmet, and kneeling in prayer before a canvas tent, perhaps consigning his soul to God before a battle. Is the sign intended to be a visual pun: "The Good In [a canvas] tent"?

By now the rain is coming down quite hard and I need a reprieve. At the end of the road, where it hooks around a small knoll, rises the village church. I thread a lych-gate, the kind of roofed gateway found at the entrance to many traditional English churchyards, designed to shelter pallbearers from downpours such as this, and ascend a short flight of stairs to the church porch. I am relieved to find the church unlocked. By now, I have come to appreciate the English custom of leaving churches unlocked for the spiritual refreshment of travellers. You would never find this in Canada. We would be afraid of vandalism. Inside the empty church, I remove my pack and shake the rain from my jacket. I have determined to pause for a while to see if the rain will slacken its pace and am just starting to relax when the door opens and two scholarly looking gentlemen enter carrying heavy cases, much like salesmen's sample cases only larger, which they begin to unpack and assemble next to the church organ. As the one man, an expert technician of some kind, plugs cables into sockets, adjusts numerous dials and taps various lighted meters with his fingernail to see if they are responsive; the other man, a rather severe-looking fellow dressed in dark clothing, approaches me and asks what I am doing in the church. Something about his manner suggests a proprietary interest in the place, and I wonder if he might be the vicar.

"Just resting for moment. I'm walking the Pilgrims' Way," I offer by way of explanation.

The man's face brightens. "Ah, then you must have stopped and visited the church at Seale, too?"

I have to admit I hadn't. Seale is a mile or so north of my path this morning. I had debated a slight detour, but because of the weather, decided against it. He seems fatally disappointed. I wonder if he might be the vicar of Seale parish as well and if I have mortally offended him with my reply. (Later, I will discover that my assumption is correct. Like many rural parishes, Seale and Puttenham are managed by a single man, though I'm still not sure if I was talking to the vicar). I'm curious to know what the two men are up to. Are they measuring the acoustics? Tuning the pipe organ? But the man's demeanour has turned so frosty I don't dare ask. Instead, I excuse myself and step back out into the rain.

It's coming down really hard now. My Gore-Tex jacket is soon leaking at the seams, and my trousers are quickly soaked from hip to ankle. The fabric clings clammily to my skin, making each step unpleasant. But I know that not too much further up the trail I will find some respite.

In 1891, the popular Victorian artist George Frederic Watts and his second and much younger wife, the Scottish artist Mary Fraser Tytler, moved to a home called Limnerslease near Compton. Watts, who was in his mid-seventies and in failing health, wanted to escape the grey smog-filled streets of London, and he hired the well-known Arts and Crafts architect Sir Ernest George to design them a comfortable brick-and-timber home in the country. Across the road from the house, they eventually built a large barn-like gallery to house G.F. Watts's work. It remains the only purpose-built gallery in Britain to celebrate the work of a single artist. The gallery is also right beside the Pilgrims' Way. I know nothing of George Frederic Watts, but the opportunity to get out of the rain for an hour or so, and wander through an art gallery, is not to be sneezed at on a day such as this.

The path to Compton passes under a bridge that has been decorated with crosses. Later, I learn these had been placed there by Mary Watts to celebrate the rediscovery of the Pilgrims' Way. The gallery is located just above the trail, up a steep rural crossroad. I buy my ticket in the gift shop and climb the drive to the Arts and Crafts-inspired gallery. Entering the gallery and shaking the rain from my coat on the threshold, I apologize to the elderly docent for my bedraggled appearance. She smiles warmly and offers to take my rucksack and wet jacket somewhere where they can dry. As I have noted above, I really know nothing of George Frederic Watts, though he was one of the most popular and commercially successful painters of his age. It is interesting to see a wide range of his work together under the same roof, from his early polished genre pictures to the looser Pre-Raphaelite-inspired canvases he painted later in life. There was even a period when he tried impressionistic landscapes after the manner of Turner. But Watts's fame rests on his large symbolic paintings with sombre titles like

"Hope," "Mammon," and "Time, Death and Judgement." "Hope," which hangs in the gallery (and which is apparently one of Barack Obama's favourite pictures), features a weary, blindfolded woman sitting atop a darkened world and plucking the single remaining string of a broken lyre. These allegorical pictures do nothing for me. I much prefer his portraits. In fact, there is one whole gallery of small portraits of eminent Victorians, people like John Stuart Mill, Florence Nightingale, and Sir Richard Burton, and these are really quite good. They are honest and probing. What I find most interesting about the Watts Gallery is its comment on the fickleness of reputation.

With the exception of certain artists like Turner, Whistler, and the group known as the Pre-Raphaelite Brotherhood (Rossetti, Holman Hunt, Millais, and Burne-Jones), Victorian painting is largely forgotten today. It wasn't that the Victorians lacked talent. They had that by the bucketful. What they lacked was vision. There was something very bourgeois in the Victorian temper that didn't translate well onto canvas. They tended to paint sentimental subjects or genre paintings that, today, we find cloying. What failed as art, however, succeeded as literature. Somehow the Victorian novel, perhaps because it was such a new and vigorous art form, rose above its middle-class concerns. Try this as an experiment. Imagine Charles Dickens as a painter and imagine the death of Little Nell as a picture hanging on your wall. It's a bit too earnest, isn't it, a bit too melodramatic? It tries too hard to play on your sympathy. And that was the problem with Victorian painting. Watts, at least, never fell prey to sentimentality. In that, and in his willingness to evolve, he was admirable.

In the same way, much Victorian architecture was solid and respectable, consciously reflecting a past they hoped to live up to. There were many impressive Gothic Revival buildings erected, like the new Houses of Parliament, buildings that were substantial, reassuring, awe-inspiring even, but stylistically derivative. One of the exceptions to this trend is the building I hope to visit next.

The celebrity of George Frederic Watts tended to overshadow the accomplishments of his wife, Mary, but she was a considerable artist in her own right, a designer and potter, rather than a painter or sculptor. Mary subscribed to the ideas of the Arts and Crafts movement, the notion that people's lives could be improved through art education and training. One of the things that John Ruskin had protested about in the Victorian period was the ugliness of the mass-produced items coming out of Victorian factories. Sure, a factory-made chair was less expensive than one made by a single craftsman, but it was also soul-destroyingly ugly. He believed the things we surrounded ourselves with should be beautiful as well as functional. To this end, the followers of this arts and crafts ethos believed that people could be trained to create their own pottery, their own furniture, and that they would be better off for it. Mary Watts was a firm believer in this idea.

So when the nearby town of Compton decided that their old graveyard had become overcrowded and decided to open a new one just down the road from the Watts Gallery, Mary approached the town council and offered to design and build a mortuary chapel for their new cemetery. Not only did Mary offer to design it, but she offered to train local people in the decorative arts and employ them to do the work. Her husband offered to pay for its construction and to contribute the altarpiece. The result was the amazing Watts Mortuary Chapel.

I leave the gallery and head back down the hill, retracing my earlier route, until I come to the cemetery, which is located in a woody hollow. The chapel is up a rise, visible through a scattering of yews and marble monuments. The colour of the chapel is uniform—soft red brick, scalloped red clay roof pantiles, and bands of decorative terracotta tile. At first glance, the chapel appears taller than it is wide, but as I ascend the winding cobbled lane, I realize that this is an optical illusion created by the strong verticals in the design. The floor plan is a Celtic cross—a circular chapel superimposed upon a crossing with equal arms.

The alcoves created by the crossing form the door and the three bays of narrow stained-glass windows. Each of these openings is surmounted by recessed barrel-vaulting framed with terracotta tile. As I draw closer, the decoration on the tiles leaps into relief. They are amazing. Each tile is like the illuminated page of a medieval bible, an explosion of swirling lines, Celtic knots and fantastic creatures. What is more amazing to me is that this fine decoration is the work of local amateur potters, not professionals. The design is unlike any other English chapel I have seen. The style has been called Celtic-influenced Art Nouveau, but to me it feels more Romanesque—Italianate, even, and it stirs a memory of something else I saw many years before.

As I step through the door into the richly decorated interior, the feeling of familiarity grows stronger, until I remember where I have encountered this sensibility before: San Vitale in Ravenna, Italy, which I visited in my youth. Though San Vitale is Byzantine and the Watts Chapel Victorian, and San Vitale octagonal where the Watts Chapel is more circular, they share the same compact design in simple brick. They also have the same kind of exuberant interior decoration. When you walk into San Vitale, you are astounded by the many human figures staring down at you from the sparkling mosaics high on the walls. You feel like you have entered an antique operating theatre, and that you are the patient under examination. Similarly, when you enter the Watts Chapel, you are surrounded by a host of ethereal angelic figures with folded wings, set against a pattern of intersecting twigs and branches painted in gesso. The difference is that, while San Vitale is flooded with light, the Watts Chapel feels dark and somewhat gloomy, especially on an overcast day like this. This gloom is largely due to colour choice. The palette here mimics the palette of the Pre-Raphaelites, who in turn mimicked the palettes of the medieval masters they admired: reddish earth tones and gold highlights set against a dark background of mossy green and muddy blue. The effect is rich and vibrant, but too dark for such a small space. Despite the angels, the decoration isn't strictly Christian either. The esoteric symbolism of the chapel decoration was Mary's invention, a private spiritual code. Mary's penchant for the esoteric was not that unusual for the time. This was, after all, the same era that saw the rise of Madame Blavatsky and theosophy, and a renewed interest in Rosicrucianism, spiritualism and a belief in fairies. So I suppose I should not be too surprised at the unusual artistic choices on display in the Watts Chapel. This sort of eclectic spirituality was part of the Victorian temper.

Exiting the chapel, I discover that the rain has returned in force. Looking around for a sheltered place to rest, I spy a stone loggia up the hill, another feature designed by Mary Watt, one intended to hold her husband's ashes. I mount the hill, up a snaking gravel path, and am pleasantly surprised to pass the tombstone of the novelist Aldous Huxley surrounded by markers for other members of the Huxley clan. Later, I learn that the Huxley family had a villa in the neighbourhood. If you've read *Brave New World*, you may recall that the novel's hero, John Savage, disillusioned with a society he'd once thought utopian, ends his days in a lonely tower in Puttenham with a view of the Weald and the Hogsback. Perhaps Huxley had pickled his liver at the Good Intent?

In the shelter of the stone cloister, near the marble memorial to G.F. Watts, I find a wooden bench and sit down to eat an apple and a couple of granola bars and wait out the rain. Neatly carved across the back of my bench are the words "Here and now, boys!" A plaque informs me that the bench was donated by the Aldous Huxley Society in 2013. The words are taken from Huxley's 1962 novel, *Island*. If *Brave New World* is Huxley's vision of a dystopian future with its genetically engineered class system, *Island* is his vision of a lost Eden, destroyed by exploitive capitalism. In the novel, the words on the bench are spoken by trained mynahs, which fly about his island paradise reminding the inhabitants to live for the moment. It isn't a bad admonition, I think, as I munch my apple.

The rain has almost stopped, so I decide to head out again. I briefly debate pulling on a pair of rubberized nylon rain pants, but it is so hot I figure it would be like walking in my own personalized sauna, so I decide against it. Within ten minutes the hard rain has returned, and I realize it was the wrong decision, but there is no point in pulling rain pants on over wet trousers, so I carry on. I intend to stop at Loseley House, an estate just south of the trail, for I have read that they allow visitors and it is my sole opportunity on this walk to visit a grand English country house.

Loseley House interests me, too, because Loseley has associations with one of my favourite poets, John Donne. In 1597, Donne was appointed private secretary to Sir Thomas Egerton, the Lord Keeper of the Great Seal, and it was at Egerton's London house that he first met Egerton's niece, Anne More, and the two fell deeply in love. Neither Donne's employer nor Anne's father, Sir George More, the owner of Loseley House, approved of the alliance. When the two eloped, More had Donne thrown in Fleet Prison, claiming the marriage was invalid, and Egerton dismissed Donne from his service. Writing from prison to tell his wife of his plight, Donne signed the letter: John Donne, Anne Donne, Un-done. Eventually, the court declared the marriage valid, and Donne was released, but it would be nine penurious years before Donne was reconciled with his father-in-law. Nevertheless, I think it was a successful marriage, if twelve children and poems like "A Valediction: Forbidding Mourning" are anything to go by. John Donne wrote Anne some of the finest love poems in the English language. (I know: I used them to woo my wife). Anne died in childbirth in 1617, and Donne, now a clergyman, was bereft. His famous poem "Holy Sonnet 17" summed up his feelings. He knew the memory of his wife's love should prepare him for the greater love he receives from God, and he should be content now to cast his thoughts on Heaven. "But," he tells God, "though I have found thee, and thou my thirst hast fed, / A holy thirsty dropsy melts me yet."[2] His grief at his wife's death, despite the comfort he takes from God's great and abiding love, is inconsolable.

Thinking of Donne's loss reminds me of the day of my father's funeral. It hadn't been raining on that day. It had been sunny and hot, very hot—so hot, in fact, that we worried people might pass out in the oven-like atmosphere of the parish church. A phone call brought a fire truck, and two burly firefighters wrestled a large exhaust fan onto the front steps of the church in front of the open doors. A small generator was set up on the sidewalk and before long the overheated air was being sucked out of the church.

"We'll turn it off once the service begins," shouted the middle-aged firefighter who seemed to be in charge. "But it should at least make things a little more bearable for the folks inside."

"That's very kind of you," I yelled.

He shrugged. "Your dad was a great guy. It's the least we could do."

As we were standing on the sidewalk shouting to be heard over the combined roar of the fan and generator, an elderly woman approached, waving a cane in our direction. You could tell from her stiff gait and clenched jaw that she was unhappy.

"Is this really necessary?" she screeched. "I live right there!" She pointed her cane at the two-storey red brick house next door. "I can't hear myself think over that contraption!"

I've always admired people who work with the public in times of crisis—people like firemen, policemen, and nurses. They never seem to lose their cool. I suppose it is part of their training.

"We'll turn off the fan as soon as the funeral starts," the fireman explained calmly. "It's over a hundred degrees in the church, ma'am. We wouldn't want to have to call an ambulance to a funeral, now would we?"

His attempt at humour didn't cut any mustard with the old woman. "It's very inconvenient," she pouted and tried to stare him down.

"As soon as the funeral starts," he reassured her, and she hobbled away, muttering direly.

No one will do this at my funeral. I simply don't have that many friends. But my father had a talent for friendship. He liked people and he was a good listener—a good listener, that is, if he had his hearing aids turned on.

For my father was very hard of hearing. He called it nerve deafness and complained that his whole adult life was accompanied by a chorus of crickets chirping in his ear. He must have been in his late forties when he got his first pair of hearing aids. When he would get home from a long sales trip, he would greet my mom, give us all a hug, and then collapse in his La-Z-Boy recliner with the newspaper propped up on his chest. Within minutes, he would be fast asleep and gently snoring, newspaper tented over his face. As kids we found this hilarious. How could anyone sleep with all of the racket going on in our house? It was only later that I realized that the second thing my dad did when he got home, after talking to my mom, was to turn off his hearing aids.

Fortunately, I did not inherit my father's hearing. (My sister got that). However, I do find myself frequently falling asleep over a book in the recliner after work, and it's still hilarious to the younger generation. More and more, I find myself looking in the mirror and seeing my father's reflection staring back. It makes me wonder how much I am like him, but it also makes him more human. My father, as much as I admired him, was a man, like me, fighting his own battles. Is it only after a parent dies that we see them as fallible and forgivable? Like me, he lived the given life, not the chosen one. He did the best he could with the hand he was dealt.

As I am woolgathering, I miss my opportunity to visit Loseley. The rain is coming down so hard and I have my hood pulled down so low that I somehow miss the turnoff and walk right past the connecting trail. By the time I realize what I've done, I don't have the heart to backtrack in the mud and rain.

The Pilgrims' Way leads me eventually to a prominent hill just south of Guildford where the ruins of St. Catherine's Chapel reside in solemn eminence. Despite the drizzle, I decide to pause and eat my lunch standing up. The grass, though clipped short by the numerous rabbits, whose many burrows threaten to break the leg of the unwary, is slick with rain. The view from St. Catherine's hill is marvellous, looking down at the river Wey at its foot and across to the wooded whaleback of St. Martha's Hill in the distance. The presence of numerous empty bottles and a pimply pattern of scorched campfire rings testifies to the popularity of the hill with local youth. I stuff my apple core down a nearby rabbit hole and head back down the hill to where a steep narrow lane leads to the old ferry crossing. When Hilaire Belloc was researching his book on "The Old Road" in 1903, he found himself stymied at this point.

> *It was now quite dark. My companion and I clambered down the hill, stole a boat which lay moored to the bank, and with a walking-stick for an oar painfully traversed the river Wey. When we had landed, we heard, from the further bank, a woman, the owner of the boat, protesting with great violence.*
>
> *We pleaded our grave necessity; put money in the boat, and then, turning, we followed the marshy path across the field to the highway, and when we reached it, abandoned the Old Road in order to find an inn.*[3]

Fortunately for me, there is now a high-arched footbridge across the Wey at this point, so I am not reduced to boat theft to continue my journey.

Crossing the same meadow as Belloc, I follow a rising path to a wooded ridge called The Chantries. The forest gets its name because it was gifted to Holy Trinity Church in Guildford to pay for a licence for a chantry there where a priest would pray for the soul of Henry Norbrigge, a fifteenth-century wool merchant and nine-times mayor of Guildford. The pilgrim road then ascends a ridge through a forest along a broad and sandy sunken track that leads up and up St. Martha's Hill. It's a shame that it's raining, for the views from the eponymous chapel at the summit are panoramic, and I'm sure they must have been stunning on a clear day. The biggest mystery to me is why such a fine chapel was constructed on this hill at all. One story is that it was constructed to memorialize some early Christians who were martyred on this spot. Indeed, the full name of the chapel in some records is Saint Martha the Virgin and all the Holy Martyrs, and, in the fifteenth century, this hill was called "Martirhill," not "St. Martha's." At any rate it is a lonely place. The nearest community is Chilworth in the misty valley far below. The chapel lies astride the pilgrim road, and so perhaps benefited from pilgrim traffic. There is apparently a window in the south wall of the chancel bearing the Arms of Canterbury and dedicated to St. Thomas Becket, but the church is locked, so I'm not able to confirm this. The early history of St. Martha's is murky, but eventually, with the dissolution of the monasteries, it was given to the squire of Chilworth Manor and gradually fell into ruin. In 1850, it was restored and became part of the parish of Chilworth. Occasional services are still held here for those fit enough to climb the hill. In the tiny cemetery surrounding the chapel, I notice a number of Commonwealth war graves, so it must have been a busy place during World War II. Descending the hill on the far side, I encounter another memory of that war, a brick and concrete bunker called a pillbox, now crumbling and overgrown, erected in those uncertain years as a last line of defense should Britain be invaded.

My walk for the day is supposed to end at a popular picnic site called Newlands Corner, just off the A25, where the highway climbs the North Downs on its way to Guildford. On my map, Derek has indicated that I should leave the North Downs Way at Newlands Corner and follow the highway for three-quarters of a mile north, until I arrive at my accommodation for the night. I stand on the shoulder of the busy highway, flinching as the traffic zips by, thinking I don't like the looks of this at all. The A25 is two tight lanes of speeding traffic enclosed by dense forest on either side.

There is no safe shoulder to walk on. I examine my map again and notice a bridleway running parallel to the highway, beginning just behind the visitor's centre on the pullout. Here's a happy coincidence, I conclude. If I follow the bridle path, I can stay off the road, and I will only have to risk my life once when I dash across the highway to reach my hotel.

I retrace my steps to the parking lot in front of the visitor's centre, and, as expected, there is a broad gravelled path leading off into the woods right where the map says it should be. As I walk into the forest, I soon lose sight of the highway, but I can still hear the traffic through the trees, so I figure I am all l right as long as I keep the highway within earshot. But after a few hundred yards the trail begins to veer left, away from the highway. I notice a smaller, less trammelled path heading off to the right. This trail isn't marked on my map, but I reason that as long as I keep turning right, I should be heading back toward the highway. So I leave the main trail, but soon come to another fork. I turn right again. Then another fork. I turn right. I quickly lose count of the turnings in the trail. By now, I am completely surrounded by dense, somewhat sinister forest, much of it rather scrubby and sickly in appearance. I can't hear the highway anymore. In fact, I can't hear anything. The forest seems strangely barren of life. The sky is overcast, and I can't see the sun. I'm heading roughly north but have no idea where I am on the map. I continue walking until I enter a clearing. In its centre stands an ancient yew with a barrel-shaped trunk and drooping branches that arch down to the ground and make it look like an enormous spider. Shades of Mirkwood Forest, I think, and shudder. I continue down the path, convinced by now that I have walked well past my destination. I push through the trees and find myself standing on the shoulder of a road. Finally.

But something is wrong. There are no cars on this road, and it is much too narrow to be the A25. Where the hell am I? I consult my map again. There *is* a road, branching off the highway, well north of the visitor's centre and well beyond where I want to be. Could

I have wandered that far out of my way? It doesn't seem possible.
But if my guess is right, on the far side of the road there should be
a golf course. I decide to cross over and see. I cross the road, crash
through a screen of trees, and, sure enough, I am standing on the
edge of a golf green, a tiny flag hanging limply in its centre. I look
at my map again. There should be another path on the far side of
the green that will lead me back to the highway. I wait for a pair of
golfers to play through, and then I dash across the neatly clipped
saucer of green and find the path I am looking for. Spirits lifting, I
plunge back into the woods. I know that once I reach the highway
I will have to backtrack, but at least I now know where I am. The
path winds on and on until I emerge once more into a clearing.
I look around. The place seems strangely familiar. Right in front
of me is an enormous spider-shaped yew. Can it be? How can I
possibly be back here without crossing a road? Somehow, I have
walked in an enormous circle. I curse my own cleverness. There
is nothing for it but to retrace my steps, remembering to take the
left-hand path this time whenever I come to a fork in the trail. In
time, I re-emerge at the visitor's centre, much chagrined. I return
to the shoulder of the highway and skirt the dangerous road as
the commuter traffic whizzes by, compressing myself as much as
possible into the scratchy underbrush to allow the speeding drivers
to pass. After an eternity I come to the front lawn of the impressive Manor House Hotel. It is, I hasten to point out, a motor lodge.
Nobody in their right mind would ever walk there. In all, I add
another half hour's walking to my day and another two to three
miles to my route.

   I trudge up the long drive, my feet sloshing about in my wet
boots. There is a large white tent on the lawn, and the hotel lobby
is full of rented tuxedos and peach-coloured bridesmaids' dresses. I
feel horribly out of place and very conscious of my slovenly appearance. But I am too tired to care much. I retire to the bar and order
a thick hamburger with fries and try to sit in an inconspicuous
corner where I won't offend the wedding guests with my funk.

Three small children tear around the bar dressed in their wedding finery, shrieking and playing tag amongst the tables and chairs. Their mother is seated on a barstool in a bright red minidress with her back to the bar, fixated on her cellphone, thumbs tapping madly. The long-suffering bartender pleads with her. "Please madam. We have guests trying to enjoy their meals."

"Wotcha want me to do?" she snaps without looking up. "The manager had a fit and threw us outta the ballroom."

I finish my burger and retire to my room. I strip off my damp clothes and climb into a hot shower. After towelling off, I sit on the edge of the bed to lance my blisters, rub them with Polysporin, and tape my feet.

Would my father have enjoyed today's walk? He taught me to read a map, so perhaps, if he had been with me, we wouldn't have gotten lost. On the other hand, he was never one for sticking to a plan, so maybe we would have. Sometimes getting lost or going deliberately off map leads to a wonderful adventure. And sometimes it just leads to getting lost. Upon reflection, I'm glad I didn't drag him along for all those extra miles in the rain.

Exhausted, I crawl under the covers. I'm sure I will have trouble falling asleep with the noise from the wedding banquet echoing down the hallway, but before I know it, I'm out.

6

Newlands Corner
to Dorking

---

*[O]ur matter...consists in this: whether the things we speak of,
such as praying to saints, going on pilgrimage, and worshipping
relics and images, may be done for good, not whether they may
be done for evil. For if they may be done for good, then although
many may misuse them, that does not diminish the goodness of
the thing itself. For if from the misuse of a good thing and from
the evils that sometimes grow out of its abuse, we should utterly
do away with the whole use of something, we should then have to
make some marvellous changes in the world*

—THOMAS MORE, *A Dialogue Concerning Heresies*

THE NEXT MORNING, I decide to leave my perch on the North
Downs and descend the long grassy slope to the valley below,
where I can rejoin the old pilgrims' road. I will be doing a lot of this

in the coming days. The Pilgrims' Way and the long-distance hiking
path known as the North Downs Way follow roughly the same
route. In places where walking the old pilgrims' road is no longer
feasible, where it has become a paved highway or where the route is
closed to pedestrians, the North Downs Way defaults to the crest
of the chalk escarpment. Occasionally, as happens today, they
follow different but parallel routes, and I have to make a choice.
This morning, I choose to follow the older road.

There is a wonderful sweeping view from Newlands Corner, of
woodlands and farms in the low ground, surmounted by the rolling
hills of the South Downs far away. Just below me, in the middle
distance, I can see the squat spire of the church of St. Peter's and
St. Paul's in the village of Albury.

Until about the middle of the nineteenth century, the village of
Albury was known as Weston Street, and was much smaller, but
the owners of the large estate of Albury Park to the east wanted to
relocate their tenants off the estate, and so created the new settlement of Albury where we see it today. The man who purchased
the estate in 1918 was a London banker and Member of Parliament
named Henry Drummond. The relocation of the village of Albury
had already started in the 1780s, long before Drummond's tenure,
but it was he who completed the process. Since the villagers had
attended the old Saxon church on the estate, which was now in
rather poor condition, Drummond offered to build them a new
place of worship, a red brick church in the Romanesque style (some
say modelled after the medieval church at Thaon, near Caen in
France). This was the church whose spire I could see below me.
Drummond also hired the architect Augustus Welby Pugin, best
remembered today for remodelling the Palace of Westminster and
for designing Big Ben, to repair and remodel the Saxon church,
so that it could start a new life as the Drummond family mauso-
leum. But Drummond also built a third church, one for his own
use, and this is the one I really want to see. This church is called
the Apostles' Chapel, and it was meant to serve as the headquarters

of a new Christian sect called the Catholic Apostolic Church, which Drummond supported.

The late Christopher Hitchens, who made no bones about his atheism, wrote in *God Is Not Great: How Religion Poisons Everything*, that the reason there are so many religions and religious sects is that everyone fashions a god in his own image:

> *God did not create man in his own image. Evidently it was the other way about, which is the painless explanation for the profusion of gods and religions, and the fratricide both between and among faiths, that we see all about us and that has retarded the development of civilization.*[1]

Hitchens makes a valid point, but I would hasten to remark that God's existence or nonexistence is not predicated by our poor understanding of Him. Just because we create a god in our own image does not mean that God does not exist. Hitchens is too clever to stretch his argument quite that far. Instead, he reasons that, since any proof for the existence of god must depend upon (quoting Kierkegaard) a "leap of faith," then it makes more sense to dismiss the whole notion as absurd. It is also a short step from believing in a god of one's own devising to believing one knows just what that particular god wants from us. I would suggest that if you ever meet a man on the road who tells you he knows the mind of God, run.

On the other hand, I find the subtitle of Hitchens's book, *How Religion Poisons Everything*, curious, if not a little disturbing. It is an echo of something Mao Zedong said to the young Dalai Lama. Had Hitchens meant to quote Mao approvingly or was he unaware of the attribution? The story, found in the Dalai Lama's autobiography, tells of the Dalai Lama's last visit to Beijing before his flight to India in 1959. The Dalai Lama is invited to a private meeting in Mao's office, where he is lectured on how to govern the now prostrate province of Tibet. Towards the end of the interview, Mao leans forward and whispers, "Religion is poison," in the Dalai Lama's ear. Up until that point, the young Tibetan ruler had been attempting to work with the Chinese communists, even to learn from them. But at this declaration, he feels a sudden chill of horror and thinks, "So you are the destroyer of the dharma after all."[2]

But back to Albury and Henry Drummond.

Drummond was a follower of a renegade Presbyterian minister named Edward Irving whose radical interpretation of the book of Revelation had drawn quite a following from those who were disaffected with the established Christian churches. Drummond convened a study group of like-minded individuals at Albury Park to explore Irving's message. Out of a series of conferences grew the new Catholic Apostolic Church, of which Drummond became a leading member. At first, the vicar of Albury Park, the Reverend Hugh McNeile, attended these conferences and even moderated the discussions, but he soon became alarmed by the doctrines he heard espoused and began preaching against them. This was awkward, for Drummond, as the owner of Albury Park, held the appointment of the benefice. He might have dismissed McNeile. Instead, Drummond mediated by offering to build the two new churches as noted above: one, in the village of Albury, for Reverend McNeile and his parishioners, and another, closer to Drummond's country home, for the followers of the new Catholic Apostolic Church.

While the village church was constructed in red brick in the Romanesque style, the Apostles' Chapel was constructed in stone in the newly fashionable Gothic revival style, a style that would dominate church architecture in Britain and her colonies for the next hundred years. The Apostles' Chapel was hardly a "chapel." Instead, it is a grand structure with an impressive Norman tower at one end and a beautiful rose window at the other. Drummond intended it to be imposing, for it was to be the nerve centre of his new religion.

The Catholic Apostolic Church, sometimes called the Irvingite Church, was an evangelical sect that believed in the imminent second coming of Christ. They practised faith healing and speaking in tongues, and believed in the possibility of rapture (the bodily ascension to Heaven without dying). They erected a complicated church hierarchy of apostles, bishops (whom they called "angels"), priests, and deacons, with the priesthood further divided into elders, prophets, evangelists and pastors. Leadership of the new sect was vested in twelve latter-day "Apostles," and the Apostles' Chapel was to serve as their "college."

At its height, the Catholic Apostolic Church claimed two hundred thousand adherents, with close to a thousand parishes worldwide. They attracted followers who were impatient with the traditional churches, who wished to recapture the excitement and immediacy of the first followers of Jesus. They wanted to live lives charged with spiritual energy, for they expected Christ's kingdom to arrive at any day.

But time passed. Christ did not return, and the leadership of the Catholic Apostolic Church began to die off. There was no succession plan for the Twelve Apostles, who were appointed for life, because it was never thought that such a plan would be needed. The last of the Twelve died in 1901, and the membership slowly dwindled. The writer Gavin Maxwell, whose family were followers of the Catholic Apostolic Church, and who stayed briefly in the cottage next to the chapel when Maxwell was a young boy in the 1930s, remembers the followers as "a veritable colony" of whom the greater number were spinsters.[3]

I am curious to see the Apostles' Chapel, and am hoping I can find someone, a caretaker perhaps, who will let me in. As I descend the hill on a diagonal path through the trees, I come upon a clearing, and there, across a low meadow and surrounded by a high hedge, stands the Apostles' Chapel. From a distance it looks pure white, but as I approach it mellows to a sandy brown, for it is constructed, as are many local churches, of flint, with all of the fine detailed work, the window frames, buttresses, and door frames, picked out in local sandstone. It looks ancient, but it was only constructed in 1840. I cross a water meadow, then a quiet road, and approach the abandoned church up a long walled drive to an iron gate. The gate is locked. No one is around, though there are piles of sand and gravel to one side of the church, which suggests that some repairs are underway. It's peaceful and shady in the lane, birds warble in the trees overhead, and I linger for a while. What am I to think of Drummond's folly? Is it a monument to an evolutionary dead end on the road to true religion? So many religions start out with brave enthusiasm but end up like this. Where are the cultists of Mithras today, the worshippers of Baal, the bull-leapers of Minos, the Elect of Mani, the horse sacrificers of Tengri? Gone and turned to dust.

Disappointed, I hoist my rucksack and rejoin the Pilgrims' Way. I soon come to a shallow ford in the Tilling Bourne and cross over a narrow footbridge to the village of Shere. Shere is often called the prettiest village in Surrey, and it has that kind of cozy Tudor ambience, a combination of weathered brick, red pantiles, timber-framed stucco, and window boxes stuffed with geraniums, that delights the eye. Not surprisingly, the village has featured in a number of Hollywood movies, starting in 1918 when it posed as an embattled French village in D.W. Griffith's World War I propaganda film *Hearts of the World*. More recently, Jude Law wooed Cameron Diaz here in *The Holiday*, and lovely St. James' Church, at the centre of the village, was featured in both *Bridget Jones: The Edge of Reason* and *The Wedding Date*. It is to St. James that I now direct my steps.

The path to the church has often been painted by artists in search of the picturesque. First you enter the broad market square, which grows narrower as you approach the church, then pass under Edwin Lutyens' lych-gate (Lutyens—perhaps the greatest architect of the British Empire, who designed much of New Delhi, including

Government House), before crossing the ancient churchyard towards the Norman spire of St. James'. The church is renowned for its brasses and monuments, some surviving medieval glass, and a curious two-inch high bronze Madonna and Child that once topped either a pilgrim's staff or a bishop's crozier. The tiny sculpture was discovered, quite by accident, when a dog dug it up on nearby Juniper Hill in 1886. But the thing I am most curious to see is the remains of an anchoress's cell.

In 1329, a girl named Christine Carpenter petitioned the Bishop of Winchester to be permitted to take a vow of "continence and perpetual chastity and allow herself to be shut up in a narrow place in the churchyard adjoining the parish church of Schire, that therein she may be enabled to serve Almighty God the more worthily."[4] The bishop was a cautious man. He wanted to be assured that she was not running away from something, that she was not married or promised in marriage, and that her vocation was true, and not a passing fancy. To this end, he directed the parish priest and the parishioners to question Christine to see if she "is likely to make a success of this proposal for a more saintly life." He must have been convinced, for on August 14, 1329, he granted Christine's wish. A stone cell was constructed against the west wall of the church near the altar. Two holes were cut through the wall: one, a trefoil window, allowed her to receive communion, the second, a narrow slanting aperture called a squint, allowed her to see the altar as she knelt in prayer. Food was apparently passed through a barred opening on an outside wall. You can still see the twin openings through which Christine viewed the world, and if you walk around to the outside of the church, you can see the outline of the anchorite's cell where it had once adjoined the chancel wall, though the cell was demolished long ago. It would have been a very small damp space, not tall enough to stand up in, nor long enough to lie down at full length—a good place to park a bicycle perhaps, but not a human being. Cool in the summer, an icebox in winter, it would have tested the girl's resolve. A second letter from the Bishop of Winchester, dated November 10, 1332, showed that it was more than the girl could bear. At some point, Christine had left the cell. Now she was petitioning the bishop to allow her to return. By leaving the cell and breaking her vow, Christine laid herself open to strict censure, even excommunication. The bishop directed the Dean of Guildford to impose a penance upon Christine, in proportion to her offence, that "she may learn at your discretion how nefarious was her committed sin."[5] Afterwards, she could be once again walled into her cell to fulfill her vows. These two letters are all that we really know about the life of Christine Carpenter. Did she spend the rest of her life as an anchorite? What prompted her to seek the life of solitude in the first place? These sketchy details have inspired both a mystery novel and a feature film, but we shall never really know what went on in her head. We can only speculate.

I met Buddhist monks in Bhutan who took similar vows, who meditated for a period of three years, three months and three days while walled up in a mountain cave. These men seemed remarkably sane to me after their ordeal. The famous Tibetologist Giuseppe Tucci described a similar holy man, Lama Tsampa Tendon, whom he met in Tibet before the Second World War. Tucci was an astute observer of humankind, amused but not gulled by fakes and charlatans; so when he said that Lama Tendon was the "strongest personality" he'd met in his travels, we believe him. Lama Tendon lived in retreat in a small cell on a mountainside above the city of Gyantse. He had not left his cell for eight years, and his only contact with the outside world was through a small triangular window. After meeting Lama Tendon, Tucci remarked that solitude works differently on different people. For some, it is a poison, but for others it is a "flame." Lama Tendon was of the latter sort. Solitude had a "purifying effect on him." He "emanated peace and benevolence almost as if they were physical realities; he radiated inner light." He had developed a "reputation for sanctity" and pilgrims came to his hermitage hoping for a blessing. Tucci too felt blessed to have met him and reflected: "Any religion can be a vehicle between God and man, just as any religion can deteriorate into magical or commercial practices, or be turned into an instrument for tormenting one's fellow-men."[6] I suppose the same could be said for economic or political theory. Athens of the Golden Age gave us a great idea, democracy, but Athens was also a slave state. Do we reject an idea because its practitioners are human and fallible?

I suppose I am attracted to the story of Christine Carpenter because I have always been attracted to the monastic life and to a life of solitude, but her choice seems extreme, even to me. Religious life is full of ascetics—Christian saints who sit atop stone pillars or Hindu sadhus who stand for years balanced upon one leg—all seeking salvation through hardship. But this kind of penance can so easily slip into narcissism, a kind of spiritual showing off. Lord Buddha, it must be remembered, tried this route and ultimately rejected it, seeking instead the Middle Way. The Anglican Church, the most Catholic of the Protestant sects, also claims to follow a middle way, the *via media* between the Pope and Martin Luther. I suppose that's why I've always been comfortable with Anglicanism: it is a religion of compromise rather than confrontation. But it also represents a stance that is more likely to breed spiritual poets—churchmen like Donne, Herbert and Traherne—than spiritual heroes.

From Shere, I decide to climb back up the chalk escarpment to the North Downs Trail. According to historians like Belloc, this would have been the pattern for medieval pilgrims too—walk high, sleep low. The trail along the Downs was dry and sheltered, but everyone lived at the base of the chalk escarpment, for here was the flat, fertile land needed for cultivation and the water needed to support a settlement. The trail up to the top is miserable— steep and muddy and churned up by the wheels of tractors and ATVS—but once at the top the walking is easy—wide, level drove roads along woodland lanes, once used for livestock, but now, as I discover, popular with cyclists, dog walkers and horseback riders. During the Second World War, a portion of this road had also been used by Canadian troops preparing for the Normandy landing on D-Day, and so it is also known as the "Canadian Road." The Canadian troops have left large concrete water tanks, shaped like above-ground swimming pools, at regular intervals along the road, now filled with trash, and I am at a loss to discover what they might have once been used for.

Just below the trail, I see another WWII pillbox and decide to investigate. Some twenty-eight thousand were constructed during the war, to be manned by the home guard as a line of defense to protect London. About six thousand remain. The pillboxes are all of a pattern—squat hexagonal structures of brick and concrete with five firing slits and a flat roof that could be camouflaged from enemy bombers by strapping brushwood to protruding steel loops. The entrance to the pillbox is narrow and low. I squeeze through. Inside, it is dark, damp and claustrophobic, and smells of rotting leaf mould. Peering through one of the firing slots, I try to imagine an enemy invasion force creeping up the slope through the trees. Despite the thick layer of concrete, I don't feel safe in the pillbox; I feel trapped. In the event of an invasion, I think I would much rather be outside in the woods and take my chances. It's a relief to step outside into the sun.

As I continue along the trail, I begin to meet scattered groups of high school students coming the other way. They are all heavily burdened under backpacks. One strapping young man, who could have been a model for a Greek statue of Apollo, is—instead of wearing his backpack—carrying it under his arm like a sack of groceries, which suggests to me that (a) it is borrowed and doesn't fit properly, or (b) he is trying to impress the girls in his group with his rugged manliness. Oh, how I do not miss adolescence! If you are a teenager and reading this book, let me reassure you: it gets better.

At Blatchford Downs, the trees disappear, and the world drops away beneath my feet. I feel like Gulliver in the land of Lilliput.

The prospect from Steer's Field, a little further along the trail, is, if anything, more breathtaking. From here I get my first real view of the Weald, the lowlands that stretch between the North and South Downs. Far below, I can see a train speeding east, and, through the heat haze, I can see its destination, which is also my destination for the day, the town of Dorking.

I have now reached the edge of the Denbies Estate and the village of Ranmore Common. Little remains of the village but the rather impressive church of St. Barnabas. The church is a beautiful example of the English perpendicular style and clearly no expense has been spared in the workmanship or the materials. The stone carving and stained glass are all first rate. But I wonder how often it is used today. It was designed by the eminent Victorian architect Sir Giles Gilbert Scott for the use of the Cubitt family and the more than four hundred workers who were employed on their estate. The Cubitts had earned their fortune in the building trade (much of Belgravia and Buckingham Palace was their work), but a tax sale following the Second World War destroyed the closed paternalistic world of the estate, and the great country house was torn down. Today, the land is owned by Biwater, a water treatment company (a sign of the times in an era when clean water is more precious than oil), and the sun-warmed, south-facing slopes of the Downs have been transformed into a vineyard. It is interesting to note that Dorking was once a Roman town and that the ruins of a Roman Villa have been found in Abinger, not far away. I wonder if the Romans cultivated grapes here as well.

As I leave the church and round a corner, the valley of the river Mole opens up below me. Here the Mole cuts through the North Downs and forms a broad, flat valley. Across the river, the Downs rise steeply to the top of Box Hill, which I will be climbing on the morrow. Dorking lies a little to the south. As I walk further onto the estate grounds, the trail becomes groomed and asphalted, and I have to step aside occasionally to make room for an open-sided bus that gives visitors tours of the estate. No doubt each tour ends with a wine tasting in the gift shop.

My path zigzags down the slope to the valley floor and then south through rows and rows of carefully cultivated grape vines. At a crossroads, I meet a group of eight schoolboys, red-faced in the heat, and grousing amongst themselves. A few have flung themselves on the grass in defeat. Their backpacks are enormous and poorly packed. Pots and pans are tied to the outsides and clank as they move. One wonders how much useless extra weight each boy carries. One boy, small and bespectacled, breaks off from the group and approaches me.

"Excuse me, sir? Could you help us?"

"Sure."

"We can't decide which trail is the correct one."

"We've already wasted an hour walking in a complete circle," grumps another.

A third, a rather fat boy with a face like a red harvest moon, says, "Don't blame me, you all agreed—"

I look around the circle of boys, small and spotty-faced, overweight and sweating, skinny and asthmatic, and think, these are not the popular boys at school. They are the ones nobody picks for team sports. They are members of the tech crew, the chess club, and the math league. They probably play some contemporary version of Dungeons and Dragons and have endless conversations about Middle Earth or its modern equivalent. They can probably quote whole Monty Python skits by heart. In other words, they are me at fourteen years of age.

"Okay," I say, pulling out my map and laying it on the ground. "Gather round. Here is where you are at the moment. ('Told you,' says the second boy, elbowing the fat one in the ribs). Where were you hoping to go?"

Within a few minutes I have them straightened out and send them on their way, clanking in unison like a tinker's van.

"Thank you, sir," the boys chorus, while the two continue to bicker—"Useless." "Moron." "Twat." "Idiot."—until they fade from earshot.

I am soon walking through the suburbs of Dorking. (What would you call a resident of Dorking? I wonder). I will be spending the night in the White Horse Inn right on the high street in the centre of town. The White Horse is one of the oldest hostelries I will be patronizing on my trip. Parts of the hotel date back to the sixteenth century. The original inn on the site, dating back to 1215, was called Cross House, suggesting that it had been a stopping place for travellers on their way to the Holy Land during the crusades. (As an aside, the first crusaders referred to themselves as *peregrini* or "pilgrims." It wasn't until the Third Crusade that the term *crucesignati* came into common use. *Crucesignati* meant "those signed with the cross," because of the red cross sewn on the knights' surcoats. *Crucesignati* eventually became the English word "crusader.").[7] The current incarnation is a traditional English coaching inn with an arched pull-through for stagecoaches and a large courtyard for discharging passengers and stabling horses. Today this courtyard is used as a car park. Local legend has it that Dickens used the White Horse as the model for the Marquis of Granby in *The Pickwick Papers*, and it was here that the imperturbable Samuel Weller first met his indomitable stepmother. It was, Dickens observed, "a model of a roadside public-house of the better class—just large enough to be convenient, and small enough to be snug."[8] The front of the hotel is the same as it would have been in Dickens's day, and you can imagine the author warming his britches before the massive fireplace after a cold, damp coach ride from London.

I check my backpack and decide to explore Dorking. The church with its enormous spire makes a convenient landmark around which to orient myself, and it is my first stop. The church is late Victorian English perpendicular, but the interior is decorated with marvellous golden mosaics in the Arts and Crafts style. I wander over to the concert hall to visit the statue of Ralph Vaughan Williams, who lived in Dorking from 1929–1951. I have always loved "The Lark Ascending" and his "English Folk Song Suite" (which would make a pretty good soundtrack for my pilgrimage, come to think of it), but I am surprised to learn that one of his late compositions was an opera based on *Pilgrim's Progress*, a book he admired and a project he laboured over for forty-five years.

I walk up High Street, which has probably changed remarkably little since Dickens rode up in his coach. One side is higher than the other with a raised sidewalk lifting pedestrians above the mire. I look in the old bow windows and stop at an Oxfam shop to browse old books. As I approach the hotel, I notice that the new public library is located in a modern shopping plaza across the street. Being a librarian by trade, I can't resist having a peek.

Everything inside is brand new. The shelves are low, sinuously curved, and sleekly modern, nothing like the old-fashioned library stacks I am used to. Even the books look new and crisp, and the shelves aren't packed tight, so that many of the books sit face-out in attractive eye-catching displays. There are lots of people in the library, sitting comfortably in plush seats or browsing the shelves. There is no traditional circulation desk with librarians checking books in and out. Instead there are several self-check kiosks near the door, and next to the kiosks, I note, are several racks with items for sale—bookmarks, stationery, earbuds, that sort of thing. In fact, the library reminds me of a bookstore. I have heard that libraries have fallen on hard times in the U.K., but this library looks to be well-funded and very up to date. I look around for someone to ask, but I can't find any staff. Everything seems to be set up for self-service. In fact, it strikes me that the thing that is missing is a traditional reference desk staffed by a librarian. Indeed, I can't see a traditional reference collection either, for all of the non-fiction titles are popular current bestsellers—biographies, narrative histories, travel memoirs, self-help books—the sort of thing you might find in a well-stocked bookstore. I finally find an employee near the back of the library, hidden behind a freestanding partition. She is assisting patrons on a bank of public access computers, sorting out who is next in line and helping those who are having difficulty navigating the Internet or who are frustrated in their attempt to print off some government document to apply for social assistance. She is very busy and a bit distracted, but I introduce myself as a visitor from Canada.

"Are you looking for a computer?" she asks. "They are all busy at the moment, but I can put your name on the waiting list."

"No, no. I was just curious. I had heard that libraries in Britain were facing a real funding crisis, but your library looks well-stocked and very modern. And very well used, I might add."

She brushes a long strand of hair out of her eyes and speaks without ever losing sight of the bank of computers she is monitoring. "Well, we have been fortunate. The local community has been very generous. Not all libraries are as lucky. Some...well, many, have been closed in recent years."

"Why some and not others?"

"It's the old story. Wealthy communities have the funding to support public libraries. Poor communities do not."

It's true. Almost eight hundred public libraries have closed in Britain since 2010 and eight thousand seven hundred paid library staff have been laid off, resulting in approximately 89 million fewer visits in 2019 than in 2009.[9] Five hundred libraries are now run entirely by volunteers with varying levels of local support.[10] It's the old vicious circle: cut the funding and libraries can't offer the same levels of service they used to, so people stop coming. Then funding is pulled altogether because attendance is down. And of course, the areas that are most affected are those with the poorest economies, where the libraries are most needed.

Our conversation reminds me of Derek's comments over dinner in Alton where he had lamented the decline of social services in Britain. "Growing up in England," he had said, as he twirled his pasta on a fork, "I'd always taken it for granted that certain social services were our rights as Englishmen, that there were certain lines that would never be crossed, no matter what, like publicly funded health care. But I have lived to see it all dismantled—health care, state schools, even the post office. In the modern world, it seems, the market trumps the public good every time." Public libraries, it seems, are another casualty of government cutbacks.

Later, back in my room at the White Horse, I decide to dip back into *Pilgrim's Progress.*

Since Christian passed through the wicket gate, his path has been constricted on each side by tall stone walls designed to keep him on the straight and narrow, but he is surprised when two men clamber over the wall and join him on his pilgrimage. They are called Formalist and Hypocrisy. Christian warns them that they cannot enter the Celestial City unless they come in by the Gate and unless they have a Coat, Mark and Roll as he does. Formalist and Hypocrisy look at each other and laugh. "What does it matter how we got in?" They reason: You came in by the Gate and we came over the wall, but all have arrived at the same place. We have been taking shortcuts all our lives. Why stop now?

They arrive at the bottom of the Hill of Difficulty. This looks too strenuous for Formalist and Hypocrisy, who part ways with Christian and seek an easier route. Christian's lonely path up the Hill of Difficulty is so steep that in places he is forced to crawl on his hands and knees. Halfway up, he reaches a comfortable arbour and stops to rest and to read his scroll. Overcome with weariness, he falls asleep. Awakening later, he hears a voice saying, "Go to the ant, thou sluggard; consider her ways and be wise."[11] Ashamed of his weakness, he leaps to his feet and speeds up the hill, only to meet two men coming down. These two, Timorous and Mistrustful, have given up and warn him that the path ahead is impassable, for two lions guard the road. He reaches the top just as it is growing dark and sees a stately palace off the path guarded by the two lions. He hesitates but is bid forward by the porter at the lodge, who assures him that the lions are chained. As long as he keeps to the centre of the path, they cannot harm him. It is a test of faith. He arrives at the Palace Beautiful and, led by four grave and beautiful virgins, is assigned a place to sleep for the night, a bedroom called Peace.

I set the story aside and I too fall asleep, dreaming of virgins who are also beautiful, though perhaps not so grave, little realizing that I will soon be facing my own Hill of Difficulty in the morning.

7
Dorking to Reigate

Does the road wind up-hill all the way?
Yes, to the very end.
Will the day's journey take the whole long day?
From morn to night, my friend.
　—CHRISTINA ROSSETTI, "Up-Hill"

IT RAINED ALL NIGHT, so everything is wet when I leave Dorking. As I retrace my steps from the day before, the vineyards, which had reminded me of Tuscany in the bright sun of the previous afternoon, now look gloomy and dismal. I have to walk up one side of the busy A24 to find an underpass, and then back down the far side to find a place to cross the river Mole. A slight detour takes me to the Burford Bridge Hotel, an old inn with many famous associations. Lord Nelson bade Lady Hamilton goodbye here before Trafalgar. Robert Louis Stevenson stayed here while he was writing his *New Arabian Nights*.

Perhaps the most celebrated visitor was the poet John Keats, who was staying at the inn during a famous case of writer's block in late November of 1817. He had been struggling to finish the last movement of his long poem *Endymion*, which he said was "wanting five hundred lines."[1] He came to Burford, he told his friend Benjamin Bailey, because he needed a change of scene and a change of air to give him a spur to wind up his poem. It seemed to work. He wrote to another friend, John Hamilton Reynolds, that he liked the place "very much": "There is hill and dale and a little river. I went up Box Hill this evening after the moon [then]...came down, and wrote some lines."[2] The legend has sprung up that Keats, inspired by his moonlit walk on Box Hill, came back to his room and quickly wrote the last five hundred lines of his poem. I have serious doubts about this version of the story. Nobody writes five hundred lines of complicated iambic pentameter in a sudden fit of inspiration. That only happens in the movies.

The Mole has inspired a number of poets. This is mostly due to its curious habit of disappearing under the ground for a spell and then reappearing further downstream. Spenser, in *The Faerie Queene*, wrote:

> Mole, that like a nousling mole doth make
> His way still underground, till Thames he overtake.[3]

Milton and Pope both refer to the Mole as "sullen" because of this habit of hiding underground. Nevertheless, my problem with the Mole is not how to celebrate it in poetry, but how to cross it. My map indicates some stepping stones just south of the Burford Bridge Hotel, but I wonder if they will even be visible after the past two days of rain, or if they will be underwater.

I needn't have worried. I reach a landing that slopes down to the river beneath the shade of several large chestnut trees. The stepping stones, though slick with rain and algae, rise proud above the surface of the river. Crossing the stones isn't going to be the problem; getting down to the water is going to be the problem. The broad path leading down to the river is wet clay and as slippery as a children's playground slide. I try to avoid the clay by stepping on tree roots, but this proves to be a mistake. The roots are, if anything, more slippery, and my feet shoot out sideways and down I go. It will be the first of many pratfalls that day.

Once over the Mole, I am faced with the prospect of climbing Box Hill. Box Hill is named after the many box trees that once covered its slope. (Box, for the uninitiated, is a tight-grained wood beloved of wood carvers, particularly those making printing blocks). It is also a National Trust property, covered by a confusing network of hiking trails, and frequented by day-trippers seeking the beautiful views from the top of the hill. My path is a steep zigzag of rustic steps carved into the slippery clay. It's humid, and the temperature is already becoming uncomfortably hot. I am overdressed. Before long I'm drenched in sweat and short of breath. Up and up I trudge, carefully placing one foot in front of the other.

"Morn-NING!"

I look up to see a middle-aged jogger quickly descending the slope, two steps at a time, a terry towel sweatband wrapped around his balding head. I grunt a reply.

Up and up grinds the path.

"MORN-ning!" chirps my jogger, as he passes me yet again, this time coming up the hill from behind.

Forward I trudge, step by bloody step, up this infernal muddy staircase. Then, overcome by fatigue or carelessness, I place a foot on one of the roots crossing my path, and down I go a second time.

"Oops. You want to be careful of those roots," warns my cheerful jogger, descending the hill in bounding leaps. "They can be slippery."

I nod wordlessly, lying on my back and gasping for air. Thank you, Captain Obvious. I roll to my knees, pull myself to my feet, and carry on. Stomp, stomp, stomp, stomp.

"Pardon me, coming through," pipes my nemesis, springing up the slope yet again. I begin to fantasize ways of crippling him: piano wire garrote, bamboo Punji stakes smeared in strychnine, rabid sheepdog.

I am hunched over, grasping my knees and gasping for air when he passes me again.

"Almost there," he says, bouncing down the stairs. This guy isn't even breathing hard.

Rot in hell, I think.

Eventually, I reach the summit, but not before being lapped a sixth time by my cheerful companion.

"There you go. That wasn't so hard now, was it?"

I would like to say that I respond with a remark so cutting, so devastatingly clever that it leaves him gob-smacked, but I don't. It's tempting, but I hold my tongue. What purpose would be served by lashing out? It would temporarily mask my shame, but at what cost? One of the Desert Fathers of the early Christian community in Egypt, Abba Tithoes, was famous for saying, "To be on a pilgrimage is to be silent" (*peregrinatio est tacere*), meaning silence is an important part of the pilgrimage process, not just because silence leads us into contemplation, but because silence keeps us from harming others.[4] Biting back a cutting remark, no matter how tempting the target, is always a virtue. My jogger strikes me as a condescending type, but perhaps I am misreading the situation and he really is trying to be encouraging. So instead of replying, I simply nod in assent and try to smile. As soon as he is out of sight, I collapse onto the nearest park bench and down half the contents of my water bottle in a single gulp.

Box Hill was regarded as a beauty spot even in Jane Austen's day, and Austen sets a crucial scene here in *Emma*. The principal characters in the novel decide to go on a picnic to Box Hill (though the women travel by carriage and the men on horseback, not on foot as I did). The picnic is supposed to be a gay affair, but everyone seems to be out of sorts and dull, so one of the party, the young and handsome Frank Churchill, proposes a game to raise their spirits—everyone must tell Emma what is on their mind. If they say "either one thing very clever, be it prose or verse, original or repeated—or two things moderately clever—or three things very dull indeed" then Emma "must laugh heartily at them all."[5] Miss Bates, an impoverished and feather-headed spinster, who up until now has served as comic relief, volunteers to go first, saying, "I shall be sure to say three dull things as soon as ever I open my mouth, shan't I?" To which Emma rudely remarks: "Ah! Ma'am, but there may be difficulty. Pardon me—but you will be limited as to number—only three at once." Miss Bates is hurt, and apologetically withdraws. Mr. Knightley, whom Emma holds in very high regard, takes her aside and scolds her: "How could you be so unfeeling to Miss Bates? How could you be so insolent in your wit to a woman of her character, age and situation?—Emma, I had not thought it possible."[6] For the first time in her life, Emma is ashamed of her behaviour. It is a turning point. She later apologizes to Miss Bates and begins to see how much harm she has caused by her over-bearing, if often well-meaning, interference in the lives of those around her. Emma, who has always had a very high opinion of her own opinion, must learn some humility before she can be happy. Kindness, it would seem, not charity or wisdom, is the greatest virtue in Austen's world.

For me, though, my chief concern is to remain upright. For the rest of day is more of the same, with every tree root threatening to sweep my feet out from under me. I have to stop frequently to scrape accumulations of clay from my boots. Just before Brockham Quarries I see a large tombstone through the trees and leave the trail to investigate. "Quick," reads the chiselled stone, "An English Thoroughbred." Some pun about the quick and the dead suggests itself, but I am soon too busy trying to stay right-side up to be witty.

Coming down to the quarry is treacherous. The trail has worn a shallow trough along a sloping knife-edge of chalk, and, with the constant rain, it is more like a waterslide than a walking trail. I fall twice on my ass, hard. The quarries hold several abandoned lime kilns, the chimneys of which are, so the signpost informs me, now the home for eight species of bat, and so, somewhat ironically, this industrial scar has become a protected area of natural and scientific interest. I rejoin the Pilgrims' Way at the bottom of the hill and startle two green parakeets in a yew tree near the tiny village of the Coombe. Or rather, they startle me, for I had not expected to encounter a species so brightly hued and exotic in southern England, but apparently the ring-necked parakeet has become naturalized in Surrey and Kent, probably introduced by negligent pet owners. The wind picks up as I walk along a quiet farm track, and hawthorn blossoms drift down like snow. But it's a brief respite. Soon I have to climb the Downs once again. It's as bad as Box Hill.

I'm exhausted by the time I reach the top of the hill, but the wide-open views from the top of Colley Hill are worth it. There are lots of dog walkers, so clearly, it's a popular spot. There is a giant red brick water tower at the top of the hill with crenellations like a castle keep, and at the far side of a pasture filled with cattle, a folly, like a small Greek temple, called Inglis Folly, after Lieutenant Colonel Sir Robert William Inglis, v.c., who donated the pavilion to the Borough of Reigate in 1909. It originally housed a drinking fountain, but the cattle have murdered that. However, under the dome of the roof is a curious mosaic called a celestial clock, showing the night sky with the emptiness of space hollowed out with Prussian blue tile.

A little further down the trail, I come to Reigate Fort, an earth-ditched fort on the top of the Downs, complete with red brick barracks, storehouses and a magazine built into the hollow of a rectangular ditch to protect them from artillery fire. The fort was constructed in 1890 when a widespread fear of French invasion led the government of the time to construct a series of defensive installations along the Downs as a line of defense for London, just as the pillboxes were constructed in the Second World War. Reigate was one of thirteen depots—not really "forts" because they were not staffed, just defensible positions containing shot, powder, and entrenching tools. For many years, Reigate Fort was used as a campsite by the Boy Scouts, but recently it was acquired by the National Trust and now only sheep graze its ramparts. Just past the fort, I follow a bridleway down the hill to a modern motor hotel on the outskirts of Reigate.

There has been a lot of climbing up and down in the last two days, and I record some of the elevations:

St. Martha's Church 573 feet/175 metres (above sea level)
Box Hill 682 feet/208 metres
Colley Hill 738 feet/225 metres
Reigate Fort 754 feet/230 metres

After checking into the hotel, I walk to a service station up the road and buy some sandwiches, a couple of apples, and a large bottle of Coke, and retreat to my room to Skype my family.

To my surprise, they aren't at home, but are using a computer at the nearby public library. Our modem has died, I am informed. And my wife's car is leaking gas and will need a new gas tank. "But don't worry about us," she assures me. "How is your trip going? Do you feel like a pilgrim?"

Good question. After today, my answer would have to be, no. So far, this trip has not been life changing. It has been a diversion, an entertaining diversion, but nothing more. I say goodnight to the kids and log off, feeling guilty, and reflect that all of my problems will still be waiting for me when I get home. What am I doing with my life?

This may be one question my father could *not* have helped me with, for my father never really settled down to anything. Oh, his faith was rock solid. I don't mean that. But his work life was always in turmoil. He never stuck with a job for very long, and in that sense, he was not a great role model. When he finished high school, he joined Hayes Steel in St. Catharines, Ontario, as an apprentice tool and die maker, but the steel industry soon went into a slump, and he was laid off. As a newly married man with a baby (me), he needed to find a job, and fast. He did, working as a laboratory technician at a government-run experimental farm. The job even came with a small white clapboard cottage for his young family. (The farm is now Lester B. Pearson Park in the heart of St. Catharines, but the cottage was torn down long ago). He enjoyed the job. He even helped to co-author a paper on new ways to inoculate rabbits for laboratory experiments, of which he was extremely proud, but it was hard to raise a family on a lab tech's salary. One day, the Tempter entered in the form of a travelling salesman.

"Sales," this slick devil crooned, "that's the way for a young man with ambition to get ahead. A bright young fellow like you could make a killing in sales."

So my father quit his job, joined a laboratory supply firm, and moved us to Ottawa. For the next thirty-five years my father was a travelling salesman, a job for which he was temperamentally unsuited. He was a kindly, soft-spoken man and lacked the killer instinct needed to close a sale. When the economy was booming, he did okay; when the economy tanked, we ate casserole. Over the course of his career, my father sold laboratory supplies, audiovisual equipment (overhead projectors, 8mm film projectors, slide projectors and the like), school textbooks, school uniforms, welding supplies, and God knows what else. Each new position promised greater prosperity, a better salary and a chance for promotion; but after a few years, each, in turn, proved a disappointment, and he would accept a new position in a new territory. For one job (school textbooks), his territory was Alberta, Saskatchewan and northern British Columbia, an area roughly the size of western Europe, and he was often on the road for as much as six weeks at a stretch. We moved, on average, every four years.

In retrospect, I realize this must have been very tough on my mother. Most of the child-rearing fell to her. She was a strict disciplinarian and broke many hairbrushes and wooden spoons across my backside over the years, but there came a time when I was too old for her to bend over her knee, and all she could do was threaten: "Just wait till your father gets home!" This was a crazy threat and my three siblings and I knew it. Not only was Dad the biggest softy in the world, but it might also be weeks before we saw him again. When he returned, tired and dispirited, my mother would haul us out and reel off our many misdeeds, expecting my father to do something immediately. We would stand before him, heads bowed, silent. He would sigh.

"Follow me." He would herd us into his office, sit us down, close the door, and try his best to look stern.

"Is this true?" he would ask.

"Yes, sir," we would answer, looking as repentant as possible.

"Do you realize what you've done was very wrong?"

"Yes, sir."

"And do you promise never to do it again?"

"Yes, sir."

"Okay, now buzz off and play."

In his fifties, my father inherited a small sum of money, quit his latest sales job, and started his own business, an investment firm that quickly failed. The stress nearly killed him. He gained weight and had a series of mild heart attacks. At fifty-eight, he was broke, unemployed and almost unemployable—a position I found myself in a few years ago at a slightly younger age. (I'd quit my job as a librarian to become a full-time writer with equally dismal financial success). My father learned that a local factory, manufacturing veterinary medicine, was hiring, so he rewrote his resumé, leaving off the three decades of sales experience, and applied. He was granted an interview. The interviewers were surprised—they had expected a much younger man from his sparse resumé—but they gave him the job, and he quickly rose to become lead hand. He rode his bicycle to work every day, lost weight, grew healthier, and died happy, if poor.

In many ways I am like my father. For the first part of my life I was constantly changing jobs. Those early positions were all contract jobs, and so I would have had to change anyway, but this didn't bother me much. Everything I owned could be packed in a trunk, and I was able to see much of the world this way: Bhutan, India, China, Europe, and the Canadian Arctic. But once married with children, I needed to settle down, so I found a long-term position as the director of a public library. I put down roots. My children have grown up in the same small town, attended the same small school, had the same small circle of friends, and have never known the constant uprooting of my childhood. I think they are happy and secure as a result, but it's killing me. I get itchy feet every few years. I want to chuck everything and hit the road. But I can't. I have a mortgage and three kids who depend on me, so I stick with the job I have now, even if it depresses the hell out of me.

My biggest fear is that I will cease to care. At the moment, I am a very conscientious public servant. I make endless to-do lists and work my way through them diligently. I think I am a good boss. I try to do the best I can, but I am miserable. Like my father, I have fallen into a line of work for which I am temperamentally unsuited. At heart, I am a doer, not a manager. I spend my days attending meetings, writing reports, answering emails, drawing up budgets, writing planning and policy documents, supervising other people while they do their work (usually far more interesting work than mine), and I hate it. I feel like I am wasting my life, and I am constantly aware of the existential clock ticking.

I want to walk away from my desk, from my worries, from my job. I want to place a pack on my back, put the road beneath my boots, and tramp away from my troubles like a scholar gypsy. So I find myself here, on the road to Canterbury, desperately hoping for a cure to my utter despair.

8

Reigate to Godstone

By all means use some time to be alone.
Salute thyself: See what thy soul doth wear.
Dare to look in thy chest; for 'tis thine own:
And tumble up and down what thou find'st there.
Who cannot rest till he good fellows find,
He breaks up house, turns out of doors his mind.
　　—GEORGE HERBERT, "The Church Porch"

I LEAVE REIGATE IN A GREY DRIZZLE and climb the intermi-
nable hill up a muddy bridle path to Gatton Park, once the grand
estate of mustard king Jeremiah Colman. The grounds, designed by
Lancelot "Capability" Brown, now house the Royal Alexandra and
Albert School, founded in 1864. I had hoped to see the inside of the
old church on the estate. The fifth Lord Monson decorated it with
architectural curiosities pilfered while on the Grand Tour in 1830,
and it is apparently quite something to behold; but I arrive as a

service is in progress, so turn my attention to the "Town Hall" instead.

At one time someone erected a folly, a small Greek temple, on the grounds, calling it Gatton's Town Hall. The intention was either ironic or self-serving, for Gatton was one of the most notorious rotten boroughs in England, a riding with only seven voters, but which nonetheless returned two members to parliament at each election. Cobbett was scathing in his scorn for Gatton and the wealthy "tax-eaters" who thus controlled seats in what was supposed to be a democratic institution. Cobbett supported Sir Francis Burdett's motion in parliament to abolish rotten boroughs. "Will you still cling to the rotten-borough system," recorded Cobbett approvingly in the *Political Register*, "the creature of innovation, nursed by usurpation and matured by corruption?"[1] Is it reasonable, Burdett argued, to convert into private property, "that which the constitution has declared to be a public trust—to permit a usurped local sovereignty, independent of the king, independent of the people and destructive to both?"[2] Under the roof of the open Doric pavilion is a stone urn on a plinth with four lines of Latin incised around the bowl. These translate as:

> *When the lots have been drawn, the urn remains*
> *Let the well-being of the people be the supreme law*
> *The place of assembly of Gatton 1745*
> *Let evil deception be absent.*[3]

Is there a touch of deliberate cynicism here, or did the seven voters of Gatton really believe they were acting in the best interest of the people? At any rate, the Reform Act of 1832 did away with the rotten boroughs. Today, Gatton, once the haunt of the privileged, is a state-run boarding school for children.

From Gatton Park, it is a short walk to Merstham. My path takes me down the hill and through the local golf course. I see an agitated man abandon his friends on a golf green and trot stiff-legged in my direction. I've seen that walk before on enough toddlers to know the cause, and, sure enough, as he rounds a small copse on the edge of the green, the golfer turns his back to me, unzips his fly, and strikes the pose. His sigh of relief is almost palpable. No sooner has he exposed himself than up walks a middle-aged woman with her golden retriever from the other side of the trees. The dog sniffs the golfer's sagging trousers, the woman changes colour, and his friends burst into raucous laughter. Welcome to Merstham.

I enter Merstham by way of the village cricket pitch. Youngsters are warming up by jogging around the field in their cricket whites, while parents, paper cups of takeout coffee in their hands, stand blearily in the bleachers, clearly wishing they were still in bed. This could be Sunday morning at any hockey arena back home.

Merstham is a pretty place that the motorcar has destroyed. The village has been sliced and parcelled by motorways into almost unbridgeable parts. I walk up Quality Street, a row of attractive seventeenth and eighteenth-century cottages, constructed in a builder's manual of styles in brick, stone and timber. The street gained its name in the early twentieth century, when the stars of J.M. Barrie's play *Quality Street* lived in the Forge at the top of the quiet lane. In 2014, these picturesque cottages are the homes of wealthy commuters with the average cottage selling for £600,000 (or about $1 million Canadian). Struggling actors must look elsewhere for accommodation these days.

A scary overpass crosses the M25 and takes me to St. Katherine's Church. Merstham's early wealth was built on the strength of the limestone quarried nearby, and St. Katherine's is built of that stone. Merstham stone was of excellent quality and had the reputation of becoming harder with age. The country's first public railway linked Merstham with the Thames, so that stone quarried in Merstham could help build the city of London. However, those early Merstham stone boosters hadn't anticipated acid rain. The stonework on this eight-hundred-year-old church is peeling off in brittle layers like the skin on a sunburned nose.

I cross under the lych-gate and climb the shaded slope to the church, now cut off from the village by several major highways. It's quiet, and despite its being a Sunday morning, there appears to be no one about. Approaching the porch under the bell tower I hear the mutter of voices. Turning the corner, I spy a pair of legs encased, sausage-like, in pink fleecy track pants. The upper part of the body is hidden in shadow, and I realize that the speaker is reading the notices on the noticeboard under the stone arch, or pretending to, for the words that emerge are nonsense.

"Hmm, yes. Mustn't eat the cat. Pretty cat. Pretty, pretty cat. Hmm, yes...."

"Excuse me," I ask. "Is the church open for visitors?"

"Hurry, hurry, eat your curry. Hmm, yes. Must hurry, yes...."

"Sorry, I don't understand. May I go into the church?"

"Church, yes. No. No one at home."

"Pardon?"

The speaker steps into the sunlight and I see her face. She has Down's syndrome, and I realize she has been trying to tell me the church is empty. Thank you, I say, and she waddles away, ignoring me, still muttering to herself, locked in private conversation. I try the door. It too is locked, which seems a shame on a Sunday morning.

A quiet lane through characterless suburbia takes me to a long, sinister passage under the M23 that is littered with trash and empty bottles. Spray-painted graffiti covers the damp concrete. "Vandalism is an art," someone has scrawled in letters stretching from floor to ceiling. I remain skeptical. Soon I am out in the open fields again and climbing.

My plan today is to take another detour. Several miles to the north of the trail rests the tiny country church of St. Peter and St. Paul in Chaldon. In 1869, workmen renovating the church discovered an early thirteenth-century mural hidden beneath a layer of whitewash at the back of the nave. The mural was carefully uncovered and is the oldest and most complete example of a Doom mural in existence. It is a depiction of the Day of Judgement, illustrating the various punishments exacted for each of the seven deadly sins. I'd first encountered the mural as an illustration in a magazine article. The cartoony monochrome illustration fascinated me, and when I learned that the original was just a few miles off my route I was determined to visit it.

Today is also my second Sunday and remembering my disappointment in Winchester, I approach the church of St. Peter and St. Paul with trepidation. After a week of walking in the sun and rain, I am not very presentable. My boots and trousers are spattered with mud and cow dung, my backpack is sweat-stained, and when I remove my baseball cap my hair remains plastered to my skull with perspiration. As I push open the heavy oak door and enter the tiny parish church, twelve heads turn in my direction from the last two rows of pews.

"I'm sorry," I sputter. "Have I interrupted choir practice?"

A tall man in tweed with a neatly trimmed grey beard unfolds himself from the near seat and beckons me in. "Yes, but not to worry. We've just finished. Come in and have a peek around. But don't linger," he warns me, with a twinkle in his eye, "or you will have to stay for the sermon. Service starts in fifteen minutes."

"Reg," chides a female chorister, possibly his wife, "Perhaps he *wants* to stay for the service. Can't you see he's a pilgrim?"

I needn't have worried about my reception. I am made welcome and the ancient church is soon packed with parishioners of all ages. The choir sings with gusto, the Sunday School students proudly exhibit a flock of cotton ball sheep, and the minister preaches a thoughtful sermon larded with references to the "dim sheep" in a Monty Python sketch. Following the service, I am invited into the parish hall for coffee and refreshments, but observing the friendly gathering through the glass panel that separates the ancient church from the hall, I feel like a gate crasher at a family wedding, so I retreat to the nave to get a closer look at the mural.

The mural is enormous, taking up the entire back wall of the church and is painted in muted shades of red and yellow. It is possible that the mural was more colourful once, but that the colours have faded with time. The schema is simple. The wall is divided into two layers, like a two-storey doll's house, with a ladder extending top-to-bottom in the middle, effectively cutting the picture in half and creating four equal quadrants. There are figures climbing the ladder to a cloudy eminence, which I presume to be Heaven. There are also figures descending the ladder, sometimes falling off the ladder, to the lower level, which represents Hell. The upper floor of this curious doll's house represents Purgatory, and in the top left-hand corner stands an archangel, possibly Michael, weighing the souls of the recently dead, who are portrayed as little doll-like figures who stand in a line awaiting their turn to be judged. A large demon stands to one side of the scale, slyly poking a finger in one pan to sway the judgement in his favour. Other angels are ushering the saved to the ladder to begin their ascension. On the top right, Christ stands above a supine Satan, spearing him in the mouth with a staff that is topped with a cross. Other doll-like figures are emerging in prayerful attitudes from a bed of flames near Satan's head, perhaps representing those ancient souls whom Christ redeemed at the time of his death and resurrection.

In many ways the lower level, Hell, is the more entertaining. It is populated with giant demons and smaller imps who are prod-ding and herding the damned with pitchforks, and who seem to be quite enjoying their work. Half the fun is trying to decide what the sinners have been condemned for. There are figures tossed in a boiling pot—gluttons, perhaps—and another figure who squats over a fire while coins pour out of his mouth—a usurer? Three small figures, whose feet are gnawed by a dog, may represent sloth. And there are other figures that could represent pride, envy and lust. There is also a curious bridge of spikes that various figures cross carrying the tools of their trade. One commentator has read this as an illustration of the hopeless and unending travail of Hell;

for example, a potter tries to form a pot without a wheel, and a blacksmith tries to forge a shoe without an anvil. Finally, in the bottom right hand corner stands the tree of knowledge from the . Garden of Eden, complete with a cunning serpent, the source of all this sin.

I wonder what the modern parishioners make of all this, especially the children. In the Middle Ages, when this mural was commissioned, you were held accountable for the choices in your life. There would be a reckoning. But today: What standard am I held to? This was a question my father might have answered.

You have to remember that the men who commissioned this mural believed in the doctrine of original sin. St. Augustine (354–430 CE), an early church father from Hippo in North Africa (not to be confused with the later St. Augustine, who died in 604 CE and was the first Archbishop of Canterbury) defined original sin as the inclination we have to follow our base desires against our reason, which he ascribed to the fault of Adam and Eve who ate the fruit of the Tree of Knowledge against God's will. Because of this "original sin," human beings have, ever since, been hard-wired for selfishness, sensuality and violence, and that it is only through the sacrifice of Christ that we can be redeemed.

Of course, not everyone agreed with this formula. By contrast, Jean-Jacques Rousseau, a philosopher of the Enlightenment, believed the opposite to be true. He wrote, "Man is born free, and everywhere he is in chains."[4] Men and women living in a state of nature, Rousseau asserted, are essentially good, but society corrupts them. Even liberal Christians dislike the doctrine of original sin. They argue, "Why would a loving God create us with a deliberate design flaw or deny us our humanity?" But if we are by nature sinful, and history would seem to suggest that we are, a mural such as this would be useful. It would warn us of the consequences of allowing our worst impulses to guide our behavior.

As I turn to leave, a memorial catches my eye. It is dedicated to a poor woman who had survived a shipwreck while emigrating to

Jamaica with her second husband. Her husband died, the climate ruined her health, but she endured the vicissitudes of life without complaint, and is buried here, a model of virtue for all to follow.

My trip to Chaldon has taken me a little out of my way, but a couple of local footpaths soon put me back on the Pilgrims' Way. Before I know it, I am descending the North Downs, crossing the busy M25 and following a local footpath into the village of Godstone. As has become my pattern in the last few days: I walk high on a ridge during the day and sleep in the valley.

Godstone is lovely. Constructed around a triangular green, now the village cricket pitch, it is surrounded by picturesque inns, suggesting that it was always an important stop on the way to somewhere else. One, the White Hart, is very old—said to date back to the reign of Richard II—and famous. It is mentioned by Cobbett, who passed through on January 8, 1822: "At and near Godstone the gardens are all very neat; and at the Inn, there is a nice garden, well stocked with beautiful flowers in the season. I here saw last summer some double violets as large as small pinks and the lady of the house was kind enough to give me some of the roots."[5] I am staying in the Godstone Hotel next door—also lovely and dating back to the reign of Elizabeth I (so a relative young-ster by comparison), when it was originally a coach house called the Greyhound Inn. My room is around back in what used to be the stables. Because I arrive with time to spare, I dump my bag in my room and decide to explore the neighbourhood.

A wooded causeway leads me over the earthen dam of an artifi-cial pond, called Bay Pond, east of the town. An explanatory plaque erected by the local town council tells me that this pond was constructed by the grandfather of the diarist John Evelyn to power his gunpowder mill. The Evelyn family had been granted a patent by Elizabeth I to supply the Crown with gunpowder, which became the foundation of the family fortune. Once the site of busy manu-facture, today it is bucolic. A woman with a stroller and a passel of children passes me walking one direction, while a mallard and her ducklings paddle by in the other. The path leads me to a smaller but even more attractive village with cottages in zigzag brick, a Norman church with a tall tapering spire, and an impossibly picturesque timbered almshouse designed to house eight of the deserving poor. The almshouse is deceiving though, for I learn that it is not nearly as old as it looks but was actually constructed in the nineteenth century at the height of the Arts and Crafts movement in faux-Tudor style. The church is open and empty, and I wander around exploring. On the path through the churchyard leading up from the road I spy a weathered grave marker bearing a skull and crossbones. Local legend says that it is the grave of a notorious pirate and smuggler, John Edward Trenchman, but it is impossible to glean any details from the weathered limestone.

Born in the London dockyards, Trenchman ran away to sea at the age of twelve and joined the crew of the notorious pirate Henry Morgan. Many years later, Trenchman returned to England and captained a smuggling boat that operated along the southeast coast. Betrayed by one of his crew, Trenchman and his gang were ambushed one night in 1687 by customs officers while carrying a cartload of contraband up Tilburstow Hill, just south of Godstone. All were killed but Trenchman, who managed to drag himself to the Fox and Hounds Inn, where he expired. He was buried in an unmarked grave in this churchyard, but repeated hauntings by a nautical ghost convinced the locals to exhume his body and give him a proper Christian burial and erect this headstone, at which time the ghostly visitations ceased. Or so the story goes.

I return to my hotel and decide to splurge. It has been a good day, so I dine in the hotel restaurant on paté and chutney on toast, with roast pork, beets and potatoes in an apple-apricot sauce. It is delicious, but when I go to pay for it, my credit card is declined. We try again. Declined a second time. This is embarrassing. I excuse myself, return to my room and rifle every pocket and pouch until I assemble enough stray cash to pay for my fare. This could be serious. I am only halfway through my walk. If my credit card has stopped working, I'm screwed. I return to my room in a funk. I don't have a phone, there is no Wi-Fi, no way at all to contact my bank at home. I decide to trust in Providence and hope this is just a glitch.

The night has turned cold. My room is, in fact, a converted box stall and the wind whistles around the poorly fitting door. So, with nothing better to do, I curl up in my bed under an eiderdown and return to Bunyan's tale of pilgrimage. Christian has now crossed the Hill of Difficulty and enters the Valley of Humiliation. The virgins in Palace Beautiful have given him armour to protect him on his journey, and he soon has need of it, for he is confronted by the demon Apollyon. Apollyon tells Christian that he is the lord of the town Christian is fleeing, and he has not given him leave to go. Christian says that he has switched his allegiance. He no longer recognizes Apollyon as his ruler, but instead follows Jesus. Apollyon is furious and attacks Christian, battering him to the ground in a battle that must have thrilled early readers before the invention of moving pictures and CGI technology. Christian somehow prevails and continues his journey, entering the Valley of the Shadow of Death, a place of deserts and pits, teeming with hobgoblins and other fearful creatures. The path here is treacherous. A single misstep could cost him his life, especially as he edges past a burning pit that is the open mouth of Hell. Up ahead he hears a voice shouting, "Though I walk through the Valley of the Shadow of Death, I will fear none ill, for Thou art with me."[6] Hurrying ahead, Christian is overjoyed to overtake Faithful, a friend from back home, who has also undertaken the journey to the Celestial City.

The two meet a tall man upon the road called Talkative, who preaches well, and Faithful is quite taken with him. But Christian draws Faithful aside and cautions him, for he knows Talkative of old, and says he is a man who talks much about faith but doesn't practise it. He is "a saint abroad, and devil at home," for he treats his family, his servants and his neighbours shamefully. Hearing and saying don't make a good man, says Christian. Practising what you believe does, for there is a vast difference between a talker and a doer. He reminds Faithful of St. Paul's admonition to the people of Corinth: "Though I speak with the tongues of men and of angels, and have not charity, I am become as sounding brass, or a tinkling cymbal."[7]

Why is it that I always recognize myself in the villains of this piece?

9

Godstone to Otford

Stand at the crossroads, and look, and ask for the ancient paths,
where the good way lies; and walk in it, and find rest for
your souls.

—JEREMIAH 6:16

DESPITE MY FINANCIAL WORRIES, I sleep well. Buried deep
beneath my eiderdown with the cool country air nipping my nose,
it is the most peaceful night so far. After breakfast (fortunately
included in my pre-booked accommodation), I slog back up the hill
to the North Downs Way—hundreds and hundreds of carved
steps—and am back on the main trail by nine o'clock. The first
stretch is depressing, lots of garbage strewn throughout the
forest—plastic bottles, trash bags, a mattress, some blankets, and a
torn and faded nylon tent. It looks as if someone had been living
rough in the woods at one time and had just walked away from
their gear. I cross a busy road and drop into a deep wooded dell.
The sun moves behind some clouds, and suddenly I feel a chill that

has nothing to do with the temperature. Crows call direly from the trees overhead, seeming to mock my slow progress through the twisting muddy trail. Once I am past this section and climbing the hill again, I immediately feel better and tell myself that this sense of dread is all in my imagination. (Though later, when I consult the map, I discover that this feature is called the Devil's Hole).

As I continue my climb through Marden Woods (donated to a grateful nation by the conductor Sir Adrian Boult), the sun comes out once more. I spy a fox and dozens of rabbits. As the woods open up onto bare chalk slopes, hundreds of large yellow butter-flies surround me, landing on my hat and shoulders. Perhaps they are attracted to my bright red T-shirt. At one point I see a railway line disappear into the hill beneath my feet, as I cross over a tunnel that cuts right through the Downs. Stretches of the old Pilgrims' Way follow, and then once more I am climbing the Downs. My map tells me this is the Titsey Estate and I am hoping to catch a glimpse of Titsey Manor, but the woods are too dense. Up and up I slog, endlessly it seems, finally emerging at a car park at the top of the hill only to discover from a large visitor map that any of the cross paths labelled "Titsey Estate" I stepped over on my way to the top would probably have taken me to Titsey Manor. Oh well, too late. Also, at 853 feet, this is the highest hill I will have to climb on my journey.

Leaving Titsey Estate, I follow the aptly named Chestnut Avenue, quite a long stretch of road, walking past large gated suburban villas. One of the houses, called Mole End, has silhou-ettes of Mole and Ratty from *The Wind in the Willows* painted on the wall, while next door an old-fashioned gas-powered lamppost is fixed at the end of the drive, like the one found in Narnia. These lend an air of whimsy to a neighbourhood that is otherwise quite forbidding—iron gates, high walls, CCTV cameras, keypad secu-rity and aggressive signage like "Flytippers Beware! See You In Court!" At one razor wire-topped gate, a pair of Alsatians do their best to eat me through the wire barrier. It is all very depressing, the overwhelming presence of CCTV cameras especially. Britons, I later learn, have more of these closed-circuit TV cameras per capita than any other nation on earth. It seems ironic that the country that gave us George Orwell should be so amenable to such constant and all-pervading surveillance. Big Brother indeed. What are the rich so frightened of? It also strikes me that if this had been Canada, these villas would have been fronted by beautifully-landscaped, but never used, front lawns; whereas here, everything is surrounded by high security fences—not so different from the rich in the middle ages who surrounded their homes with high walls, moats and guarded gatehouses.

I am glad to escape the stockbroker belt and re-enter farmland, though it means passing through field after field of cattle. In a corner of one field I see an interesting sight: two mature beech trees with plum-coloured leaves flanking a large brick entrance gate—but there is no drive. Wherever it had once gone, it is now grown in and leads nowhere. The trail continues along the North Downs as I enter Chevening Estate. Suddenly there is a gap in the trees by a trailside bench—an aperture cut like a gun sight— that perfectly frames Chevening House. It is very dramatic, a real Brideshead moment. I decide to leave the North Downs Way, descend the hill on a public footpath, and visit the estate's chapel, which, according to my map, lies just south of the Pilgrims' Way. I'm glad I do, for as I emerge from the trees on a broad grassy slope, I am rewarded again with a marvellous view of Chevening House, which, though not open to the public, may be as close as I come to fine English Country House on this walk. The central block was constructed in 1616–1630 to a design by Inigo Jones, the great Restoration architect and stage designer, for the seventh Earl Dacre. The estate was sold in 1717 to James Stanhope, one of Marlborough's generals, who became the first Lord Stanhope, and foreign secretary under George I. Stanhope added the two wings, turning the Jacobean manor into a Palladian-style mansion. In 1959, the seventh Earl Stanhope donated the house to the nation with a sum of money for its upkeep, hoping it would become the country residence of the prime minister of the day. However, maintaining such a residence was more than most politicians could afford, since it came with a substantial tax burden, so it remained empty for almost two decades. A special Act of Parliament eventually dealt with the tax problem, but it continued to remain untenanted until 1974, when Prince Charles announced it would become his country house. But the Prince only stayed for six years before he transferred his residence to Highgrove in Gloucestershire. Once again, the house sat empty, an embarrassing situation for Parliament. In 1987, the amended Chevening Estate Act made it the Prime Minister's responsibility to nominate a resident, usually a cabinet minister. In 2014, it is occupied by the Foreign Secretary—a nifty coincidence, since that had been its original purpose under the first Lord Stanhope back in 1717.

In the centre of the little village of Chevening, just down the road from Chevening House, is the Church of St. Botolph's. St. Botolph is the patron saint of travellers, so it seemed appropriate that I drop in and pay a visit. It is a beautiful little fifteenth-century Norman church with a square battlemented tower and, in a side chapel, a marvellous collection of memorials to the Stanhopes and Dacres, who sleep atop their tombs in sculptured alabaster torpor. The tomb of Lady Frederica Louisa Stanhope is particularly moving for, though she died in childbirth, the sculptor has portrayed her asleep atop her chest tomb, in her nightgown with the baby tucked snugly in the crook of her arm. Leaving the church, I walk through the churchyard and pause beside the simple grave of the last Earl Stanhope, generous donor to his nation, who probably never realized how much trouble his generosity would cause.

The last stretch of walking is the worst. Leaving Chevening, I am forced to walk along the side of a busy highway, with no shoulder, to reach a bridge where I can cross over the M25. After a number of near misses with traffic whizzing by in both directions on a long curve, I arrive at Donnington Manor where I am to spend the night—perhaps the strangest of the places where I will sleep on my journey. The front of the hotel is a black-timbered Elizabethan manor, but the back, hidden from sight, is a modern North American-style Best Western Hotel. It is in the middle of farmland, near a busy highway, with no village close by, so without a working credit card I am forced to dine on cookies and apples, with a cup of courtesy tea brewed on the little kettle in my hotel room. I go to bed ravenous, determined to gorge myself on the free English breakfast the following morning.

On the whole this has not been my favourite day—too much slogging up and down hills, too many busy roads, too much stock-broker suburbia to traverse under constant video surveillance. Once again, I ask myself: What I am doing this for? Historically, there are any number of reasons for undertaking a pilgrimage. Historian John Ure in his *Pilgrimages: The Great Adventure of the Middle Ages*, lists five.

The first was to seek a cure for some affliction that medical science (which, let's face it, wasn't much of a science back then) had failed to address. Many pilgrims travelled to a holy shrine to seek the intercession of the saint, who might plead their cause in Heaven. Even today, some six million pilgrims visit Lourdes in France each year, many of them seeking a miracle cure. Many of those pilgrims believed that the relics of a saint—the jewelled skull, finger bone or scapula—could transfer wellness by their very proximity. In Winchester Cathedral, as we've seen, pilgrims used to crawl beneath the tomb of Saint Swithun, hoping that some of the saint's mojo might rub off.

Pilgrims began to come to Thomas Becket's tomb almost immediately after his death, some claiming miraculous cures caused by the intercession of the Saint on their behalf. The monks in Canterbury began a lucrative trade in small lead ampoules of the Saint's blood, which they claimed to have sopped up at the time of his murder, and which pious pilgrims could purchase as keepsakes that would protect the bearer. Becket's official sanctity was proclaimed remarkably quickly. In just two short years after his death, the Pope declared Becket a saint—a rather quick turnaround considering that, in addition to leading an exemplary life, a sanctified person must perform at least two confirmed miracles.

The second reason for pilgrimage, at least in the early days, was to atone for a sin or a crime. Penitential pilgrims were often assigned a pilgrimage by their confessor as a measure of atonement. This was not always the soft option you might think, especially if the penitent was travelling to Jerusalem. A pilgrimage to the Holy Land was fraught with dangers, like bandits, plague, shipwreck and war. Many set out; some never returned.

A third reason was to seek an indulgence, a church-sponsored shortcut to Heaven. In a violent age when the idea of everlasting punishment was considered a very real possibility, the idea that you could somehow buy forgiveness through the Church's indulgence was a welcome alternative. In other words, a sinner, by making a pilgrimage, might bypass Purgatory or at least shorten one's stay there significantly. Pope Boniface VIII, for example, declared that the year 1300 CE would be a special jubilee year and promised that pilgrims who visited Rome in that year would be granted a plenary indulgence. This was the Pope's guarantee that, through the prayers and intercession of the Church, all the pilgrim's sins, accrued over the course of a lifetime, would be forgiven. When a pilgrim arrived in Rome, all he needed to do was, first seek confession of his sins from a priest, and then to visit the basilicas of St. Peter and St. Paul at least once each day for fifteen days in a row. If this was done, all sins would be erased. As a result of the Pope's announcement, thousands of pilgrims flocked to the Holy See that summer. The roads were choked with pilgrims, inns and hostels ran out of beds, and Romans who catered to the pilgrim trade grew very rich.

Of course, then as now, some pilgrims were simply travelling in search of a change of scenery. Today, we would call them tourists. Many of Chaucer's pilgrims fell into this category. The Wife of

Bath, we are told, had been to Jerusalem three times, as well as to Rome, Compostela, and (perhaps for the sake of rhyme) Boulogne and Cologne. She had also outlived five husbands. If she were alive today, we would probably find her dancing in the conga line on the Lido deck of a Caribbean cruise ship, seeking husband number six.

Others used pilgrimage as a cloak to escape trouble, for pilgrimage gave common people the right to travel in an age when getting permission to leave home was difficult. Most people in the Middle Ages were not as free to pick up and go as we are today. Serfs and peasants needed permission from their local lord or priest to leave the parish of their birth. Pilgrimage was seen as a worthy reason to travel, and so it was condoned for the good of the soul. Some "pilgrims" were undoubtedly criminals or people on the run from the law. A host of sins could be hidden under the guise of piety.

However, the last and most enduring reason for taking a pilgrimage was spiritual. There is a sense that certain places, because of their association with a saint or other holy person, are charged with spiritual significance, and that a journey to these places can help the pilgrim's own spiritual progress.

Pilgrimage was also big business. Saints drew pilgrims, and pilgrims left offerings at shrines. A shrine containing the relics of a popular saint could benefit the local economy, bringing welcome donations that could assist with large building projects, like the construction of a cathedral. This economic benefit also led to a certain amount of shrine raiding. The people of Galatia, for example, stole the body of St. James from Jerusalem and brought it home to northern Spain, where it eventually found a home in Santiago and drew hundreds of thousands of pilgrims each year. Venice stole the body of St. Mark from Alexandria. Italian merchants from the city of Bari stole St. Nicholas (yes, Santa Claus!) from Myra in Turkey. When legitimate relics could not be had, illegitimate ones were invented. Chaucer's Pardoner travelled with a whole peddler's pack of false relics and indulgences to sell to the gullible—chicken bones purporting to be the finger bones of saints, falsified papal documents promising to shorten the sinner's stay in Purgatory, and chicken feathers plucked from the wings of the archangel Gabriel himself. This was why pilgrimage detractors scorned the veneration of relics as superstition at best and fraudulence at worst.

When Erasmus, on his way to visit Canterbury, entered Harbledown in 1514, riding with John Colet, the Dean of St. Paul's, they were pursued by a leper who sprayed them with holy water and then held up an old piece of shoe leather into which a piece of glass had been set, like a gem. Colet, who was much put out by this assault, asked the old beggar what he meant by it. The beggar replied that the object was the shoe of Saint Thomas Becket, and he would let Colet kiss it for a small fee. Colet flew into a rage, saying to Erasmus, "What would these brutes have us do? Do they mean that we should kiss the shoes of all good men? Why do they not give us their spittle and other bodily excrement to kiss as well?" Erasmus felt sorry for the old leper and gave him a coin, though he quotes the story as an example of the sort of fraud that was frequently practised on pilgrims.

Not surprisingly, exponents of the Protestant Reformation would use scams like these to cast pilgrimage in a bad light, and the practice of pilgrimage would die off after 1500 CE, though surprisingly the language of pilgrimage would remain. John Bunyan's *Pilgrim's Progress*, for example, adopted the language and form of pilgrimage to speak of an inner transformation cast in the form of a travelogue. Even today, the language of pilgrimage comes up in the most surprising contexts. We speak of people making a pilgrimage to Graceland or worshipping at the shrine of capitalism. Words like "penitence," "indulgence" and "atonement" are still a part of everyday speech, though their usage and meaning has shifted in six hundred years.

My own reasons for going on a pilgrimage are mixed. On the one hand, I am completing the journey my father and I would have made, if he had lived, as a way of honouring his memory. It is my way of saying goodbye. On the other hand, I am seeking something for myself as well—call it spiritual renewal or finding a sense of life's purpose, but this is harder to articulate. I am now the same age my father was when he had his first heart attack, the same age as Thomas Becket when he was martyred. When people ask me why I am going on a pilgrimage, I tend to dodge the question. It makes me uncomfortable. But if pressed, I usually say that I am going on a journey to do something constructive for the sake of my soul. Surprisingly, most people seem to find this answer satisfactory. I say "surprisingly," because I am still not entirely sure what I mean when I make this statement.

Think about it for a moment. We bandy about the word "soul" quite freely, as if we all know exactly what it means. But do we? Most of us have a general sense of the word's meaning. By "soul" we mean something that is separate from our body. Most of us feel that we are more than just mere mechanisms and that if the body is just a clockwork shell, then there is something that is in charge, which we might call the soul. But this soul/body split is a relatively new concept. It wasn't familiar to medieval theologians in Western Europe. Otherwise, why would they worry about the resurrection of the body? St. Augustine, for example, called the soul the "rider" of the body. It was the thing that gave us our sense of self, but it couldn't exist independently of the body. The modern idea that soul and body can exist separately is our inheritance from Descartes. He saw mankind as a union of body and soul, but that each existed as a distinct substance acting upon the other. He equated the soul (or "mind"—he used the terms interchangeably) with consciousness: "I think therefore I am." But is the mind even the same thing as the soul?

Eighteenth century rationalists like John Locke considered the mind, at the moment of birth, a blank slate or *tabula rasa*. Locke believed that everything we know we learn from our senses. But if Locke is right, if we all begin in infancy as blank slates, then we are born without a soul. It is something we construct as we go along (if it exists at all). On the other hand, if we buy Locke's argument, then we all have an equal opportunity to be useful, honest, productive citizens, as long as we are all given the right stimuli when young. There would be no such thing as original sin (a Christian concept dating from the late Roman period) or a criminal nature.

More recent thinkers have thrown doubt on Locke's theory. How is it that infants are able to master the complicated rules of language, asked Noam Chomsky, if their minds are a blank slate? We no doubt learn some things by experience, but other kinds of knowledge seem to be innate. Perhaps instead of a blank slate, we are more like a computer. In this model, we are all born with the same operating system, but our memory is empty, and we add data and programs as we grow and learn.

Why am I bringing this up? I am raising the issue to suggest that the mind and the soul cannot be the same thing. If our mind is an operating system, perhaps our soul is our sense of self with its associated systems of morality and unique identity. But if our soul is simply our sense of who we are, does our soul die when our body dies?

The cognitive psychologist Steven Pinker believes it does. Sort of. Pinker defines the soul as "the locus of sentience, reason and will," but he also believes it is a false concept.[1] It is part of the fallacy the philosopher Gilbert Ryle called the false dogma of the "ghost in the machine." Descartes divided man into mind and body, but Pinker asserts that "we have every reason to believe that consciousness and decision making arise from electrochemical activity of the neural networks in the brain."[2] In other words, our sense of self separate from our body is an illusion. The attributes we assign to the soul, Pinker believes, can be explained biologically. Even our sense of self is an illusion. It evolves over time and is a self-deceit.

Each of us feels that there is a single 'I' in control. But that is an illusion that the brain works hard to produce, like the impression that our visual fields are rich in detail from edge to edge. (In fact, we are blind to detail outside the fixation point. We quickly move our eyes to whatever looks interesting, and that fools us into thinking that the detail was there all along.) The brain does have supervisory systems in the pre-frontal lobes and anterior cingulated cortex, which can push the buttons of behavior or override habits and urges. But those systems are gadgets with specific quirks and limitations: they are not implementations for the rational free agent traditionally identified with the soul or the self.[3]

However, even Pinker acknowledges some of our decision-making processes are still a mystery: "But how moving molecules should throw off subjective feelings (as opposed to mere intelligent computations) and how they bring about choices that we freely make (as opposed to behavior that is caused) remain deep enigmas to our Pleistocene psyches."[4] In time, Pinker asserts, our brains may evolve to the point where we understand how they work, but until then we must take his theories on faith.

Other cultures had other definitions of the word "soul," which may or may not be more helpful. Gnostics and Buddhists believe that outside of our world there is a divine world, and that our souls are calling us back to that divine world. For the Gnostics our world is a prison, and the divine spark in each of us is trapped in a human body. In the Christian Gnostic tradition, it was Jesus who came to show us the way, who possessed the secret knowledge required, to return us to this divine realm. In Buddhism, our world is an illusion, and the teachings of the Buddha exist to help us to break free of this illusion and achieve transcendence. But in both cases, our souls are rather impersonal and seek to break free of the individual ego. The goal of the individual soul is to be reunited with the divine and hence erased.

Plato, and later Cicero, seemed to feel that the soul was that part of us that told us who we should be. When we are born, we forget who we are, but we each have a soul companion, which Plato calls our *daimon* and Cicero our *animus*, that prompts us to find our true calling. Perhaps this is more helpful. It is a more useful story, even if it can't be proven scientifically. For after all, a pilgrimage is a physical journey that is also an inward journey. Perhaps the point of the journey is to come face to face with oneself. If so, what does this mean? Does it mean finding one's true purpose?

Fortunately, there is a precedent for going on a long walk. Walking and thinking have always gone hand in hand. Nietzsche (perhaps not the best role model under the circumstances) wrote one should "never trust a thought that didn't come by walking."[5] Kierkegaard, who, like me, suffered from depression, added: "Above all, do not lose your desire to walk: Every day I walk myself into a state of well-being and walk away from every illness; I have walked myself into my best thoughts."[6] Bruce Chatwin, quoting Robert Burton, also noted: "Movement is the best cure for melancholy... 'The heavens themselves run continually round, the sun riseth and sets, stars and planets keep their constant motions, the air is still tossed by the winds, the waters ebb and flow...to teach us that we should ever be in motion.'"[7] So like these other sufferers, I strap on my boots and hope to walk myself into a better frame of mind and to discover something along the way that I might bring home, some boon that I can share with others or that will make old age bearable.

10

Otford to Addington

...You are not here to verify,
Instruct yourself, or inform curiosity
Or carry report. You are here to kneel
Where prayer has been valid.

— T.S. ELIOT, "Little Gidding"

WHEN I WAKE IN THE MORNING, I'm surprised to see Derek waiting for me in the lobby. He looks anxious.

"Listen," he says. "Something's come up. I'm really sorry, but I've been hired to give a guided tour to a group walking from Rochester to Canterbury, which means I won't be able to see you again. But," he hastens to add, "if you run into any trouble, you can always reach me on the phone I gave you."

I reassure him that I will be fine. But when he continues to look worried, I ask him if something else is bothering him.

"Well," he says, "my publishers have set me up on Saturday for a radio interview. I'm a bit nervous."

"Why? Haven't you done a radio interview before?"

"No, it's not that. It's a jazz station, and my book's about the Blues. I don't know anything about jazz. I'm afraid they'll ask me about John Coltrane and I'll just look daft."

I tell him of my own scary experiences with live radio and reassure him that he will be fine. "Just redirect the questions back to your book. Keep control of the conversation. I'm sure you'll do great." We shake hands and part. I'm sad. I had looked forward to more chats with Derek, but truth be told, if I've learned anything so far, it is that I am quite capable of doing this walk on my own.

After breakfast, I pack up and leave Donnington Manor. It's a short walk to Otford over muddy fields and a railway overpass. It's garbage day, and municipal workers are out with large malodorous trucks emptying bins. Children wait in clumps for the school bus. The main road through Otford follows the old Pilgrims' Way, and I will walk beside it for much of the day. In Otford I make a slight detour to visit the ruined archbishop's palace. There is not much left: a three-storey wing of what must have been a much larger building, all fenced off to protect it from further vandalism. The brickwork is Tudor, so I suspect it postdates St. Thomas Becket. I mention this because Otford was apparently his favourite of the many palaces attached to the See of Canterbury. There is a local legend that Becket, unhappy with the poor water in the palace, walked down the road, stuck his crozier in the ground, and like Moses, caused a spring to rush out of the earth with the freshest water imaginable. On my map, "Becket's Well" overlays "Roman Villa, Ruins," so my guess is that the truth of the matter is much more prosaic.

I guess it is time to address the elephant in the room. The whole reason to make a pilgrimage to Canterbury is to visit the shrine of

St. Thomas Becket, a shrine that no longer exists, because Henry VIII's agents destroyed it and seized the gold and jewels for the royal coffers in 1538. Yet during the great age of pilgrimage in Europe, which historian Jonathan Sumption dates from the millennium to the Reformation, a period when Europe was, by medieval standards, relatively peaceful, the shrine of St. Thomas was the third most popular site to visit after Rome and Santiago.[1] Yet I must confess I find Thomas Becket rather unlikable.

When Henry II ascended the throne of England in 1154 CE, he inherited a mess. The country had suffered through almost two decades of civil war while the two grandchildren of William the Conqueror—Mathilda, Henry's mother, and Stephen, Henry's uncle—tried to claim the kingdom. When Henry gained the crown of England upon the death of Stephen, he was already the ruler of much of present-day France, from Gascony in the south to Normandy in the north, but he knew little of England, indeed barely spoke the language. He needed people with local knowledge to assist him. When Archbishop Theobold of Canterbury recommended his clerk Thomas Becket as a likely candidate, Henry accepted him at once, making Becket first his councillor, and later Chancellor of England. Becket became Henry's right-hand man and friend.

The two men were a study in contrasts. Henry was the head of one of the most powerful noble families in Europe, while Becket was a commoner, the son of a successful London merchant and landlord who had sent his son to the Church to receive a good education. Henry was stocky, red-haired and freckled, and was fiercely intelligent, with an excess of energy that everyone who met him remarked upon at once. Becket was thirteen years older than his monarch, tall and pale with a shock of black hair. Henry was active and outgoing, loved feasting and the hunt; while Becket was austere, was a talented administrator, and loved ceremony and fine living. If Henry always dressed with calculated nonchalance, Becket was always dressed in the finest clothes money could buy.

The civil war had weakened the English crown. The barons had used the conflict to boost their own power within the Kingdom by playing one side against the other. It was a great period of castle building, as the new Norman barons created private armies and used the chaos to seize land and settle private scores. Similarly, the Church grew fiercely independent of the Crown. Henry wanted to restore things to the way they had been under the Conqueror, and his first target was to bring the Norman barons to heel. He became known as "Henry, castle-breaker." Henry was also interested in legal reform. He wanted every man, or at least every freedman, to have the right to appeal to the Crown. His major obstacle here was the existence of separate church courts. Anyone who was clergy or who could claim the benefit of clergy (that is, they could demonstrate they were literate, a virtual monopoly of the clergy at this time), had the right to be tried in a church court. Often the penalties were very uneven. For example, a murderer who was convicted in a royal court was executed, while a murderer who was convicted in a church court was more often dismissed from his position in the church and sentenced to do a penance. This drove Henry mad. He wanted a centralized state, where no one was exempt from royal control. What Henry needed was an inside man, someone to help him reform the English church from within, and when Archbishop Theobald died in 1161, Henry thought he had the perfect candidate: his good friend Thomas Becket. With some arm-twisting, Becket became the next Archbishop of Canterbury, the new leader of the English Church.

Henry had several reforms in mind. First, he would make the church courts subordinate to the royal courts. Second, the crown would have the right to approve appointments to senior posts in the English Church. Third, the Crown reserved the right to approve the act of excommunication for royal officials. Excommunication, the act of banning an individual from the services and sacraments of the Christian church, was the Archbishop's most potent weapon against spiritual transgressors. This punishment, which might seem inconsequential in our secular age, was taken very seriously in Henry's day, for banishment from the sacrament of Baptism, for example, could consign an individual's soul to eternal damnation. All of these reforms Henry outlined in a document called the Constitutions of Clarendon, after the place where Henry announced his new policies in 1164. To Henry's great surprise, Becket, who had always seemed the most worldly of men, suddenly became the Church's most ardent champion. The Church answered not to the Crown, declared Becket, but to the Pope. At Clarendon, Becket refused to back Henry up. Henry was furious. To escape punishment, Becket fled to the Cistercian abbey of Pontigny in France. It is important to note that not everyone in the English Church agreed with Becket's stance. A number of bishops and archbishops, including those of London, Salisbury and York, considered Becket's position too extreme, and felt there was no harm in a little compromise, if it led to peace in the realm. A further quarrel grew between the two men when Henry asked Becket to anoint his eldest son as King of England, and Becket refused. Enraged, Henry asked the Archbishop of York to preside over the ceremony instead, and York was supported by a number of other senior churchmen. This angered Becket, who believed that only the Archbishop of Canterbury had the right to anoint the new king. He excommunicated the offending prelates. And so it went. There were a number of attempts to reconcile the two men, but both were too strong-willed to meet the other halfway. When Becket eventually returned to England in 1170, he began once more to stir the pot. Henry, who was across the channel near Bayeux at the time, moaned, "What miserable drones and traitors have I nourished and promoted in my household, who let their lord to be treated with such shameful contempt by a low-born clerk!"[2] Four knights—Reginald fitzUrse, William de Tracy, Richard le Bret, and Hugh de Morville—overheard this outburst and jumped a boat to England, determined to settle the Becket affair to their lord's satisfaction. At first, it seems they just intended to arrest Becket, but things soon spiralled out of control. Becket was just sitting down to a meeting with his closest advisors when the four knights forced themselves noisily into his presence, and he treated them with the contempt he felt they deserved, further enraging them. They withdrew to rethink their options and to further fortify their courage with alcohol—for arresting an archbishop was no small thing. Becket's household pleaded with him to hide or flee, but he was determined to go about his business as usual, and walked to the cathedral, unguarded, to attend vespers. After entering the cathedral, his attendants begged him to bar the door behind him, but Becket refused, saying he would not bar the door of the house of God to any man. It was almost as though he wished to force the issue. You must picture too, that although vespers began at half past four in the afternoon, this was December 29, and the sun had already set. The church would have been cold and dark, with only the light of a few flickering candles holding back the shadows. When the four knights, now roused to a drunken frenzy, burst into the cathedral, armed, and with their faces hidden behind their helmets, all but two of Becket's followers fled in terror.

"Where is the traitor?" shouted the knights.

"Here I am," replied Becket coldly. "No traitor but a priest of God. What do you want?"[3]

FitzUrse tried to grab Becket and force him onto de Tracy's back to carry him away, and a most undignified wrestling match took place. "Panderer," taunted Becket as he struggled with fitzUrse. This was more than the knight could bear. Up came his sword and down it crashed onto Becket's head. A visiting clerk named Edward Grim tried to shelter Becket from the blow, and the sword sliced Grim's arm to the bone before it took off the top of Becket's skull, exposing his brain. (Grim survived the blow and became one of Becket's first biographers). A second blow, possibly by William de Tracy, brought Becket to his knees, where he murmured, "For the name of Jesus and the protection of the Church, I am ready to embrace death."[4] A third savage blow, probably delivered by Richard le Bret, cut through the crown of Becket's head. This last blow was struck with such violence that the sword shattered as it connected with the stone floor. Another knight stood upon the archbishop's neck and plunged his sword into Becket's skull, scooping his brains onto the floor and stirring them around with the tip of his sword. "Let's be off, knights," he said. "This fellow won't get up again."[5]

As the knights fled the scene, the local congregation began to drift in and surround the scene of the crime, as crowds always do. I would imagine that more than one bystander was thinking, "If only he hadn't been so stiff-necked, all of this might have been avoided." Then a strange thing happened. As the monks were preparing Becket's body for burial, they discovered that under his elegant robes of office he wore a rough hair shirt that was crawling with lice. Becket, it seemed, had lived a secret life. On the surface, he was a flashy prince of the Church, but underneath, he was an ascetic who mortified his own flesh. In the nonce, Becket the proud was transformed into Becket the pious. And as the word of this revelation spread across Europe to Rome, Becket the troublemaker became Becket the Christian martyr. Within two years, Becket would be canonized, but even before that date pilgrims were rushing to his tomb and witnessing miracles. Somewhat surprisingly, two of Becket's greatest champions after his death would be the senior clerics he had excommunicated, the Bishop of London and the Archbishop of York, who, while they may not have liked Becket as a man, could see the value of Becket as a symbol.

Though Becket is a hero to many, I find it hard to warm up to him. He was brave and principled, but he was also unbending. Righteous men have always made me uneasy, for a righteous man is never wrong. A righteous man can never see anything from another's point of view, because he will always be convinced that his opinion is the same as God's. In the modern world, many of our heroes, particularly our environmental heroes, are uncompromising, but my heroes have always been the peacemakers, who are by necessity brokers of compromise.

Leaving the ruins of the bishop's palace, I decide to follow a footpath to Kemsing, rather than walk along the shoulder of the modern road which follows the course of the old Pilgrims' Way. By this time, I've grown tired of walking on a concrete sidewalk by the side of a busy road. The footpath takes me past a train station and through a modern suburb of brick and stucco. Here, I think, is white-collar England in all its drab uniformity, like Privet Drive in Harry Potter. But the centre of old Kemsing is charming. There is a pub and a tiny post office, and raised sidewalks lift the pedestrian above a quiet roundabout that surrounds a war memorial and the ruins of St. Edith's Well. Edith, the daughter of the Saxon King Edgar, was born in Kemsing, and the well that bears her name once had the reputation for curing sore eyes. I head up a quiet lane hoping to visit the village church, which my guidebook informs me is "full of the work of ancient craftsmen, rich, beautiful and colourful," including several ancient brasses, a magnificent altar canopy and what may be the oldest stained-glass window in the country.[6] But it is not to be. The church is locked up tight, perhaps because the old vicarage next door is a burnt-out shell with yellow caution tape still strung through the trees. Half-burnt pages from a dismembered book blow up the path before me like autumn leaves. I stoop to pick one up. The heading at the top of the page reads "The Tenderfoot's Oath." It is a page torn from an old Girl Guides manual.

Rising straight up the hill from Kemsing, I rejoin the North Downs Way just below Otford Manor where a gaunt grey Norman tower stands sentinel through the trees. The trail leads me through a patchwork of woods and fields along the top of the ridge, crossing pastures full of sheep. Crossing a stile, I frighten a caramel-coloured cow that is resting in the shadow of the hedgerow. When she sees me descending from on high, she starts and lumbers heavily to her feet, galloping away with a startled "moo-wah." This strikes me as rather funny—the thought that I could terrify something as large as a cow seems hilarious; but then I hadn't read Bill Bryson's latest book on Britain yet, and I didn't know that "cattle trampling" was a major cause of death on British country trails. I kid you not. Read *The Road to Little Dribbling*, you'll see.

I pass through a number of horse pastures too. Most of the horses ignore me, but one pair, near Cotman's Ash, canter over and make a nuisance of themselves, nuzzling my back and my jacket pockets. I suspect other walkers have been feeding them. They are friendly but a bit too young to be aware of their own strength. They nearly knock me off my feet in their enthusiasm. Imagine you are Gulliver in the land of Brobdingnag and they put you in charge of the nursery. Then imagine that the giant toddlers decide to play a game of "pile on the nanny." That's how I feel with these youngsters. Finally, I take a long stroll down an open meadow and rejoin the Pilgrims' Way, which leads me along a muddy lane into Wrotham.

As I approach Wrotham, I meet five older women walking in the opposite direction. All are tricked out in colourful Gore-Tex jackets and stride along purposefully, flexing rather business-like Nordic walking poles.

"Lovely day!" I call out as I approach, exuding the milk of human kindness.

They seem perturbed to find me there and huddle close together, eyeing me warily and muttering to each other out of the corners of their mouths as I pass by. I blush and excuse myself as I squeeze past in the narrow lane. I don't understand their reaction. Do I look disreputable or dangerous? Do I have the face of a villain on a wanted poster? The hedged-in lane *is* rather tunnel-like and lonely, but how menacing can I be, really? I mean, there are five of them, grasping ten sharpened aluminum ski poles. If I were a masher, I wouldn't stand a chance.

St. George's Church in Wrotham is unique in that the attached bell tower has a tunnel passing through it for pedestrians. My guidebook says that this was created so that the annual Corpus Christi processions could circle the church without ever having to leave consecrated ground. Inside the tunnel, there are several deep grooves carved in the stone. These are thought to have been created by archers stopping here to sharpen their arrowheads on their way to the practice butts on the village green. It's details like this that make history come alive. I try to imagine some English archer, longbow slung over his shoulder, honing the edge of his broad-head here before leaving for Crécy or Agincourt.

I enter the church to find that I have arrived just in time for a charity tea. So have the five elderly ladies I passed earlier, who must have taken a circular route. They sit at a table in the back of the church and glare at me suspiciously over their Spode china teacups. A large man with a shaven head and a tan uniform enters the church and greets the women heartily. They talk quietly for a moment and then all turn to look at me. I turn quickly away and try to look interested in the memorial brasses. There are a lot of them, the memorial brasses, I mean, and most seem to be dedicated to members of the Peckham family. The church is full of peculiarities, I learn, like a circular staircase inside a pillar which once led to a nun's walk atop a vanished rood loft, but which now would probably lead to your death if you tried to ascend it. The church carillon is one of the oldest in the country and can play five songs apparently—four hymns and a catchy tune from 1745 which begins, "The Captain with his whiskers took a sly glance at me...." When I turn to look back, the women are hunched together in conversation and the big security guard (for that is what I take him to be) is no longer there.

I exit the church and begin to walk back up the main street to rejoin the Pilgrims' Way. As I pass a small car parked on the shoulder, a voice growls in my ear, "Gotcher tea up at the church, did ya?"

Startled, I turn to the open driver's side window. It's the uniformed man nodding amiably and chewing on an egg salad sandwich made with thick slices of white bread. He opens the door and struggles to emerge. I say "struggles" because it is a ridiculously small car for such a large man, like one of those clown cars you see in the circus. As he straightens up, he towers over me. He is not just tall, he is enormous. Thickset and broad-shouldered, he has a massive potato-shaped head set atop a thick neck. His nose is broken, his ears are tiny shells recessed into the side of his skull. I wonder if he was ever a boxer. He has the build. He is wearing a tan uniform with epaulets and a large Maglite flashlight in a holster on his belt. He offers his hand and I shake it. My hand vanishes inside his calloused paw. I am six feet tall, but I feel like a three-year-old next to this man.

I lie and tell him that the tea was lovely.

"Canadian?"

"Yes, how did you know?"

"The accent. I used to be a London Bobby. You meet lots of tourists, get to learn the difference. Now I'm retired. Got this job with County Council, walking a beat. Not bad, eh? Walk around. Talk ter people. Pretty soft."

He asks me where I'm going, and I tell him about the Pilgrims' Way. He cautions me not to miss the Coldrum Stones. "And did you see the donkey wheel?" When he sees the blank expression on my face, he points across the road to where a red brick hexagonal tower with a slate roof rises from an unseen yard. "Some years back, they were going to tear it down, then someone realized it was the last of its kind, so now it's a designated monument."

"What is it?"

"A water tower. In Queen Victoria's reign it was what you might call state of the art. A donkey, you see, walked round-and-round a wheel in the bottom of the tower, drawing up water from a deep well to the reservoir at the top. Gravity did the rest."

"Cool."

Wrotham, I learned, was synonymous with the Gordon family. They owned the large white manor house I'd passed on my way into town, which was in the process of being carved up into luxury flats. They apparently owned a famous hotel in London too. "You know the one I'm speaking of," he said, "It's very posh. Kate's family stayed there during the royal wedding."

"He's a strange one," said my new friend, meaning the present head of the Gordon clan. "Always going around in three-quarter pants and sandals, no matter what the weather. And she's mad about horses. Never mind. They're all right."

Wrotham, I tell him, is very pretty.

He wrinkles his nose. "Pretty. I suppose, but the motor bypass killed it. I remember when there was a butcher's, a bank, several grocer's shops and a couple of pubs along here. Now what do we have? *Boutiques*, that's what. See the old school." He points across the way. "That's public housing now. The whole street is public housing."

I mention all the school children I met on the trail. He brightens at this. "Aye, that's for the Duke o' Edinburgh Awards. The kids have to do outward bound stuff and public service to earn enough credit to win an award. They comes in bronze, silver or gold. Started in the fifties, I think. Did it in my day too. Mind, I wasn't in no school like these kids. I was in a naval cadet school. Hard discipline, but it din't do me no harm and I learned how to sail. Mind, some of the things we did back then, well, they wouldn't be allowed today, would they? They'd be afraid o' being sued."

We chat some more, and he discovers I'm a librarian. We chatter about books. He recommends a book he is rereading, *The Letters of Private Wheeler*, a collection of letters written during the Napoleonic wars.

"That fellow who wrote the Sharpe novels, he used 'em for research."

"Bernard Cornwell?"

"Aye, an' if you like Cornwell, you should try a fellow called Captain Curling—though he was recordin' what another fellow called Harris was telling him, so it's not really his story. An' there's another fellow called Bourgogne too, though he was French. Still, it makes fascinating reading. You know who is underrated?"

I shake my head.

"Forrester."

"The fellow who wrote the Hornblower novels?"

"Aye, but you should read *Death to the French*. That's his best. All about this soldier—an infantryman—who gets cut off behind enemy lines. Read it. It's first class."

I ask him if he's read the naval fiction of Patrick O'Brian, my current favourite.

"I tried him. He's not bad, but he doesn't hold a candle to Forrester. Read *Death to the French*. You'll see what I mean. But look at us. We're talkin' about work." He laughs. "Hey, don't let me keep you. I could stand here all afternoon talking, and you've a long way to go."

We shake hands again, and somewhat hesitantly I ask, "Say, did you ever do any boxing?"

He laughs. "The nose? Aye, I was school champ." He shrugs. "I had the build. People look at me and think: There goes a boxer. But you want to know something? I never really enjoyed it. I never liked hitting people."

Hitching my pack up on my shoulders, I wave goodbye and turn to continue my journey.

I climb the hill to rejoin the Pilgrims' Way, but first have to cross over the busy M20 on a pedestrian overpass, high above six lanes of buzzing traffic, which makes my head spin. Given a choice between climbing the escarpment to follow the North Downs Way and staying at its foot to follow the Pilgrims' Way, I decide to follow the older route along quiet leafy lanes, turning off on a bridleway to visit Trottiscliffe and the church at Trosley Court. I should mention that the weather has been unsettled all day. It started gloomy and wet, and it has been a battle between sun and showers ever since, with the result that I am constantly either donning or shedding my Gore-Tex rain jacket. By the time I reach Trottiscliffe Church, the rain has returned with a vengeance, so I decide to spend a few moments quietly in the church on my own. I take off my wet jacket and leave it by the door along with my dripping rucksack. There is beautifully carved wooden pulpit rising from a narrow stem and flowering to an impressive canopy, just like a jack-in-the-pulpit flower, a flower name I never really understood before, because they don't have pulpits like this in Canada. The pulpit seems a little outsize for a church this small. The story is that the pulpit came originally from Westminster Abbey and was removed in 1821 to make room for the coronation of George IV. Somehow it was forgotten and has remained here ever since. Above the altar is a lovely wooden carving of the Holy Family on their flight to Egypt. The church is small and narrow, built for the people who worked on the estate, which was originally deeded to the Bishop of Rochester. Indeed, the Norman chancel was designed by the first Norman Bishop of Rochester, of whom I will have more to say later. Today the church is empty. The rain outside beating on the stained glass guarantees privacy—no one will be moving about on a day like this. I can see that I will not be disturbed. I decide that it is time to try prayer once again.

I kneel in the empty church. The cross-stitched hassocks waffle about on the flagstones under my knees. I am used to a different arrangement back home, a wooden kneeler, like a low bench, fixed to the back of the pew in front. I find kneeling on a moving pillow an impossible balancing act. I try to focus, but my mind won't settle. The long narrow nave, the dull polished wood, the uneven floors, the dust, the whitewashed walls, and the musty smell of the place all speak of abandonment. The church feels forsaken, and so do I. I give up and sit back in the pew. I'm not sure what I expected, but nothing has happened. I am so long out of practice that the form of prayer feels hollow.

Part of the problem is that I am not exactly sure what prayer is. I asked this question to my brother-in-law, a clergyman and a man

I greatly respect, before I left on my pilgrimage, and he loaned me a book called *Prayer* by Richard Foster that lists twenty-one different kinds of prayer. Far from clarifying the issue, the book simply made things more complicated. For one thing, Foster includes meditation as a kind of prayer (number fourteen on his list). Prayer, I had always assumed, was a conversation with God, whereas meditation…what was meditation exactly? I asked my brother-in-law. He thought for a moment and said, "Well, I guess if prayer is talking to God, meditation is listening." The writer Anne Lamott said that there were just two basic prayers: "Thank you! Thank you! Thank you!" and "Help me! Help me! Help me!"[7] whereas the early church father Clement of Alexandria defined prayer as "keeping company with God." All of these definitions are useful, I suppose, but until prayer is heartfelt, they are just academic. My fear is that I may have left things too late, that it may be impossible now to recapture the faith of my youth.

On the other hand, Carl Jung, in *Memories, Dreams, Reflections*, felt that it was healthy to pay attention to the religious impulse, especially in the second half of one's life. He felt that our psyche was "by nature religious" and that ignoring this fact led to a number of serious neuroses.[8] There is a nice tradition in India that when a man is old enough to relinquish his duties as a husband and father, he is free to set off in search of enlightenment. And what is a pilgrimage, if not a working vacation where you give yourself permission to abjure life's normal responsibilities (family, work, community) so that you might do something constructive for your own soul. The problem, as I've noted before, is the word "soul." If you don't believe in the concept of the soul, can you still be a pilgrim, or are you just a tourist?

The rain isn't letting up, so I pull on my rain pants and jacket and head once more into the storm. I haven't walked fifty yards when the rain suddenly clears. The sun comes out, the foliage begins to smoke, and it grows tropical. Nevertheless, I decide to leave the rain gear on, for everything—the bushes, the tall grass—is dripping wet, and I know that just brushing against them is going to soak me through.

Not far from Trottiscliffe are the Coldrum Stones. I am now on the edge of the Medway Gap, where the river Medway carves a several mile-wide gap through the North Downs on its way to the sea. Here, on both sides of the river, are found an impressive collection of Neolithic stone monuments, of which the Coldrum Stones may be the most impressive. The stones are just that—massive slabs of sarsen stone set in the earth in a rough circle surrounded by a deep earthen ditch. It was once a tomb and covered with earth, but the earth has washed away revealing the stone skeleton beneath. An excavation in 1910 uncovered the remains of seventeen people interred here, dating from about 2000 BCE.[9] There is a well-worn path from a small car park at the end of the lane that dips down a wooded tunnel to the stone circle. Coloured ribbons and knotted strips of cloth dangle from the overhanging branches— offerings to the ancestors perhaps, or charms for good fortune. From the platform of the Coldrum Stones, you can look directly across the Medway Valley to the continuation of the North Downs, a route I will be walking in two days' time. I know that if I had a good telescope, I would see more Neolithic monuments on the far side at roughly the same elevation.

My bed tonight is a fair distance off the Pilgrims' Way. I journey south from the Coldrum Stones on another path, called the Wealdway, to Addington. The Wealdway is a nightmare of sticky mud, especially where it passes through a forest called Ryarsh Wood, where the cattle have churned the trail into a gloppy soup of wet clay, viscous algae and cow pat. The Angel Inn in Addington is nice though, worth the extra effort. I'm sleeping in a quiet second-storey room in an old wing surrounding the car park. After a nice hot bath, I repair to the pub, the only place in Addington to grab a bite to eat. I ask the server to check my credit card first to see if it will work. It does, thank goodness. Godstone, it seems, was an anomaly.

My neighbours at the next table are celebrating a birthday. There is a lot of good-natured teasing and banter. The celebrant, a loud red-faced man in his early sixties, complains of feeling a bit off, but calls for another round. "The hair of the dog," he roars, "that's all I need." Cheers all round. I finish my meal and leave them to it.

Back in my room, I decide to catch up with Christian and Faithful. They have entered the town of Vanity Fair, a place where everything is for sale, including "houses, lands, trades, places, honours, preferments, titles, countries, kingdoms, lusts, pleasures, and delights of all sorts."[10] The pilgrims' strange attire attracts unwanted attention, and soon merchants are aggressively seeking their custom. When every offer is rejected, one merchant asks, "What will ye buy?" "Truth," is the response, which so outrages the merchants that Christian and Faithful are arrested as madmen and locked in a cage in the marketplace to be made sport of. However, the pilgrims' mildness and obvious sincerity wins the hearts of a few sympathetic bystanders and a violent argument ensues. The pilgrims are charged with disrupting trade and brought before the town's judge, Lord Hategood. Faithful is tried first, convicted and sentenced to death. He is scourged, beaten, lanced with knives, stoned and then burned at the stake for good measure. They are very thorough in Vanity Fair. Christian somehow manages to escape and is comforted by the thought that Faithful has become a martyr to the Faith (like Thomas Becket) and has ascended directly to Heaven.

I hear sirens, slamming doors, and raised voices. I part the blinds and look down to see two paramedics wheeling the birthday boy out of the pub on a gurney and into a waiting ambulance. He is wearing an oxygen mask and his red face has grown damp and pasty. His wife is wringing her hands and generally getting in the way. His friends huddle quietly to one side in a worried little group, smoking cigarettes.

I decide it is time to email my wife and children.

11

Addington to Rochester

The struggle itself toward the heights is enough to fill a man's heart. One must imagine Sisyphus happy.

—ALBERT CAMUS, _The Myth of Sisyphus_

DESPITE THE RUDE REMINDER of my own mortality the night before, day eleven is a turning point. It's the day when I stop thinking about the past or worrying about the future and start living in the present. Every good holiday reaches this tipping point where you realize that you have discarded the baggage you have been carrying along with you, and you begin to exist in the present tense. It's a beautiful morning—cool, the grass wet with dew. It will be a long day, perhaps the longest of my journey, but I know by now that I am capable of covering the distance required and that there is no hurry really. My room tonight is booked. I will show up when I show up.

I begin each morning now with sore feet. My blisters chafe. Walking is painful. But after a few miles, the pain disappears, or perhaps I just get used to it. My boots don't fit quite as well as I thought they had in the store. They pinch my toes. I'm developing new blisters each day, and each night I drain, swab, and bandage them. It's not a big deal really, just annoying—a little irritation, like the prick of conscience, something to remind me that I'm not on vacation, but on a pilgrimage.

I start my day by visiting the ruins of a dolmen just off the square in Addington, a jumble of vast stones in a green field. Not as impressive as yesterday's Coldrum Stones. There is apparently a second circle close by and I walk down the quiet lane indicated on my map, but discover this ruin is on private property, and a hand-made sign advertises tours for a price. I debate the cost of a tour briefly but decide to pass. I return to the road, careful of the early morning commuter traffic, and cross a stile into a field, retracing my route of the day before. I trudge through a very wet field and the cuffs of my trousers are soon soaked through. I can smell the clay before I even enter the forest. Green water still pools in the multitude of cattle tracks. Jumping from one hummock to another, I do my best not to lose a boot in the heavy clay. Once through the forest, the path pulls me back to the Coldrum Stones. I take off my jacket, roll it up and put it in my pack. I have a swig of water and try to take a few pictures in the crystal-clear morning light. There is no one around. The hum and buzz of insect life fills the air, punctuated with trills and chirps of songbirds. I now follow a new trail, constricted by high banks of dew-laden cow parsnip and nettle, so that I have to raise my bare arms above my head to avoid getting a rash. Entering a field of buckwheat in full bloom, I am soon drenched with dew. I spy a butterfly on a bloom—one of the jewel-like orange butterflies with four bright eyespots on its wings that have accompanied me for days now (a peacock butterfly, I later learn)—and try to get a photo. But each time I lean in and am just about to snap the shutter, the butterfly flits away, further down the path. I stalk it again, and again it eludes me. I do this a dozen times, determined to get a picture, but its timing is uncanny. Just as I get ready to press the shutter release, off it goes again.

The butterfly leads me to the tree line on the edge of the North Downs, and I climb to the old pilgrim road and turn east. The road is deeply cut into the chalk, a tribute to its great old age, and deeply shadowed by trees, so that it forms a green tunnel, but it *is* dry underfoot, in contrast to the Wealdway, as Hilaire Belloc said it would be in *The Old Road*.

My destination today is Rochester, and I will soon have to leave the old road and climb the chalk escarpment to rejoin the North Downs Way on its crest. Earlier travellers would have continued on this road until they reached the river Medway and crossed the bridge at Aylesford or perhaps taken one of the many ferry cross-ings. Travelling north to Rochester would have put them out of their way, adding many hours to their journey. But today the old pilgrims' road has been lost beneath railway yards and factories—not an easy or attractive route for walkers—though a monastery still exists near the Aylesford bridge and continues to offer hospi-tality to travellers. So reluctantly, I will head north and cross the river at Rochester, adding miles to my route, though I comfort myself with the knowledge that it was at Rochester that Chaucer's pilgrims, riding south from London, would have crossed the Medway, and that from tomorrow I will be joining their company.

There have been numerous wildflowers blooming in the hedges, even wild roses in the bounds of the Way, but as I climb through the forest I notice that the bluebells are fading, turning brown, and I realize that I have walked through spring and into summer. I have also walked through two counties: first Hampshire, then Surrey, and am now in Kent.

Once I reach the top of the slope and rejoin the North Downs Way, I make good time. For the next couple of hours, I walk on cart tracks through woodlands with names like Holly Hill, Great Buckland, Horseholders, Scrub, Wingate, and Ten Acre. Looking at the map, I marvel over names like Longbottom Bank, Home Bavins, Paddlesworth and Snodland. The only place I've ever been that has more picturesque names than southern England is Newfoundland. There is logging going on in the woods, but even so I see a lot of wildlife: the usual wood pigeons racketing about, but also a little mouse that could have fit in the palm of my hand, a large raptor who casts his shadow across my path, perhaps pursuing the many doves whose cooing fills the green air, and a whole flock of pheasants—more pheasants today, in fact, than on any other day in the rest of my life. At one point I have to wait while a backhoe with a giant steel claw shifts brush from one side of the cart track to the other. The operator has his back to me and is unaware that I am waiting to pass. To call out would be futile—he would never hear me over the roar of the diesel engine—and to try and scramble by would be foolish and dangerous, so I must be patient and wait until he finally catches sight of me out of the corner of his eye and waves me through. I wave my thanks in return, and hop-and-skip past the throbbing engine over the deeply rutted road. He is the first human being I have seen for hours.

Crossing over a valley above Dean Farm I pause to take a photograph of an oast house, the first I've seen, but a sight that will become more and more common as I walk through Kent. Oast houses are round barns with cone-shaped roofs, used for drying hops. The little hamlet of Upper Bush near Cuxton is lovely, with a postcard perfect old Tudor-style cottage. I bypass Cuxton proper by climbing a steep diagonal path behind the houses to a train overpass. Then I arc through Ranscombe wood, a part of the Cobham Estate, down a lane to a major highway interchange. I tunnel beneath the highway using a pedestrian subway and emerge high above the river Medway, from where I catch my first glimpse of the Medway Viaduct.

This will be my crossing point over the Medway, and I must confess that I am both looking forward to, and dreading, the passage. As a piece of engineering, the Viaduct is jaw-dropping. A kilometre long and rising a staggering thirty-five metres above the surface of the river at its apex, it is actually three bridges constructed side-by-side-by-side: two carrying motor traffic and one carrying the high-speed train from London to the Channel Tunnel. Even from here, I can see that traffic on the viaduct is non-stop and very fast—the Eurostar high speed train was once clocked crossing the viaduct at 337.4 kilometres per hour, a UK speed record. I descend the hill and enter the hum and roar of traffic.

The broad lane reserved for pedestrians and cyclists is on the downstream side of the three bridges, facing Rochester, and doubles as a lane for emergency vehicles. I have it to myself this afternoon. A fierce dry wind is blowing up the Medway Valley, and the first thing I do, as I step onto the bridge, is remove my hat for safekeeping and stuff it in my rucksack. I feel very lonely and exposed. Peering over the rail into the brown water swirling below, I spy a smoke-blackened barge full of sand creeping upstream and hugging the shore. I start to cross the enormous span, feeling like an ant on a tightrope. A solid barrier separates me from the motor vehicle traffic. All the same, my ears are filled with the steady roar of traffic and with the hum of rubber tires on asphalt. My lungs are choked with car exhaust. This is not an environment that welcomes a pedestrian. The trek across the bridge seems endless. I pause in the middle and look downstream. On a small hill, a pimple really, where the Medway makes a sharp right turn toward the English Channel, stand Rochester Castle and Rochester Cathedral. At this distance, I can cover them with my thumb.

I set down my rucksack and extract my camera to take a couple of photos. I snap the pictures and then, panning around and following the rise of the hill behind the town, my viewfinder finds a long wooded ridge that stretches along the crest of the North

Downs. Somewhere beyond this, I know, squats Her Majesty's Prison Rochester, formerly known as Borstal Prison.

In 1902, Borstal Prison became England's first detention centre for juvenile male offenders. It was an experiment—a place to reform rather than punish young men who had fallen into a life of crime. It was soon followed by other juvenile detention centres across the United Kingdom and the Commonwealth, all called "Borstals" after the original—there was even one in India. Thinking about Borstal Prison brings to mind Brendan Behan's marvellous memoir of life as a seventeen-year-old inmate, *Borstal Boy*, with its masterful evocation of the rich and varied slang used by the teenage prisoners. All of these thoughts are passing through my mind as I look through the viewfinder of my camera—Borstal, Borstal Prison, prison slang—when my eye is caught by movement on the bridge and I adjust the focus of my camera. I am no longer alone. A solitary cyclist is approaching me from the Borstal shore. I lower my camera to examine him.

As he grows closer, I begin to make out more details. He is a big lean man, scrawny but well-muscled, with tattoos down both of his bare arms. He wears old jeans that are cut off at the knees and a stained white T-shirt with the sleeves ripped off. He rides a rusty old ten-speed with racing handlebars. He is bare-headed, with long, kinky, graying hair that is thinning on top. As he draws closer, I can see he has a deep tan beneath his unshaven chin and deep wrinkles at the corners of his eyes. His mouth looks like it might have been carved on his face with a sharp knife and a cigarette juts from one corner. Our eyes lock.

"Oi!" he shouts.

Now "oi" can mean any number of things, but in my experience all of them are bad. "Oi" can be shorthand for "What you lookin' at?" or "Piss off!" "Oi" is usually a grunted prelude to a violent confrontation. I brace myself, thinking of the aggressive pissing contests Behan describes in his book, as the inmates sort out who is going to be top dog in the prison system. As the cyclist draws abreast, he continues to stare at me; then he nods in a friendly fashion and carries on. I realize I have been holding my breath and smile in relief, gulping in the smoggy air.

"Oi," I reply.

Borstal has a down-at-heels feel that is not helped by the fact that it's garbage collection day and bins of rotting garbage clutter the sidewalk; or by the fact that the gas company is ripping up the main road into Rochester to lay new gas mains and I have to step around piles of sand and gravel; or by the fact that I am tired and no place looks its best when your feet hurt. That said, Borstal looks depressed, there is more stucco than brick in evidence, and I hold my breath as I try not to asphyxiate on a combination of backhoe diesel and cat-scavenged garbage. And when I do pass a row of well-proportioned brick villas, each named after a different saint, most are run down and subdivided into poor tenements. There are few people on the street, and the only places open for business are an off-licence, a pub, a Chinese takeaway, and a Baptist church with an active outreach program.

But as Borstal merges into Rochester the atmosphere becomes tonier. Here the city slopes down toward the castle and the river crossing with fine views of the harbour. My bed and breakfast is located on a quiet Victorian street. Here all of the brick villas are tall and narrow, each looking a bit like its neighbour with well-maintained front gardens bounded by low brick walls and wooden latch gates, many with little nameplates, plates that list not the name of the householder, but the whimsical title with which the owner has dubbed his villa, names like Rose Cottage or Lavender Hill. I find my destination for the night, push open the gate, climb the brick walk to the front door, and ring the bell. My hostess, Janet, opens the door and beckons me in. The inside is bigger than the outside, and the builders did not skimp on materials. There is fine trim work in the hall, while frosted glass panels adorn the pocket doors. She leads me up the stairs to a quiet room at the back of the house. My room is huge and bright with a bay window overlooking the garden. I ask Janet if there is a coin-op laundry nearby, but she volunteers to do some washing for me, thereby solving my biggest problem: I have no clean clothes. I empty my luggage on the bed, have a quick shower, and, after a sniff test, put on the cleanest clothes in the pile before setting out to explore Rochester.

I hadn't expected to like Rochester. I'd pictured a grubby seaport with a depressed economy—some place with rusting cranes leaning out over decaying piers and empty warehouses. But as I descend the hill into the well-preserved heart of old Rochester, I am pleasantly surprised.

Rochester is the lowest bridgeable point on the Medway. The Romans built the first bridge here and a fort to guard it. This bridge allowed for the construction of a direct road from London to Dover. The Roman bridge was later replaced by a medieval one, and the Normans built a castle over the ruins of the old Roman garrison to defend it. The road continued to be important and was known as Watling Street in Chaucer's day. His pilgrims crossed the river here. Today the old Roman road still runs through the heart of Rochester as High Street, though the architecture is more Victorian than anything else. Dickens was fond of Rochester. In fact, he grew up not far away, in Chatham, where his father was a clerk in the Royal Navy, and Rochester figured in many of his novels. Young David Copperfield crossed this bridge in the 1830s, and the facades of many of High Street's shops would still feel familiar to him today. The medieval bridge was replaced by a Victorian one in 1856. It is incredible to think that traffic still crosses the Medway here, following a road constructed by Roman legionaries and trodden by medieval pilgrims.

I pause to rest on a low stone wall opposite the west door of the cathedral. Behind me bulges a grassy median containing a collection of weathered headstones laid flat above a boneyard that threatens to explode with the remains of Rochester's ancient dead. Over the road and up the hill lie the ruins of Rochester

Castle, guarding the estuary. It was just about here, I remember, just outside this cathedral door, that three men, one of whom was Mr. Tope, the verger of the cathedral, stood and speculated on the health of the opium-addicted choirmaster, John Jasper, at the beginning of Dickens's final and unfinished novel, *The Mystery of Edwin Drood*:

> 'And Mr. Jasper has gone home quite himself, has he?' asked the Dean.
>
> 'Your Reverence, he has gone home quite himself. And I'm glad to see he's having his fire kindled up, for it's chilly after the wet, and the Cathedral had both a damp feel and a damp touch this afternoon, and he was very shivery.'
>
> They all three look towards an old stone gatehouse crossing the Close, with an arched thoroughfare passing beneath it. Through its latticed window, a fire shines out upon the fast-darkening scene, involving in shadow the pendent masses of ivy and creeper covering the building's front.[1]

To my delight, the cobbled lane, which runs before me and down the hill in front of the great west door of the cathedral, passes beneath a medieval gateway—Jasper's lodging, just as it is described in the book! And crouched beside the old gateway, in which the fictional villain had lived, is a half-timbered house—now a restaurant—called Topes. How wonderful!

A modern conversation breaks into my thoughts. "If you look up at the tympanum above the great west door, you will see the figure of Christ Triumphant, seated on the throne of judgement." A tour guide, leading a small group of middle-aged visitors, is using a furled umbrella to point to the weathered stone carvings around the entrance to the cathedral. "And if you look on the arch above his head, you can see a series of figures. There are some angels and four unusual winged creatures. These creatures represent the authors of the four gospels: Matthew, you see as a winged man;

Mark, as a winged lion; Luke, as a winged bull; and John, as an eagle. The figures on either side of the door are thought to be of Solomon and Sheba, and one figure on the niche high up on the left, with the long robes and pointed hat is Gandalf, the creator of this cathedral—"

"—did he say Gandalf?"

"Something like."

"Gandalf? The wizard? Like in *Lord of the Rings*?"

"Aye, that's what 'e said."

"He looks a bit like a wizard, but he can't really mean…"

The group drifts away, drawn by their energetic guide to a new point of wonder. I walk closer to investigate. Gandalf? Well, he *does* look like a wizard with his long robes, flowing beard and tall hat, but a closer look at the base of the statue reveals that his name is not Gandalf, but Gundulf, and that he is a not a wizard, but a bishop, though I later learn that he was something of a wizard when it came to military engineering and architecture. I note, too, that he is not holding a wizard's staff, but a crozier, and tucked under his right arm is a miniature castle, a model of the Tower of London. For Gundulf was not only responsible for building the Romanesque nave and western front of this cathedral, but also a series of Norman fortifications, including the castle behind me and the famous White Tower of London. William the Conqueror made good use of this churchman's architectural skills to protect his new dominions. Today, Gundulf is remembered as the father of the Corps of Royal Engineers. A capable man then, if not exactly magical.

You enter the cathedral today, not from the large west door at the front of the building, but from a smaller side door in the south transept. Here, there is a gift shop and a reception area. An older woman, conservatively dressed in a pleated skirt and cardigan, stands with hands clasped as if she is a conservatory-trained singer awaiting her cue.

"Hi," I say. "Is it okay to come in?"

"Yes, by all means. Is this your first visit? Yes? Then I would recommend you take one of the maps."

I thank the woman who returns to her waiting pose, drop a few coins in a donation box and pick up a simple folded brochure that leads me on a merry steeplechase around the cathedral. The map directs me up the south aisle and the first thing that catches my eye is a brass memorial plaque for three cadets from the Royal Military College in Kingston, Ontario, Canada. They died in Africa during different expeditions in the nineteenth century. I begin to notice that there are more military monuments, dedicated to soldiers who died in remote places all over the globe: Sierra Leone, Bechuanaland, the Sudan, the Gold Coast (Ghana during the Ashanti Wars), Afghanistan, the Malay Peninsula, China, various locations in India, and one young lad who was "murdered by the Bedouin" while crossing the Sahara. Many, I notice, are military engineers, which makes sense, given the cathedral's association with Bishop Gundulf.

My map leads me up a set of stone steps that are so scalloped by age and wear that planks have been laid over them to make them useable. My guide tells me the steps were worn away by the knees of countless pilgrims ascending to the shrine of Saint William of Perth. Saint William of Perth? Here's a new one.

St. William, it turns out, was a wealthy baker from Scotland who died in Rochester—was murdered, in fact—while on his way to the Holy Land by way of Canterbury. William had a reputation for piety—it was said that every tenth loaf he baked, he donated to the poor—and the story goes that one day on his way to his parish church in Perth he found a baby abandoned on the church steps. William decided to adopt the little mite, make him his heir and train him to run the family business. When the boy came of age, William decided that the two of them would make a pilgrimage to the holy places of Europe and then Palestine. The boy must have found this prospect unbearable, for as they were leaving Rochester, he murdered his adoptive father and stole his purse. A mad woman came along, and finding William's bloody corpse, decided to grace his brow with a crown of flowers. No sooner had she performed this charitable deed than her sanity returned. Hearing of this miracle, the clergy of Rochester Cathedral declared William a saint and installed his body in the cathedral. A miracle-working saint brought a lot of pilgrim traffic and associated income. In his heyday, William's shrine vied with Becket's and Swithun's in popularity and was credited with hundreds of miraculous cures. Ironically, William is the patron saint of adoption.

Thinking of William made me realize that, although Becket was the draw for most pilgrims, he was not without his rivals along my pilgrimage route. After all, Becket was a hard saint to warm up to. He was rigid, proud, and ambitious. He was also famously efficient and hard-working, but these are hardly the traits that make a man beloved or godly. The thing is, there were more likeable saints to be encountered along my road.

Take St. Dunstan, for example. Dunstan was a reluctant saint. He was, for a time, the Abbot of Glastonbury and later the Archbishop of Canterbury, but he preferred a life of quiet contemplation. He was also a renowned blacksmith, and it is in this context that he is best remembered in the popular mind. The devil apparently saw the pious Dunstan as a challenge, and hung about the saint's forge constantly, offering him one temptation after another. Fed up with the constant interruptions, Dunstan caught the devil by the nose with a pair of tongs and wouldn't release him until the devil promised to leave him alone. Another version of the story tells how the devil brought his horse to Dunstan to be shod, but the saint grabbed Lucifer by the heels and nailed a red hot shoe to the devil's cloven hoof instead, saying, "I will remove it when you promise that you will never enter a house where there is a horseshoe hanging over the door."[2]

Then we have Saint Anselm, another early archbishop of Canterbury and the author of the famous ontological argument for the existence of God, which begins (echoing Psalm 14:1): "The fool says in his heart, 'There is no God.'" Anselm set himself the philo-sophical challenge of refuting this proverbial fool, a man who can both conceive of God and yet deny his existence. Anselm's rather elegant argument begins by defining God as "that than which nothing greater can be conceived."[3] He then proposes that if you can conceive of a being than which nothing can be greater, then such a being must be possible, even probable, since it would be impossible to conceive of a being that is greater than the greatest being you could possibly imagine. Every philosopher worth his salt has taken a crack at this one, from Thomas Aquinas to Descartes, Hegel, Leibnitz, Kant, Hume, and Bertrand Russell. Even modern mathematicians and physicists have tried variations on Anselm's proof.

But my personal favourite is Saint Swithun, whom we encoun-tered back in Winchester, whose symbol is a broken egg, because he once took pity on a woman carrying her eggs to market whose basket was overturned by a pair of ruffians as she crossed a bridge into town. Swithun, who witnessed the incident, told her to dry her eyes and pick up her basket. When she looked inside, all of the broken eggs had become whole once more. One can't imagine Becket even noticing a poor widow's anguish, let alone restoring her lost income. In the Anglo-Saxon period, Swithun was such a popular saint that most of the pilgrim traffic on the Pilgrims' Way was moving westward, toward Winchester. Once again, I wonder if I am walking in the wrong direction.

Nevertheless, Becket's reputation eclipsed his rivals' and, within a few years of his death and canonization, his shrine at Canterbury became one of the most popular pilgrimage destinations in Christendom.

I ascend the stairs to St. William's shrine, which, of course, is no longer there, removed like all of the others of its kind during the Reformation. In its place sits a small chapel for quiet prayer. Following the directions on my map, I visit the sanctuary with its high altar and turn to visit the choir.

On the east wall in the choir, near the front of the cathedral, I discover a depiction of the wheel of fortune painted by an unknown artist sometime in the fourteenth century. Only half of the mural survives. On the part that remains I can see the ascending side of the allegorical wheel, with the Queen of Fortune standing in the middle, turning the spokes, while a poor man lies helplessly at the bottom and a better-dressed yeoman in a red hood climbs the wheel to better fortune. A rich man in his fur-lined cape sits comfortably on the top. What is no longer visible is the downfall of the rich man as the wheel completes its turn. Theoretically, the three figures could be the same man. The face is similar, and in each stage the figure is wearing a red tunic. The missing part of the mural was scraped off in a fit of iconoclastic rage during the English Civil War, but the rest of the picture was hidden behind a pulpit, and so survived. It was not discovered again until the nineteenth century when the architect Gilbert Scott was doing renovations on the cathedral. The mural offers a fascinating glimpse into the medieval frame of mind. The allegory is a warning to the proud, but also a succour to the poor. For if the proud can be cast down, so too can the poor be raised up. If fortune is circular, men's fortunes may be mended.

In the *Canterbury Tales*, as the pilgrims approach Rochester, the Monk is called upon to tell his tale. After invoking Fortuna and her wheel, the Monk recounts the stories of famous men who were overthrown by pride, ambition or complacency. After listening to seventeen wearying examples, the Knight calls a halt to this litany of woe, saying, "Enough already. You're bringing us down" (or words to that effect in Chaucerian English). Perhaps Chaucer had seen this mural when the paint was still fresh, and it inspired the Monk's moralistic sermon?

But if fortune is fickle in the medieval world, the world itself lay in God's hands and remained remarkably immutable. I experienced something of this same sense of certainty when I lived in Bhutan thirty years ago. I lived in a small village in a remote mountain valley in the eastern Himalayas where constant prayer was as natural as breathing, and where men and women, though incredibly poor, were not wracked with existential doubt. I envied them their certainty.

We don't share this certainty today in the secular West. When did this change? Certainly, by the late nineteenth century our faith in an ordered universe had become shaken. Matthew Arnold's "Dover Beach" (1867) is a wonderful expression of this sense of doubt. Listening to the waves at Dover, the poet hears the "melancholy, long withdrawing roar" of the "Sea of Faith." In its place he finds fear and confusion:

...for the world, which seems
To lie before us like a land of dreams,
So various, so beautiful, so new,
Hath really neither joy, nor love, nor light,
Nor certitude, nor peace, nor help for pain;
And we are here as on a darkling plain
Swept with confused alarms of struggle and flight,
Where ignorant armies clash by night.[4]

By the time of the First World War any complacency we might have felt in a beneficent universe was gone. The butchery in the trenches had erased any sense that all was right with the world. The twentieth century saw the birth of Modernism, an art movement that tried to capture this sense of uncertainty, and Existentialism, a philosophy that began with the premise that the universe was meaningless.

In the twenty-first century we look to science and technology to supply us with the sense of certainty we once sought in religion. A good number of my friends assure me that every problem we are now facing has a technological solution, and that we will discover this solution eventually, even though most of the problems we are now trying to solve have a technological root cause. In other words, we are good at creating problems that we are not yet smart enough to solve. We live in an age where technicians call the shots, where utility is measured by efficiency, not by efficacy.

I remember Derek's uncertainty about his inheritance as an English citizen. He'd felt the British health care system was sacrosanct, his birthright as an Englishman, but apparently, it was not. Modern life is all about uncertainty. In fact, the only thing that is certain anymore is that change is constant, but, unlike Fortune's wheel, change is most decidedly not circular. To quote the Canadian folksinger Bruce Cockburn: "The trouble with normal is it always gets worse."[5]

Coming down the other side of the cathedral, I encounter a memorial to Charles Dickens. Dickens, who had been born just down the road in Chatham and had chosen to live nearby in Gad's Hill, had wanted to be buried here apparently, but upon his death, his public, led by the *Times*, insisted that a writer of his stature be entombed in Poet's Corner in Westminster Abbey instead.

Not far from Dickens's monument I spy a grander one to the Victorian soldier-hero General "Chinese" Gordon of Khartoum. Gordon is best remembered as the man who put down the Taiping Rebellion in China and as the man who led the doomed defence of the Sudanese city of Khartoum against the forces of the Muslim prophet the Mahdi. I must admit that Gordon was a childhood hero of mine, so I am delighted to find him remembered here. But I must also confess that my feelings for him have cooled over the years. He was another pious stiff-necked martyr like Becket. His orders were to proceed up the Nile to Khartoum and evacuate the Egyptian garrison and any residents who wished to leave, thus avoiding any bloodshed. If he had obeyed his orders, the political map of North Africa would have changed, but few would have died. Instead, he chose to disobey his orders and, Royal Engineer that he was, to prepare the city for a lengthy siege. He held out for almost a year, single-handedly forcing the British government to change its foreign policy in Egypt and to send a large expeditionary force to his rescue. The relief column arrived just two days after the city fell and Gordon was killed, thus maximizing the drama of his heroic death.

As I am wandering about the cathedral, I notice the elderly cathedral guides are giving a school tour to a group of teenagers. The students are dressed in typical English school uniforms— navy blazers with grey flannel trousers or skirts—but I can't help noticing that all of the children have brown or black skins and that all of the girls are wearing the hijab. The children are all very well behaved, talking in hushed voices, and for the most part, attending to the tour. They at least know how to behave in a place of worship. In a secular society like England, I wonder if they find this ancient church, and the piety it once represented, surprising. After all, Christianity is about six centuries older than Islam. I wonder too what General Gordon would make of it all. I suspect he would be pleased. He was always interested in the spiritual and physical well-being of children, and he spent most of his income supporting charities for orphans and children living in poverty. Once, when asked to donate to famine relief and finding himself without funds, Gordon donated a gold medal given to him by the Chinese government, first effacing the engraving, so no one would know from whom it came—though this action obviously didn't fool anyone, or we wouldn't have this anecdote to illustrate his sense of charity.

Standing in the crossing under the bell tower, and still contemplating the complicated life of Charles Gordon, I glance up. High above me, in the carved ceiling panels, I spy the faces of four Green Men grinning down in puckish amusement through a screen of fecund greenery, an echo of pagan Britain mocking all this new piety.

Leaving the cathedral, I walk up to the castle and stroll the battlements. The keep is a hollow rectangle, destroyed by King John's forces during the First Baron's War and further damaged in the Second Baron's War in the revolt against John's successor, Henry III. From the top of the castle keep, the interior of the castle is a comfortable green square of lawn, where locals toss a Frisbee or enjoy a late afternoon picnic. I have a fine view of the cathedral from here, too, and, turning in the other direction, of the river Medway. I can trace the path of the Roman road from London to where it meets the old bridge crossing the Medway. Young David Copperfield, running away from cruel servitude in London, penniless and in rags, and having pawned his waistcoat for a few coins to buy bread, crosses the Medway here, and, "footsore and tired, [he saw] one or two little houses, with the notice, 'Lodgings for travellers,' hanging out."[6] Having no money and frightened by the look of fellow tramps, Copperfield continued through town, seeking "no shelter, therefore but the sky." I am more fortunate, having arranged a comfortable room beforehand, and so my gaze into pawnshop windows is out of mere curiosity, not necessity. Walking down the hill to High Street, I stop in a Greek diner for a bite to eat and note a banner stretched high across the street advertising a Dickens Festival in two weeks' time. I do a bit of browsing in a large dusty bookshop, and then head back up the hill, passing through the arch of Jasper's gatehouse, to my room for the night.

12

Rochester to Thurnham

All men by nature desire to know.
—ARISTOTLE, *Metaphysics*

IT'S AMAZING HOW MUCH DIFFERENCE a good night's sleep, a full stomach, and excellent conversation with agreeable hosts can do to change a man's perspective. As I walk out of Rochester and retrace my route through Borstal, I find myself thinking what a lovely community it is, and how a person could live quite comfortably and happily here, and wondering why it isn't listed on more tourist maps.

My route takes me under the first two of the viaducts, and then follows a lane that passes between them and the high-speed rail line. It had once been a quiet country lane, but the countryside is now chopped up and overshadowed by the enormous expressways.

A woman approaches me leading her Labrador retriever on a leash. She stops to inform me that she has just started a deer.

"What, here?"

"Uh-huh, just back."

A compact car slowly passes me and parks on the shoulder just up ahead. A middle-aged couple emerges and releases their over-excited German shorthaired pointer from the back seat. The dog runs up to sniff me, wagging his stump of a tail, and bounds away. The couple are deeply engaged in a debate about where to spend their summer holiday, rejecting Ibiza as too crowded, Greece as too problematic, and France as, well, too French. I quickly pass them. They seem oblivious to my presence, so deeply are they immersed in their discussion. The dog adopts me and paces by my side, occasionally darting into the roadside scrub to sniff a tree or mark his territory. Having read *Pilgrim's Progress* the night before last and determined that Rochester must correspond to Vanity Fair, I turn to the friendly dog.

"If this is Vanity Fair, you must be Faithful. I'm sorry, boy, but you're doomed. It's the funeral pyre for you."

Just then, a fox darts across the road, and Faithful, all aquiver, starts to follow. I grab his collar, thinking that it won't do for him to tangle with a fox, since foxes are frequent carriers of the rabies virus. I turn and shout back at the dog's owners who are still deep in discussion.

"Hey, do you have a leash for him?"

They look at each other, and the man shouts back, "No, we left it in the car. Why?"

I explain about the fox.

"Oh, he'll be okay. Let him go."

I turn to the dog. "Mind my words, Faithful. Beware the gimcrack, the superficial, the tawdry, the showy or the merely pretty. Keep your eye on the prize, my friend." I let him go, and he plunges into the underbrush after the fox. "Good luck."

My trail leaves the lane, cuts through the sadly dismembered Nashenden Farm and over a railway overpass into ploughed fields beyond. Rabbits are everywhere, more than I've ever seen before in my life. I count five, turn a corner in a hedgerow and count four more. In the next field, there are more. I try to count them: one, two, three, four, five, six...wait, have I counted that one already? I soon give up. No wonder the fox was heading this way. This is a fox buffet.

I climb a long open slope along a fence line, and then follow a path through the woods, emerging on the far side at the top of the rise. From here, there are expansive views across the Medway Valley. I can see my route of the day before on the far side of the river. Below me, on the near bank, lies the village of Wouldham and, across the river, the village of Halling. It was here that one of the last ferry crossings of the Medway operated until 1964, when the automobile rendered it obsolete. A crossing here saved a pedestrian a long journey to the bridge at Rochester. It is possible that medieval pilgrims crossed the river here too, for the Halling ferry had been in service for at least six hundred years before the last ferryman retired.

My path takes me south, following the crest of the North Downs and the edge of the forest. The morning sun blazes down, there is no shade, and I bake, consuming water at an alarming rate, so I'm pleased when the trail enters the woods again and follows a leafy lane. I pass two cyclists and a rider on horseback, also a rather alluring pub called Robin Hood's. I make good time until I reach the car park at Blue Bell Hill, then I follow a dirty track alongside a major motorway that is littered with the sort of trash one finds along the sides of highways: plastic bottles, chip wrappers, takeout food cartons, and paper cups. The track takes me down the hill to Kit's Coty.

I have seen many photos of Kit's Coty House even before I came to England (it is one of the most photographed ancient monuments in Britain), but every photo I have ever seen makes it look like the ancient site is standing in the middle of a wide green field in a remote location, not down the hill from a dirty tangle of access roads where two major highways cross, and only screened from the busy traffic by a thin line of trees. It's true that the view from the monument is splendid, but I am constantly aware of the angry roar of traffic just over my shoulder.

Kit's Coty House looks like a giant house of cards—three upright stone slabs support a fourth laid across as a flat roof. It is all that remains of a Neolithic burial mound, of a type called a chambered long barrow. What we see today is just the tomb entrance. The barrow was once seventy metres long and covered in earth, but the other stones have been removed and the earth ploughed flat over the intervening centuries. A cast iron fence was erected in the late 1880s at the suggestion of the famed antiquarian Augustus Pitt Rivers (he of the Pitt Rivers Museum in Oxford) to protect what survived from further vandalism. If you walk around to the back of the monument, you can see why he was concerned. Numerous names have been carved into the stone, but, judging by the dates, the graffiti is all Victorian.

The source of the monument's name is lost, but the common belief is that locals thought it to be the tomb of Catigern (the son of the British chieftain Vortigern), who was killed fighting the Saxon, Horsa, at the Battle of Epsford in 455. So Catigern's Cote ("cote" is the Anglo-Saxon word for "house") became, over time, Kit's Coty House. The monument was deserted today, but it is clear that lots of people still visit the tomb on a regular basis. There are bouquets of withered wildflowers tied to the black iron bars with faded twine, and a pair of pink candles, shaped like tiny beach sandals, drip pink wax down the railings, hinting at secret ceremonies conducted by New Age druids cavorting under a Beltane moon.

England is rich in sites like this, though their original purpose and meaning is not entirely clear. Over time, layers of folklore have become attached to such places. Kit's Coty House is reputed to be haunted. Some say that on a still night you can hear the sounds of that ancient battle where Catigern lost his life. Others say the tomb is a portal to another world, where, at the full moon, if you place an object on the roof and then walk around the monument three times, the object will vanish, magically transported to another realm or perhaps to another time.

I don't really hold with any of these old tales though I think they are wonderful. Stories like these create an affinity for the landscape. Wallace Stegner, the American novelist, wrote: "No place is a place until things that have happened in it are remembered in history, ballads, yarns, legends, or monuments." He went even further: "No place is a place until it has had a poet."[1] It is significant that it was an American who wrote this. I'm not sure an Englishman would feel it necessary. In North America, we lack these stories, because most of us are newcomers, and our original peoples have been scattered and their stories lost. The literary critic Northrop Frye once remarked that Canada is a place without ghosts—the implication being that a place isn't our place until it becomes part of our story. Writers play an important role in this process. Think of how the Lake District is associated with William Wordsworth or the North York Moors with the Brontë sisters or Bath with Jane Austen or Dorset with Thomas Hardy. These authors' stories, though fictional, help us to imaginatively inhabit the landscape. They help create a sense of place.

The importance of this sense of belonging goes beyond mere comfort. If we don't feel we belong in a place, we will not value it. We will allow terrible things to happen to it, like strip mining, clear cutting, or farming the soil to the point of exhaustion. We will sell our fresh water to the highest bidder or use our lakes and rivers as places to dump mining sludge or industrial effluent. There is a difference between a place we simply live in and a place we call home. We protect our homes, we don't see them as things to be used and discarded, but as places we inhabit and value.

Saying goodbye to Kit's Coty House, I turn down the hill to seek a second barrow, sometimes known as Little Kit's Coty, but more often as the Countless Stones. Once again, I have to risk life and limb, dodging busy traffic on narrow shoulderless roads blindly hedged with impenetrable scrub. At times, I have to push backward into the greenery, actually forcing my pack into the thorny branches, so as to make myself smaller to the passing cars as their thrumming tires pass just inches from the toes of my hiking boots.

At last, I plunge through a tunnel in the hedge and emerge into a clearing surrounded by trailing dog roses. In the centre of this clearing lies a vast jumble of stones like the final failed play in a giant game of Jenga. If Kit's Coty looks like a house of cards, the Countless Stones look like a much more ambitious house of cards that has collapsed. The name, Countless Stones, comes from the belief that each time you try to count the stones, you will arrive at a different number. The clearing is quiet. The traffic noise, screened by the tall hedge, is muffled, and I hear a lark call from the surrounding field. I feel the stress of the last few minutes ooze away. I am about to fully relax and give an audible sigh of relief when I realize that I am not alone.

On one of the largest and most level of the stones, lies a young man, flat on his back, immobile, with his eyes closed, looking like the marble effigy on a sepulchre. He is thin, freckled and fair, with ginger dreadlocks tucked into a brown stocking cap. His nose comes to a sharp point, and his eyebrows and eyelashes are so pale as to be almost transparent. He looks like a pixie. He is dressed all in earth tones: scuffed brown brogues, tan corduroy trousers, and a Mayan-style hoodie woven with patches of orange, ochre and moss green. Arranged around his head and shoulders are a curious collection of objects: candle stubs, smooth stones, rock crystals, wildflowers and what appears to be an amber necklace.

Well, this is awkward, I think. I clear my throat.

The pale eyelashes flutter and open. The young man looks around; a shy smile settles onto his features. Then he jackknifes his knees neatly, and gracefully swivels into a cross-legged position on the stone facing me. "Hullo," he says with a broad North England or perhaps Glaswegian accent.

"Hi," I reply, and then, when nothing more is forthcoming, continue, "I was just up the hill at Kit's Coty and decided to come down and see these stones too. I'm walking the Pilgrims' Way, you see, and I thought I'd do a little detour. Didn't count on the awful traffic though. Not very friendly for pedestrians."

"There's a better way, safer, round back, cross the fields."

"Right. Thanks," I say.

"Pilgrim is it?" I nod. "Been to Coldrum Stones?"

"Yesterday."

"Whatcha think?"

"Nice. More complete than others I've seen this trip. But the best barrow I've ever seen was some years ago at the West Kennett Long Barrow in Wiltshire. It's still intact and you can go inside." I go on to tell him how my guide had taken my new bride and me into the damp underground chamber and informed us that it was possible to dowse for the magnetic ley lines that pass beneath the tomb.

My new companion rises to his feet. "It's true," he says. "I've done it." This is the first sign of behaviour I've seen in this supernaturally calm young man that might approximate excitement in another human being.

"I know," I reply. "As I was the skeptic in the group, the guide handed me two L-shaped copper rods and asked me to hold one loosely in each hand and to walk the length of the barrow. At one point, the rods crossed and then separated again. I repeated the experiment and it happened at exactly the same place."

"It's the ley lines," the young man says. "It's sacred geography, man." Any embarrassment he might have felt at first has now dropped away. We sit companionably on the flat stone, side by side, and he begins to explain to me about the veins of energy that connect mystical power nodes across the planet. "The ancients understood this. They built their sacred sites on places of great power, but we have lost that wisdom. We need to rediscover this stuff."

We introduce ourselves.

"Ken."

"Rab," he says, holding out a hand.

"Rob?"

"Yeah, Rab."

I'm still not sure I have heard him correctly, but it seems impolite to ask him to repeat his name a third time, so I listen instead. Rab, it turns out, is on a pilgrimage of his own, cycling around Britain with a backpack—"h'adventure cycling," he calls it—visiting all of her ancient monuments, seeking spiritual enlightenment. I ask him about the objects he has placed on the stone. "Ritual objects," he assures me. "They help to concentrate the cosmic energy when I meditate." He recommends a book by David Cowan, called *Ley Lines and Earth Energies*. Cowan asserts that these ancient sites are connected by lines of spiritual power, that they resonate with mystical energy.

"Can you feel that here?" I ask.

He nods. "But Coldrum was better. It must lie on a particularly strong intersection of ley lines." He begins to question me about sacred places in the Americas. I tell him about the Serpent Mounds I have visited and about the sacred standing stone near my home that ancient indigenous peoples believed was the entrance to the afterworld, or at least that's what the Jesuit missionary Jean de Brébeuf reported in 1636.

He sighs. "One day, I'd like to go there. See the Mayan temples, the Nazca Lines, Machu Picchu. We need to rescue this knowledge. The world is in a bad way, man. We need to reconnect with the ancient wisdom."

Strictly speaking, I think everything he is telling me is complete balderdash, but I don't have the heart to argue with him. He seems so young, so vulnerable, and I find myself feeling protective rather than critical.[2] His heart is in the right place, and his spiritual quest seems more legitimate than mine. Rab is a true pilgrim. Next to him, I feel like a poser, a fraud.

It's time to push on. Rab guides me to a safer path, indicating a right of way across a field of canola that will return me to the Pilgrims' Road.

"Thanks," I say, shaking his hand in parting.

"I hope you find what you are looking for, man," he says with his slow, shy smile.

"Yeah, you too."

I rejoin the Pilgrims' Way at an overgrown cart track. Here another giant monolith lurks in the underbrush, an orphaned menhir, known as the White Horse Stone for its horsey shape— though I can't really see it and feel a little disappointed. Past the White Horse Stone, I have to make a decision: continue along the Pilgrims' Way, an undistinguished and trash-filled farm track at this point, or climb to the top of the chalk escarpment again and rejoin the North Downs Way. I decide to remain on the lower path because I want to make a slight detour and visit the ruins of Boxley Abbey, once an important stop for medieval pilgrims.

Of the abbey's former glory, little remains. King Henry's men were particularly thorough here during the Reformation. Boxley was dismantled and the land given to the Wyatt family who had been the king's staunch supporters. Nothing is left of the grand Cistercian establishment but the enormous guest house, now a barn, and the outline of the stout stone wall that had once enclosed the abbey estate. Boxley Abbey had probably drawn the reformers' particular ire, too, because it had been the home of the famous, or infamous, Rood of Grace. The Rood of Grace was a crucifix exhibited to passing pilgrims for a fee, whose features moved and whose eyes appeared to weep real tears. It was considered a miracle by the faithful; but, like the Great and Powerful Oz, it was really an elaborate hand puppet composed of wires, rods and carefully contrived moving parts. During the Reformation, the Rood was burned in

London along with a host of other Catholic icons. The Protestants denounced it as a con, designed to fleece gullible pilgrims. Others, more forgiving, called it an aid to faith. More recent historians have argued that it was always intended to be a piece of religious theatre, and that no deception was intended.

After a rest in the shade of the vine-clad abbey wall, I head up the hill, following a series of narrow paths to the village of Boxley. It's hot and for a short time my path follows the course of a shaded brook painted with blue flag iris. A refreshing change. Boxley is a pretty little town caught in a time warp, with a narrow village green anchored by a pub at one end and the church of St. Mary the Virgin and All Saints at the other. I step into the church to get out of the sun and sit in the cool darkness to catch my breath. The monuments that line the walls seem to honour two families in particular. The more recent ones commemorate the Lushington family of nearby Park House. There is a plaque to Alfred Tennyson's sister who had married into the Lushington family, and the poet himself stayed at Park House for a time. Some say his poem "The Brook" was inspired by his sojourn in Boxley, perhaps by the very brook I had walked beside earlier in the day. The other prominent family is, of course, the Wyatts, who had been granted the estates of Boxley Abbey. One of these, Sir Francis Wyatt, was the governor of Virginia in 1621. But of particular interest to me is a monument near the back of the church to George Sandys, the Elizabethan explorer and poet.

Sandys was the son of the Archbishop of York. A faithful son it would seem, for after the death of his father he remained his mother's companion until her death in 1610, whereupon, at the age of thirty-two, he set off on a two-year voyage through Greece, Turkey, Palestine, Egypt, Cyprus, Malta, Sicily and Italy. Note the date. King James I would have been sitting on the throne. The authorized version of the Bible was in the process of being translated into English by a committee of scholars. Shakespeare had just written *The Tempest,* and Sir Walter Raleigh was still languishing in the

Tower of London writing his *History of the World*. When he returned from his travels, Sandys published his account as *A Relation of a Journey Begun an: Dom: 1610*. The book proved extremely popular, a bestseller—Walton mentions it in the *Compleat Angler*—but it is not much remembered today.

Sandys's association with Boxley comes in a roundabout way, for his niece married Sir Francis Wyatt (mentioned above), and, in 1621, Wyatt invited Sandys to accompany him to the new and struggling Virginia Colony as the company's treasurer. Life in the new colony was not easy, nor did it suit Sandys very much. The settlers were a quarrelsome lot, and they antagonized their neighbours, the local Indigenous population. In 1622, the Powhatan Confederacy attacked the settlement at Jamestown, and 347 settlers were killed, one quarter of the colony's population. While all this was going on, Sandys became reclusive and used the time to translate Ovid's *Metamorphoses* into English. After a decade of discontent, Sandys returned to Boxley and lived a quiet life, spending his final years working on English translations of the Psalms. He died in 1644. It is curious to think that in this little country church lies the body of a man who travelled most of the known world in his day.

I seek out Sandys's tomb not because I am a huge fan, but because when I was younger I read the travel books of H.V. Morton, who admitted that it was a worm-eaten copy of Sandys's *Relation of a Journey* picked up for a few shillings in Charing Cross Road that had inspired him to begin his own travels. So begins the curious afterlife of a book. You send a book out into the world, and you have no idea whose path it may cross or what the consequences such an act of folly may accrue, even four hundred years later. So tipping my hat to the remarkable George Sandys, and by association H.V. Morton, I say goodbye to peaceful Boxley.

Clambering over a stile at the edge of the churchyard, I pass through a field full of inquisitive lambs and climb once more to the North Downs Way. I follow a lane along the top of the ridge. By now, I can tell that I've had too much sun. The bridge of my nose feels like the cracked and puckered skin on a badly basted turkey, and the back of my neck is warm to the touch. I drop back down to visit Detling and the church of St. Martin of Tours. I snap a picture of the tiny red brick school, because it is exactly how I'd imagined the school in Miss Read's memoir, *A Village School*, to be. (Miss Read's stories of English village life are a secret passion of mine). Then I climb the chalk ridge once more to the trail, wondering if this day will end in sunstroke.

Then I see a most curious site. At one point, the trail leaves the high ridge and drops down a steep flight of steps into a close-cropped meadow in a hanging valley. Where the trail crosses the meadow, the way is marked with short-stemmed daisies (*Bellis perennis*, known as English daisies in Canada). Nowhere else do these flowers grow, only where people have trodden the soil. On either side of the trail there is green grass. It is the most curious thing I have ever seen. It is so striking that I take a picture of the phenomenon: a narrow path of snowy white flowers stretching for perhaps one hundred metres, from one stile to the next. If I don't take a picture of this, I think, no one will ever believe me.

The trail continues to White Horse Wood Park and across a sunken roadway to the ruins of Thurnham Castle. The castle is of the Norman motte-and-bailey design, sitting atop a slight spur overlooking the Medway valley. It was built by Robert de Thurnham in the reign of Henry II, but he probably built upon the ruins of an earlier fortress, for it was an obvious place for a defensive castle. Parts of the flint walls still stand and some of the earthworks, though the ditches have filled in with time, and the roadway has carved away some of the mound. Peering around the ruins, I meet Jan and Dave, a retired couple in their seventies. Both are tall, lean and radiate good humour and mutual affection. We sit down and swap stories. Dave was in a band, though his bandmates are now scattered to all corners of the globe, one to California and the other to British Columbia. His latest enthusiasm is his GoPro camera, which he has mounted on a remote-control helicopter. He insists on showing me footage on his smartphone. There is something so attractive about this couple that I am loath to say goodbye. I realize that it is the enjoyment they still take in the world around them, learning new things and meeting new people. They keep each other young. Reluctantly, I part with Jan and Dave and head down the hill to Thurnham, my destination for the night.

The only place to stay or eat in the tiny village of Thurnham is the picturesque Black Horse Inn, and it is hopping on a Thursday night. The parking lot is full of sports cars, and the pub is packed with bright young things, tennis sweaters knotted around their necks, waiting to be seated for dinner. I fight my way to the front of the crowd and collect my key and ask if there will be room for dinner. The tattooed young lady behind the bar frowns and says, "Did you make a reservation?"

No, I answer, didn't think I needed to.

She looks over her booking calendar. "We can squeeze you in at seven thirty. Not the best table, though," she adds apologetically and points to a single table that is wedged between the bar, the servers' station and the swinging kitchen door.

"Beggars can't be choosers," I say.

After a cold shower and a lie down, I return to the restaurant and am shown to my seat. I am careful to keep my toes and elbows tucked in, as waitresses and patrons are constantly brushing past. My waitress hands me a menu. I open it and gulp. By now, I am used to the fact that I will have to pay double in England for what I would pay for a similar meal in Canada, but this is not a pub that serves simple pub grub. This is a pub for foodies. I look down the list of exotic fare on offer and settle on the least expensive: a salad composed of figs, pigeon breast and black pudding on watercress with a honey Dijon dressing.

"...and to drink?" asks the waitress.

"Water will be fine," I say.

To be fair, the food is excellent, and I begin to see why so many people would drive so far on a Thursday night just to eat. I have never eaten pigeon before, or watercress for that matter, but I think, why not? I am in England after all. Didn't Mr. Pickwick eat squab?

13

Thurnham
to Lenham

_____

There is but one truly serious philosophical problem, and that is
suicide. Judging whether life is or is not worth living amounts to
answering the fundamental question of philosophy.
—ALBERT CAMUS, *The Myth of Sisyphus*

I WAKE EARLY and fill the time before breakfast reading Bunyan.
Christian has found a new companion in Hopeful, one of the citizens of Vanity Fair who, inspired by the example of Faithful, has
decided to mend his life and join the pilgrimage to the holy city. In
a moment of weakness, they leave the hard path to walk in a
meadow where the soft grass is easier on their feet, and they are
captured by the giant Despair, who is the ruler of these lands and
who casts them into the dungeons of Doubting Castle. The giant

tortures them repeatedly and urges them to take their own lives rather than endure endless torment. I put the book aside.

It is difficult to explain the attraction of suicide to someone who has never considered it. In my own case, something always stilled my hand: probably a sense of duty to those I would leave behind. Perhaps it was my father's example that stopped me. He suffered many setbacks in his life—unemployment, loss of income, divorce—and yet he never succumbed to despair. Instead, he took care of those around him and was always ready with a helping hand or a joke. Did his faith give him this kind of strength? I wish he were alive to ask.

When I enter the restaurant again, it's quiet. Gone are the crowds of the previous evening. I am seated in a quiet inglenook by the open fireplace, and, looking around, realize that I had been conned the night before. What I had taken to be a charming old pub is nothing of the kind. Only the front of the house is old, where you enter from the street. The rest is a modern reconstruction but done very well. The beams are repurposed, the fox-hunting prints and Dick Turpin posters are reproductions. Even the heavy plaster, which looks like it has been stained with the smoke of generations of tobacco smokers, is just artfully stained to look that way. Still, there are no horse brasses or hammered copper serving trays. Whoever designed the addition did so tastefully, and the ropes of dried hops that festoon the heavy ceiling beams are an inspired touch.

After breakfast, I climb the hill once more and rejoin the trail just below Thurnham Castle. Walking the next section of the North Downs Way is like sailing into a steep sea. Up one wave, down the next, over the crest and then plunge deep into the trough. Hundreds and hundreds of steps cut into the chalk—up, down, up, down—and completely exhausting, but the views from the crests are worth the climb. From a peak above Hollingbourne, the view across the valley of the Medway is panoramic. I can see Leeds Castle across the river, silvery in the heat haze. I decide to descend from the escarpment and visit Hollingbourne.

I like Hollingbourne. There is a stately manor house, and a delightfully squiffy timber-framed house next to a pub called the Dirty Habit, which lies at the crossroads beside the Pilgrims' Way. The church is down the hill in a pretty cottage-lined square. Someone has taken very good care of the gardens. The church is lovely, but what catches my eye and what remains fresh in my memory is a chapel to the left of the sanctuary created by the Culpepper family in 1638 as a private memorial chapel. You ascend a set of stairs to reach it, for it is set above the Culpepper family crypt. Local legend has it that the lead caskets of the Culpeppers move around of their own volition, and each time the crypt is opened they are found on different shelves. The walls of the chapel are white stone, so the tiny room is quite bright and airy, and occupying the middle of the floor is a raised chest tomb topped with the recumbent figure of a noble woman in flowing robes and veil done in spotless white marble. The sculpture is beautifully carved, and I discover later that it is considered one of the finest seventeenth-century monuments in England. The figure is Lady Elizabeth Culpepper (née Cheney) and the chest upon which she lies is inscribed *Optima Faemina, Optima Conius, Optima Mater* (best of women, best of wives, best of mothers). The most curious thing about the effigy is the snarling little beast that lies protectively at her feet. At first, I thought it was a fierce lap dog, a common addition to tombs of this sort, where the dog represents fidelity, but then I notice that the little beast has cloven hooves. Later research reveals that it is a mythical beast called a *theow* or a *thoye*, a heraldic animal specifically associated with the Cheney family. The walls of the chapel are plain white stone but covered in hundreds of blank heraldic shields. Clearly this chapel was intended to serve the Culpepper family as memorial over many generations, with a shield inscribed to commemorate each member of the family at the time of their death. But only three shields have been engraved and only two have been painted with heraldic designs. The effect of the blank walls is rather sad.

There is a monumental baptismal font near the back of the church. The octagonal stone basin is supported upon a fluted octagonal pillar which in turn rests upon a massive octagonal base. The whole thing must weigh several tons. To top it all off (literally in this case), the basin is covered by a dome-shaped wooden lid, carved in the high gothic style, that is so heavy and ornate that it requires a chain hoist to lift it off the basin. They took baptism very seriously back then.

For those of you who are unfamiliar with the rite of baptism, it is the ceremony of ritual washing used to welcome new members into the Christian Church. When I was a baby, my parents took me to their church where the priest sprinkled some holy water from the font onto my forehead and pronounced, "I baptize thee in the name of the Father, and of the Son, and of the Holy Ghost. Amen." Then, with the side of his thumb, the priest traced a damp cross on my forehead and continued: "We receive this child into the congregation of Christ's flock, and do sign him with the sign of the Cross, in token that hereafter he shall not be ashamed to confess the faith of Christ crucified, and manfully to fight under his banner against sin, the world, and the devil, and to continue Christ's faithful soldier and servant unto his life's end. Amen." Pretty heavy stuff for a mewling infant whose understanding of the world was limited to sleeping, burping, nursing and filling his diaper. And this is why, in churches where infant baptism is still practised, a pair of family friends or relatives is asked to stand in as godparents, agreeing to oversee the child's spiritual education until he is capable of understanding the pact to which he has just been committed. A second rite, called confirmation, is performed when the child is old enough to make the vow for himself, at which point the godparents' duties come to an end. The idea of infant baptism arose in an age when children often didn't survive their first birthday; for baptism was not only a rite of initiation, it was also a ritual washing away of sin, a requirement for salvation. Without baptism safeguarding the child's eternal soul, he could not hope to enter the Kingdom of Heaven. Baptism was a spiritual insurance policy, contracted by fond parents against the ever-present threat of infantile death.

Not all Christian denominations follow this pattern for the rite of baptism. At the time of the Protestant Reformation, many theologians declared that infant baptism was utter nonsense. A loving God wouldn't send innocent souls to hell just because they hadn't been baptized. Baptism, in their view, was a profession of faith and had to be made at an age when the baptized understood what it was they were professing. In this tradition, a baptism is a ritual transformation, usually involving full immersion in water, or, if not a full immersion, a pretty thorough soaking. The newly baptized emerged from this experience reborn, moving from a fallen condition to a state of grace. Baptist Churches took their name from this rite, pointing out that this had been the practice in the early church, and that Jesus himself had been baptized by his cousin John through immersion in the river Jordan.

Theological differences aside, baptism, whether as an infant or an adult, is a rite of passage, transforming the baptized from an outsider to an insider. After baptism, you are a full member of a faith community. You belong. It's like joining the Freemasons. You can go anywhere in the world and find people who are your people and who will welcome you as one of their own.

Have we lost something in the secular West by discarding this comfortable rite? Is membership in a church community necessary for a full spiritual life? Or can spirituality exist as an individual code, with practices and beliefs borrowed from many cultures and traditions? Is a do it yourself religion valid, or do we need the weight of tradition?

As I said, I was baptized into the Anglican Church as an infant. Later I received confirmation at the age of twelve. But by the time I was in my mid-twenties, I no longer believed in all of the articles of belief found in the back of my purple prayer book. Eventually I fell away and stopped attending church altogether, because the hypocrisy of standing up each week and making my profession of faith grew too much to bear. I think this probably hurt my father, who was actively involved in his parish until the moment of his death. But I can still recite the creed, word for word. It's engrained in my memory even if it no longer rings completely true. And I'll be honest: I feel robbed. The language of *The English Book of Common Prayer* is my language; the stories told each week in the liturgy are my stories. I miss the mystery and the ritual—I find them calming and aesthetically pleasing, if nothing else—and I miss the fellowship, embodied in that lovely phrase, "the communion of saints."

St. Anselm of Canterbury is remembered, amongst other things, for having written the following formula: "Credo ut intelligam," which is usually translated as "I believe so that I may understand." This is the credo of many evangelical preachers today. "Just believe," they proclaim. "Cast away your doubts and fears. Trust in God and be saved." If you take the leap of faith, we are assured, understanding will follow. Canadian theologian Wilfred Cantwell Smith of McGill, however, has proposed that what Anselm probably meant was more along the lines of "I commit myself in order that I may understand."[1] If blind belief is too difficult, Anselm seems to be suggesting, then start with practice. Commit yourself to a way of life and, in time, understanding may follow. It's like learning to play the piano. If you want to play, you must first commit to years of practice—endless hours of scales and arpeggios—until one day you sit down on the piano bench and suddenly realize, hey, I'm playing the piano. Faith is like that. If you want to be a Christian, you begin by practising things that Christians believe are important, like charity, forgiveness, compassion, humility, and loving your neighbour. Then one day it dawns on you that you've gone from practising to being. You've internalized what it means to be a Christian. It's become a part of you.

It's an attractive formula. It seems more intellectually valid than unquestioning faith, and I feel it is a program I could get behind. But for some reason, I resist.

Anyway, that seems like an awfully long digression; but, in my defence, it is an awfully big baptismal font.

I leave the church and ascend the narrow road once more to the Dirty Habit. Turning south, I continue along the Pilgrims' Way, which has become a level shaded cart track. I am relieved to be out of the sun. My nose is starting to peel, despite the visor on my ball cap. Somehow, I had not pictured England, especially England in the springtime, as the sort of place where sunburn would be an issue. After a few miles, I detour from the Way to visit the village of Harrietsham. A footpath leads me to the modern Harrietsham train station and then to the village proper. In the middle of the village, an ancient church and its surrounding churchyard stand besieged—a walled island in the middle of a modern suburban development. The churchyard is overgrown and neglected. The church looks run down too. Everything needs repointing and a dash of paint. Wooden louvres are missing in the bell tower, and cooing pigeons have taken roost in the belfry. The glass on the door is broken, and it appears that someone has tried to jimmy the lock. Despite a printed card on the door that announces, "The church is open daily for quiet reflection and prayer," the doors are bolted. I don't blame the church authorities. In stark contrast, a modern playground and playing field stand just outside the walls of the churchyard. Here the grass is neatly trimmed. A mother with a stroller watches two children larking on a jungle gym. No one else is around, anywhere. I can't help feeling that something has gone awry here, that becoming a part of the commuter belt has hollowed out Harrietsham. The vandalized church porch reminds me of the graffiti-tagged pedestrian tunnel in Merstham.

Leaving Harrietsham, I climb the hill to the Pilgrims' Way once more. I'm beginning to sense the nearness of Canterbury. I pass a Pilgrim's Lodge and a Summoner's Farm, and a little further along the path, I discover a bench designed especially for weary pilgrims. I know this to be true because there is a life-size carving of a monk, called Brother Percival, seated on the bench inviting me to join him—well, that, and the fact that the words "Pilgrim bound with staff and faith, rest thy bones" are carved across the back of the bench. Just below me, a white Sprinter van is parked. The words "Aktiva Tours" are stencilled along the side. The driver sits, smoking a cigarette and looking down at his cellphone. He blows a plume of smoke out of the open window from the corner of his mouth. Hesitantly, I approach and ask if he will take a picture of me sitting on the bench next to the wooden monk.

"Yah, sure. Everyone wants their photo taken here."

I hand him my camera and pose.

"American?" he guesses as he takes the shot.

"Canadian. Yourself?" His English is excellent, but there is something about his accent that suggests northern Europe.

"Dutch. I'm driving the bus for a tour group hiking the Pilgrims' Way, but we have lost one of the hikers. Three are about a half hour ahead of you, but one has failed to show up. He wasn't looking good this morning, and we are worried. He has a...um, a sugar problem. How you say?"

I think for a moment. "Diabetes?"

"Yah, diabetes. I'm trying to get his cell number from someone at his home, so I can call him. If he answers, we should be able to locate him through the GPS in his phone." I realize that this is what the driver had been doing when I interrupted him in the van. He pulls out his phone and checks it again. He shakes his head in despair. "Nothing."

"What's his name?" I ask. "Maybe I will meet him on the trail and can let you know."

"Wilibert. He is kind of heavy, you know." The driver holds his hands out in front of his belly, like he's cradling a basketball. "Curly red hair. Glasses. I will give you my cell number. If you see him, you will call, okay?"

He reads off his phone number, and I save it to Derek's loaner phone. Then he checks again, but no one has texted. We fall into conversation as he waits. The driver's name is Hans, and I discover that he has travelled quite extensively in western Canada, in the Rockies and along the coast of British Columbia, by boat and helicopter. He even went to visit a niece who lived just outside of Edmonton.

"It is winter," he says, "and I am not properly dressed. Just a jacket. No hat, no gloves. I do not think I will need a car, so I take a coach, but I have never before seen a country like this. It is so wide and flat. Everything is covered in snow. Suddenly, the coach driver pulls to the side of the road and says, 'Here you are.' I look. There is nothing, not a house, not a tree. Just snow in every direction as far as you can see. So flat and white. 'Where?' I ask. 'Just over there,' says the driver, pointing to the horizon. 'Unfortunately, your niece's town is not on our route. This is as close as I can go.' So I step out of the coach, and you know what happens?"

I shake my head.

"I immediately sink into snow up to my neck."

We both burst out laughing.

"The ditch?" I ask.

"Yes."

His cellphone rings. Hans turns sideways and cranes his neck as if straining to hear. The conversation is long and involved and in Dutch. I take this as my sign to leave. I catch Hans's eye and wave goodbye. He grins and waves back with his free hand. I set off once more.

I pass Marley Court above the road, an eighteenth-century farmhouse (very pretty), and the Marley works below the road, famous manufacturers of concrete roofing tiles (very noisy). Derek has marked a diagonal approach to Lenham on the map, which directs me through a field of canola in full bloom that is higher than my hat in places. I squeeze through, leaving green and yellow pollen stains in bright stripes down my clothes. My bed for the night is in the Dog and Bear, a coaching inn constructed in 1602, whose claim to fame is that Queen Anne once stayed there in 1704. Her coat of arms is still proudly displayed above the door. My room is very nice, but it backs onto the old coach yard, now a beer patio with tables set right outside my window. I have a shower, listening to the rather intimate conversations just beyond the glass. Cigarette smoke drifts in around the ill-fitting window, in tiny convolvulus clouds like the stage smoke in a Death Metal rock concert. I put on a clean T-shirt and set out to explore the town.

Lenham's market square is lovely, surrounded by lots of timbered and tiled houses, but marred by the large numbers of parked cars filling its centre. The Saxon Pharmacy on one corner is so named, my guidebook tells me, because a Saxon grave was discovered during the course of its renovations. I decide to see the church. As I am walking along the road, the Aktiva Tours van pulls up abruptly, and Hans rolls down the window. We speak as one.

"Have you seen—"

"Any word—"

But, no, Wilibert hasn't turned up yet, and I can see that Hans is worried. "Well, I have your number," I offer, but it is cold comfort. He thanks me and drives away. I never do see Wilibert, and I wonder to this day about his fate.

The church is large, and the surrounding churchyard is kept reasonably well-tended by a resident sheep, grazing among the tombstones. This strikes me as an intelligent idea. I hate mowing the lawn and wonder if I could get away with this back home. Inside, the church is large and echo-y. The tall Elizabethan oak pulpit is whimsical, with strange sphinx-like figures supporting the lectern and canopy, and a multitude of smaller creatures, including a number of small birds, peering out of the carved foliage. If I were a parishioner, I would derive hours of satisfaction contemplating this pulpit, particularly if the sermon was long and boring. The choir stalls are quite old too, as is the altar in the side chapel, a monumental piece of carved stone with an unreadable crest on the front. Near the altar is a memorial to the prolific Mary Honywood, who died in 1620 at the age of ninety-two, leaving behind an incredible number of descendants: sixteen children, 114 grandchildren, 228 great-grandchildren, and nine great-great-grandchildren. The north doors of the church, beneath the bell tower, are enormous, large enough to drive a transport truck through, and I wonder: Why so big? What purpose would they have served? I entered through a smaller side door, and it is clear that these other, larger doors haven't been opened in many years, for a CCTV camera is mounted high up, on a bracket, and the feed cables have been stapled across the door opening. I look up, smile, and wave.

Leaving the church, I walk down a quiet lane to visit Lenham's famous tithe barn. I am hoping to see inside and am in luck, for a local arts and crafts show is in progress, and I am able to stroll in and have a good look around. For many centuries, the land around Lenham was owned by St. Augustine's Abbey in Canterbury, and the tithe barn was where local farmers deposited a portion of their harvest, their "tithe" (traditionally ten percent), for the Abbey's upkeep. The large oak beams overhead resemble the keel and ribs of a ship—like Noah's Ark—flipped upside down. The beams rest on a low brick wall to keep the wood off the damp ground. Originally, the roof would have been thatched, but at some time in the past, the thatch has been replaced with red tile. There were originally two tithe barns in Lenham, but one burned down. This is a rare survival, and I'm glad. There is something about the barn's irregular-ness and eccentricity that I find appealing. There are no straight lines, every beam and post is slightly different, and reminds you of the tree from which it was hewn. It speaks of an age when everything was handcrafted and the creation of anything of value took time. I return to my room at the inn and settle in for the night.

Walking through the Kentish countryside today has reminded me of my favourite novel by H.G. Wells, a social comedy, published when the author was forty-four, called *The History of Mr. Polly*. The title character, Alfred Polly, is an inconsequential man, both in his own eyes and in the eyes of the world. He owns a failing men's clothing shop in a little seaside town called Fishbourne. Polly has plunged recklessly into trade for a lack of anything else to do and into an unhappy and childless marriage. He is in debt, and he sees no end to his unbearable life, so he resolves to kill himself. But he is honourable enough to want to see his wife provided for, so he resolves to cut his throat one night when his wife is out at church, but to disguise his suicide by setting fire to his shop first, so that she can claim the insurance. So he sets the fire, but things soon spin out of control. The fire spreads quickly, too quickly, and Polly has to delay his own death in order to rescue a neighbour, a deaf elderly woman, whom he leads across the burning rooftops to safety. His neighbours, fellow shopkeepers with whom he had been carrying on a running feud for years, congratulate him and call him a hero, each dreaming of the new start that their insurance money will allow. His wife arrives home to find her shop gutted and begins to plot anew to begin on a larger scale. But Polly has had an epiphany: "Fishbourne wasn't the world," he realizes, and "If the world does not please you, *you can change it.*"[2] One day, he quietly slips away with just twenty pounds in his pocket, abandoning the small seaside town he had always hated, and walks out into the Kentish countryside and a new life.

Wells clearly loved the English countryside, for he describes Mr. Polly's walk in glowing terms:

> *There is no countryside like the English countryside for those who have learned to love it; its firm yet gentle lines of hill and dale, its ordered confusion of features, its deer parks and downland, its castles and stately houses, its hamlets and old churches, its farms and ricks and great barns and ancient trees, its pools and ponds and shining threads of rivers, its flower-starred hedgerows, its orchards and woodland patches, its village greens and kindly inns.*[3]

Wells goes on to list the pleasantries of other countrysides in other parts of the world—places like Picardy, Burgundy, Italy, the Ardennes, Touraine, and the Rhineland—and concludes:

But none of these change scene and character in three miles of
walking, nor have so mellow a sunlight nor so diversified a cloud-
land nor confess the perpetual refreshment of the strong soft winds
that blow from off the sea, as our mother England does.[4]

No one could write like this if they did not feel it. But *Mr. Polly* is
a dangerous book to read at my age, for it is a mid-life crisis narrative, and Polly finds that the vagabond life suits him.

For the first time in many years he had been leading a healthy
human life, living constantly in the open air, walking every day
for eight or nine hours, eating sparingly, accepting every conver-
sational opportunity, not even disdaining discussion of possible
work. And beyond mending a hole in his coat, that he had made
while negotiating barbed wire, with a borrowed needle and thread
in a lodging house, he had done no real work at all. Neither had he
worried about business nor about times and seasons. And for the
first time in his life he had seen the Aurora Borealis.[5]

By the end of the book Polly has become a larger and better
man. After a number of adventures, which include rescuing an old
woman and her granddaughter from a dangerous bully, he becomes
a general handyman in a cozy riverside inn and is content.

Only in fiction do we see such happy endings, and perhaps that
is why we read fiction. And which of us has not wished that he
could just walk away from his humdrum existence, throw a rucksack over his shoulder, and become a vagabond. Richard Jefferies,
another writer who celebrated the English countryside, wrote:
"Hardly any of us have but thought, some day I'll go on a voyage;
but the years go by, and still we have not sailed."[6] Well, two weeks
might not make a voyage, but they are a start, and I must confess, I
am enjoying myself.

14

Lenham to Wye

Be kind, for everyone you meet is fighting a hard battle.
—attributed to IAN MACLAREN (Rev. John Watson),
Scottish theologian and author

I SLEEP WELL AND AWAKE REFRESHED. Leaving Lenham
under a blue sky, I cut across a field of wheat where orange poppies
bloom in profusion. On the face of the North Downs, here a grassy
treeless slope, the turf has been removed to reveal a giant white
chalk cross. It was created after the Great War, that war to end all
wars, as a monument to the fallen. However, at the beginning of the
Battle of Britain, the turf was replaced. The cross, so large and
white, so clearly visible from the air, was an obvious navigational
marker for German bombers, so it had to be covered up. At the end
of hostilities, it was restored, a monument now to two world wars.

When I rejoin the Pilgrims' Way it has become a quiet leafy lane,
which I have to myself until mid-morning when I am joined by
numerous dog-walkers and horse-riders. At this point, the Pilgrims'

Way is magically transformed into something else: the Grim-Poo Way. It is almost impossible to walk without stepping in dog feces.

I duck down into Charing for a brief detour. Charing has lots of character—tight twisting lanes lined with impressive red brick manors. There must have been a lot of money once in Charing. I follow a lane up to the consolidated remains of the ruined Bishop's Palace, which look suitably picturesque, particularly the massive old gatehouse, but as far as I can see the palace grounds seem now to be mostly used for agricultural purposes. Maybe not so different from how things would have looked in the Middle Ages: mucky and straw-strewn.

The church is curious. The tall Norman tower is topped with a golden cockerel weathervane and is much older than the attached church. I walk inside for a peek. A young woman is changing the flowers on the altar and greets me with a smile. The thick oak beams spanning the nave above my head still have the shadowy traces of ancient painted greenery. Every window in the place is in a different style. I spy a list of former parish priests on the back wall, and notice that one is the Rev. William Henry Ady, M.A. By coincidence, my Victorian guidebook to the Pilgrims' Way, the one I purchased in New Alresford at the beginning of my walk, is written by a Mrs. Henry Ady, who also wrote under her maiden name, Julia Cartwright. Cartwright was the well-travelled daughter of landed gentry, a friend of Bernard Berenson, and the author of many notable works of art criticism, including studies of Botticelli and Raphael. Henry and Julia married in 1880, after meeting on a tour in Italy. He accepted the appointment at Charing in 1888, and the guidebook was published five years later, so the timing makes sense. Her history of the Pilgrims' Way, though an uncharacteristic subject for her to tackle, was perhaps inspired by living next to the ancient trackway.

I leave Charing on a footpath which leads me past Pett Place, a long rambling brick manor with numerous chimneys, but hidden from prying eyes behind a wall of weathered brick fringed with rhododendron. A rising path carries me once again to the Pilgrims' Way. Up ahead, I see a lone walker, bent under a backpack, plodding along. I soon overtake her, a middle-aged woman carrying a walking stick and wearing a floppy Tilley hat. She has her nose buried in a guidebook.

"Hi," I say, as I hustle past. She looks up briefly, considers me grimly for a moment, and then returns to her book.

But soon I am leaving the main trail again and dropping down to visit the village of Westwell. My right-of-way takes me diagonally through a field of canola in full bloom, and by the time I reach the edge of the village my clothes are once again coated in yellow-green pollen. Winding down the narrow lane into Westwell, however, I begin to feel I am walking on familiar ground. Somewhere around here, I know, must be the setting of E. Nesbit's *The Wouldbegoods*.

The Wouldbegoods is a children's novel first published in 1899. It is narrated by Oswald, the eldest of the five precocious Bastable children. In the story, the children are sent to the Kent countryside for their holidays to keep them out of trouble, something they have a preternatural tendency to find. The children resolve to be good, though they have no talent for it, and form a club called the Wouldbegoods, with a charter and a book of golden deeds to record their accomplishments. The humour lies in the fact that every time they try to do a good deed it goes horribly awry. By the time we reach the chapter called "The Canterbury Pilgrims," the children have chucked good-deed-doing for the time-being and have decided to become pilgrims instead. They dress like the characters in Chaucer's *Canterbury Tales* and determine to walk to Canterbury, addressing each other as Sir Knight, Manciple, Prioress, Wife of Bath, Mr. Bath, etc.

Of course we knew the way to go to Canterbury, because the old Pilgrims' Road runs just above our house. It is a very pretty road,

*narrow, and often shady. It is nice for walking, but carts do not
like it because it is rough and rutty; so there is grass growing in
patches on it.*[1]

They set out, and all goes well for a time, until they notice that
one of their number, Denny, has turned pale and is limping. When
confronted, he admits to having put split peas in his shoes.

> *"Perhaps you'll tell me," said the gentle knight, with the politeness
> of despair, "why on earth you've played the goat like this?"*
>
> *"Oh, don't be angry," Denny said; and now his shoes were
> off, he curled and uncurled his toes and stopped crying. "I knew
> pilgrims put peas in their shoes—and—oh, I wish you wouldn't
> laugh!"*
>
> *"I'm not," said Oswald, still with bitter politeness...*
>
> *"You see"—Denny went on—"I do want to be good. And
> if pilgriming is to do you good, you ought to do it properly. I
> shouldn't mind being hurt in my feet if it would make me good for
> ever and ever. And besides, I wanted to play the game thoroughly.
> You always say I don't."*[2]

So the little group of pilgrims is stuck, unable to proceed, unable
to return, until they are rescued by a jolly young lady in a dogcart,
who offers to carry Denny and the little ones to Canterbury, which
she assures them is just half a mile down the road, if the older ones
will walk.

> *When we got to Canterbury, it was much smaller than we
> expected, and the cathedral not much bigger than the Church that
> is next to the Moat House. There seemed to be only one big street,
> but we supposed the rest of the city was hidden away somewhere.
> There was a large inn, with a green before it, and the red-wheeled
> dogcart was standing in the stableyard and the lady, with Denny
> and the others, sitting on the benches in the porch, looking out for*

us. The inn was called the "George and Dragon," and it made me
think of the days when there were coaches and highwaymen and
foot-pads and jolly landlords, and adventures at country inns, like
you read about.[3]

You can see where this is going. The young lady, entering into
the spirit of the thing, gives them a rattling good tour of the "cathedral," describing in ghastly detail the death of Becket and the
martyrdom of St. Alphege "who had bones thrown at him till he
died, because he wouldn't tax his poor people to please the beastly
rotten Danes."[4] She also gives the children a tour of the dungeon,
which looks remarkably like an oast-house, and the hospital, which
looks remarkably like a barn. Later, she is forgiven her deceit,
because "she had really kept it up first-rate," and when they do
finally reach the real Canterbury, the official tour isn't nearly half as
much fun.[5]

Nesbit tells us that the false Canterbury was called Hazelbridge.
The name is an invention, but from the description it could very
well have been Westwell, which indeed has a village green in front
of the inn, and, just around the corner, a large church with an oast
house and ancient barn just across the cemetery wall.

Which raises the question: Is a pilgrimage of the imagination as
good as the real thing? Take, for example, the labyrinths depicted
on the floors of many medieval churches. These labyrinths were
created so that those who wished to travel to Jerusalem, but could
not, either because they could not afford to go or the route to the
Holy Land was closed by the fortunes of war, could perform a
symbolic pilgrimage. The Cathedral in Chartres contains the most
famous example of this practice. The pilgrim follows the path on
the tiled floor of the cathedral, and mentally and spiritually makes
the pilgrimage to Jerusalem, pausing at each stage of the journey
for appropriate reflection. Is this practice as valid as the real
pilgrimage to Jerusalem? I suspect that it is; which makes my own
pilgrimage seem like a colossal waste of time and resources. On the

other hand, I could never have imagined the path of English daisies I saw on my way to Thurnham. That was a miracle, if we define miracles as surprising and welcome phenomena for which we have no ready explanation.

I try to visit the village church, but it is locked, which is a shame because although the outside is an ugly mélange of stucco, brick and flint, I have been told that the inside is quite beautiful. On a side note, Richard Harris Barham, the author of *The Ingoldsby Legends*, was once the vicar here. After a brief rest and water break on a lichen-encrusted bench in the churchyard, I hustle once more up the hill and rejoin the Pilgrims' Way.

I soon enter the vast Eastwell Estate at the point where the ruins of the estate church of St. Mary's stand. Passing through a mossy archway and entering the skeleton of the old church, I spy the hiker whom I had passed earlier, seated on an overgrown wall. She has her lunch spread out on a handkerchief at her side. Her nose is buried in her guidebook, the North Downs Way guidebook, I note—the same one I'm carrying—and she looks up suspiciously.

"Why, hello again," I say.

She regards me for a moment with narrowed eyes, then gives a slow nod and returns to her reading. Feeling awkward, I walk back through the ruins to a small car park. I set my backpack down on the grass and remove my camera. As I am shuffling around the parking lot, looking for the best vantage point to take a photo, a moist voice chirrups in my ear,

"Are you an 'istorian, surr?"

"Sorry?"

"I said, are you an 'istorian?"

The speaker is an elderly man seated in the driver's seat of a beige Ford Focus with the side window rolled down. I hadn't seen him at first. I'd assumed all of the cars were empty.

"No," I say, "but I have an interest in history."

"Then I suppose you have come to see the grave of Richard Plantagenet?"

I profess ignorance, and he proceeds to give me directions to the tomb, and then begins to relate the history of the Wars of the Roses. I sense that if I am not careful, he will keep me standing there all day, so I interrupt him and ask if he has a moment to show me the way. He seems pleased to be asked. "I'm not an educated man, you understand, but I do have an interest in 'istory." He speaks with a Kentish brogue and with the lisp of an elderly man with loose dentures. It takes him quite a long time to extricate himself from the car, and when he stands, he comes only to my shoulder. He walks toward the chapel at a slow mincing pace, as if in carpet slippers. I realize he is much older than I first thought. His skin is like crepe, his eyes red and moist, and when he speaks, a line of spittle runs from the corner of his mouth to the point of his chin where it hangs like an icicle, growing longer and more fascinating with each syllable. He wipes it away with his shirt cuff.

"I grew up 'ere, you know. Rang those bells." He indicates the ruined tower. "My grandparents lived in the lodge beside the lake." He points through the screen of trees that surrounds the churchyard, to a picturesque cottage beside a large pond. "They are buried just over there. I come here often. I like the peace and quiet."

I am puzzled. The ruins look ancient to me. "You attended *this* church as a child?"

"Certainly. There was regular services 'ere until '38 or '39."

"What happened?"

"The War. The Germans shot it up. After the war, the roof was gone and it was no longer considered safe, so they pulled it down and moved the monuments. But it was falling down even before. The last time I rang the church bell was in 1953 for the Coronation." We look up at the bell tower, which is leaking pigeon feathers like a burst cushion. There is also a small chapel to the south of the tower and the remains of a connecting wall. That is all that remains of Eastwell St. Mary's. He points into the small chapel, now an empty room. "Used to be a beautiful statue of the

Virgin in there. It's in Challock Church now. The big monuments they took to the v and A. Ah, 'ere we are."

We pause by a cube of stone protruding from the grass in what must once have been the side wall of the nave. The woman with the guidebook is still seated nearby, making a brave attempt at pretending we are not there. I bend down and read the stone: "Reputed to be the tomb of Richard Plantagenet."

"He was the natural son of Richard III, but after 'is father's death 'e 'ad to 'ide. His enemies, the Tudors, wanted 'im dead, you see, so 'e came to Eastwell. He lived in a small cottage on the estate and worked as a stonemason." I watch with fascination as another long stalactite of spittle grows from his chin. How long before it breaks? At the last moment, he swipes it away with his shirt cuff. "He lived a quiet life and died 'ere—the last of the Plantagenets. If things 'ad turned out different at Bosworth Field, why 'e might 'ave been the King of England."

I turn to the seated woman. "Imagine that!" She knits her brow and frowns. I have completely spoiled her quiet pilgrimage.

I turn back to my guide, changing the topic. "So did you live here with your grandparents?"

"No, my parents." He can see my confusion. "Back then everyone worked on the estate. My father drove the first car in 1919."

"He was the chauffeur?"

"Aye. I left school at fourteen to join 'im. I remember my first job on the estate was a beater." I must look puzzled for he continues. "The gamekeeper, you see, would release the pheas-ants out in scrub, and then we would walk up and down beating the bushes, so the guests could shoot the birds as they flew." He frowns. "I never liked that job. Don't get me wrong. I'm not against 'unting, but it seemed cruel. The poor birds spent all their lives in cages and then on their first day of freedom, they get shot." He shrugs. "But it was like that. Different times. Back then, you never knew 'o you might be serving at dinner—King George, Lord Mountbatten, even Churchill. Why, I remember seeing all three of them standing together on the roof of Eastwell Manor watching the manoeuvres."

"Manoeuvres?"

"During the war the estate was taken over by the army. They used the grounds to practise for the invasion. When the war was over and we drained the lake, we found an amphibious tank right in the bottom." He laughs. "I remember one day, my dad and I were walking across the estate, 'im in 'is 'ome guard uniform, me in my naval uniform, and this sergeant comes running up, furious 'e was, and red in the face. 'Are you crazy!' 'e yells. 'Do you want to get yourselves killed?' I guess we'd walked right into the middle of a live fire exercise."

"You were in the navy?"

"Yes, North Atlantic convoy duty. I was in a corvette—little bathtub of a boat, tossed us around something 'orrible, it did."

"I know. I've seen one, in Canada, in Halifax. It must have been pretty cramped."

"It was, but it was nice too. Everyone pitched in together. Rank doesn't mean much on a ship that small. I remember once we was near Greenland. The ice was growing so thick on deck the captain worried we might capsize, so everyone, and I mean everyone, was on deck chipping ice as fast as we could go to save the ship."

At this point the woman gives up. She has been trying to wait us out, hoping we will go away, but it is clear that the old man is in no hurry. She packs her belongings, stands up, hoists her pack to her shoulders and sets off with a stiff angry gait.

My companion, oblivious to her annoyance, is lost in reverie. He scans the quiet churchyard and sighs. "I always loved it 'ere. Brought my wife 'ere just before she died. It was her last day outside the 'ospital. That was two years ago now. We'd been married for seventy years."

"Seventy!"

"Yes, can't even remember life without 'er." He pauses. "Well... now I can."

I walk him back to his car, and we shake hands.

"Ken," I say. "I'm sorry, but I never introduced myself."

"Peter," he responds.

"I'm pleased to have met you, Peter." We shake hands again. I hitch my pack once more to my shoulders, and, waving goodbye, turn and carry on toward Canterbury.

The Eastwell Estate that Peter remembers has changed. The Great House is now a luxury spa hotel, with indoor pool, hosting weddings and conferences, and part of the estate has been transformed into a golf course. But some of the grounds are still farmed in the old way. As I leave the chapel, my steps take me through a hay field in the process of being harvested. Hay is being cut and stacked in windrows, and the chaff and dust rise up at each step. Looming up ahead is a small bent-backed figure toiling across the empty landscape. "Oh, hell," I think. It's my lady pilgrim of grim countenance. I slow my pace, remembering the jogger on Box Hill and how annoyed I'd been with him at the time. But even with a slow pace, I am gaining steadily on her. Eventually, I am dogging her heels and there is nothing for it but to forge ahead. "Pardon me," I say as I nimbly step around her. I try to act nonchalant, but I can feel her eyes stabbing me between the shoulder blades all the way across the field.

I want to say, "Get your nose out of that guidebook. Life is meant to be lived, not read about." But I don't. For I realize the impulse would be hypocritical. If you have followed my narrative so far, you will have realized that I have spent a great deal of my life with my nose buried in a book.

And maybe it's time I stopped. I've spent my life looking for answers in books, but my father never did. He read for entertainment, not enlightenment. His favourite authors were people like Tom Clancy or Nevil Shute. He was a practical man, not an intellectual. He came from working class roots and wanted his son to do better, so he sent me off to university to get an education. As the world judges these things, I ended up becoming the more

successful man. And yet, who ended up being happier? My father
didn't live in his head the way I do. I'm not suggesting that his
inner life was less complex, but his focus was usually outward to
the people around him, which is a healthier way to live. Perhaps he
found the answers to all his questions in his faith, and that let him
concentrate on more important things.

Leaving Eastwell, I soon come to Boughton Lees. Boughton Lees
is a strangely configured little town. In the centre of the village is a
large triangular village green bounded on each side by a major road.
The houses and shops all sit on the outside of this triangular ring
road looking in towards the green. As I pass through, a cricket match
is being played on the green and spectators sit outside the village
pub—the Flying Horse—watching the match across the road. I
suppose it was all very cozy in the days of horse and carriage, but
not so much in the days of the automobile. A notice is tacked to a
telephone pole advertising a free concert of the "Society of Recorder
Players—Kent Branch" at the local church that evening. I will
return to Boughton Lees on the morrow to continue my walk, but
now I need to make a small detour to Wye to find my bed for the
night. Too bad. I would have enjoyed the concert.

My path takes me through an orchard and past rows of plastic
greenhouses holding strawberries. The smell of ripe strawberries is intoxicating, and I'm briefly tempted to reach through a tear
in the plastic sheeting and snatch a handful—they are that close
and smell that delicious—but I resist. Then I pass through fields
of raspberries and onto the old medieval five-arched bridge that
crosses the Stour at Wye. I pause on the bridge. It seems a liminal
moment, a last breath on the second last day of my hike, and I
am in no hurry to bring this day to an end. On the ridge above the
village is a large crown carved into the chalk. Peter cautioned me to
watch for it. It was created by school children in 1902 to commemorate the coronation of Edward VII. There is an old mill on one
side of the bridge and a family friendly pub on the other called the
Tickled Trout. The pub is aptly named, for, standing astride the old

bridge and looking down into the clear waters of the Stour, I can see dozens of sizable trout all facing upstream in a holding pattern, each swaying from side to side in the current, each waiting in calm anticipation should a dainty mouthful of mayfly decide to drift into their open maws.

Speaking of dinner, it is time I found mine, perhaps something with strawberries.

15

Wye to Canterbury

Take more time, cover less ground.

    —THOMAS MERTON, _Reading Notebooks_

THE NEXT MORNING, I am back in Boughton Lees, ready for the last leg of my journey. As I arrive, a coach disgorges an enormous number of bumptious schoolboys with heavy backpacks. We squeeze into the lane that marks the continuation of the North Downs Way at roughly the same time. For the next mile or so, we leapfrog each other. First, they pass me at a jog. Then they pause to take a breather, while I stroll past. Refreshed, they leap to their feet and dash ahead, bumping past me—"Excuse me, sir, Excuse me, Excuse..."—as they go. When they run out of steam and flop down on the grass, panting, I pass them again. This is going to be a very long day, I think. But mercifully they turn off on the path to Dover, and I breathe a sigh of relief.

It's a warm sunny Sunday. Everyone seems to be out enjoying the good weather, and the trail is packed with people walking their dogs. In fact, just outside the village of Chartham Hatch, I pass through a multitude of dog-walkers going in the other direction, clearly a planned event of some kind. What do you call a herd of dogs walking their owners? A crowd? A pack? A crack? If this is a spontaneous social media-inspired event, does it qualify as a flash mob? In twelve days of walking, I have only met two vicious dogs in England, and that was a pair of murderous Alsatians at an electric gate in the stockbroker belt who were trying to chew their way through the steel bars to eat me. Every other dog I have encountered on my walk has been friendly. How do the English do that? In Canada, every dog I meet wants to rip my arm off or chomp on my ankle. Are the English better at raising their pets, or is it perhaps the aura I project while on pilgrimage? Perhaps they don't see me as a threat because I am so relaxed?

The sun is so hot that at first I grow concerned, worried about aggravating my sunburn further; but for a good part of my morning I walk along a lovely shaded lane atop the North Downs that follows a deer fence along the edge of the Godmersham Park estate. There is a mature forest to my left of ancient beeches, and a scenic sweep of pasture to my right beyond the tall wire fence. The forest is open, the bluebells drying up and going to seed and young ferns shooting up in their place. Mountain bikers zip by on the forest road, helmeted and goggled, in their colourful spandex. At one point, I pass an old-fashioned deer gate, a deep ditch located in a break in the fence. This ditch has a high stone retaining wall on the forest side and a gentle slope leading up out of the ditch into the pasture, thus allowing the deer to leap easily onto the estate from the forest but making it impossible for them to jump back out again. I decide to leave the trail, cross a stile, and detour down the hill to get a look at the old country house.

Back in Chawton, I mentioned that Jane Austen's elder brother Edward had been adopted by a childless couple and had inherited their estates. Chawton was one of those estates; this was the other. Jane would have visited this house on numerous occasions to see her brother and his family. No doubt the grand house in Godmersham Park was the model for a number of country homes in her fiction, including Pemberley in *Pride and Prejudice*. Coming down the slope of the Downs through the pasture, I can see the grand Palladian house from above with its flanking wings, all constructed in the same red brick. There are three distinctive oval windows in the centre block resting above a row of pedimented windows, like three winking eyes under the steeply pitched slate roofs. While it is permissible to walk through the grounds along a designated path, there is no access to the house, which is now a college for opticians. In fact, the house is blocked from the lane by a dense eight-foot hedge, so I am reduced to holding my camera at arm's length above my head and shooting blindly. Needless to say, not one of my photos is a success.

Jane loved visiting this house. She was fond of her nephews and nieces, and delighted in family gatherings. But there was another attraction as well. In such a large house, she could actually achieve a degree of privacy, something impossible in the cramped house at Chawton. In a letter to her sister, she remarks: "I am in the yellow room—very literally—for I am writing in it this moment. It seems odd to me to have such a great place all to myself."[1] Her niece, Marianne Knight, remembered her aunt at Godmersham in this fashion:

> I remember that when Aunt Jane came to us at Godmersham she used to bring the manuscript of whatever novel she was writing with her, and would shut herself up with my elder sisters in one of the bedrooms to read to them aloud. I and the younger ones used to hear peals of laughter through the door, and thought it very hard that we should be shut out from what was so delightful…

I also remember how Aunt Jane would sit quietly working [which meant sewing] beside the fire in the library, saying nothing for a good while, and then would suddenly burst out laughing, jump up and run across the room to a table where pens and paper were lying, write something down, and then come back across to the fire and go on quietly working as before.[2]

From Godmersham Park, it is just a few miles to Chilham, and I pause to watch a dressage event on the meadows below Chilham Castle. Jane and her sister were frequent visitors to Chilham Castle, her last visit occurring just before her thirty-eighth birthday, when she noted wistfully: "I must leave off being young." She had become a chaperone to the younger set, but age had its compensations, for she writes, "I am put on the sofa near the fire and can drink as much wine as I like."[3] The village of Chilham is regarded as the most picturesque in Kent, and, as a result, the quaintly timbered village square is choked with the parked cars of visiting tourists. I linger for a moment on a bench outside the village church. Taking off my pack, I consult my map and slake my thirst. There is a service in progress in the church and the double doors have been propped open because of the heat. I can hear the congregation singing, "Crown him with many crowns..." in a thin, rather reedy fashion, and I join in quietly, surprised at how much of the old hymn I can remember.

Leaving Chilham, I climb the narrow, hedged and appropriately named Long Hill to Old Wives Lees. Then I stroll through apple orchards that remind me of home. Just ahead of me a family is biking down a gravel path, and the little girl takes a spill, grazing her knee. She is perhaps five years old, wailing as blood runs down her shin while mom and dad try to comfort her. I am the hero of the hour because I arrive on the scene carrying a first-aid kit. I gently wash her knee with a splash of water from my water bottle, rub in some Polysporin and apply a couple of Band-Aids. Voilà! We wipe away the tears and part as friends.

I have passed numerous oast houses in the past four days, but none serving their original purpose, which was to dry hops. All have been converted into cottages or holiday rentals. In fact, I haven't even seen any hops cultivated either, and this is odd because Kent was once famous for its hop gardens. In August 1884, when Joseph and Elizabeth Robins Pennell set off on a tandem bicycle from London to follow Chaucer's pilgrims to Canterbury, the roads were choked with hop-pickers, streaming out from the slums of London to find temporary work on Kent farms. Whole families took to the road, carrying their belongings on their backs or in wheelbarrows. They were a rough-spoken lot and clad in rags. Elizabeth found them quite intimidating, calling them tramps and "unwanted pilgrims." Later though, as she and her husband were cruising down the hill on their boneshaker from Harbledown to Canterbury, her attitude seemed to mellow: "All the way into the town we passed groups of pickers: women with large families of children, small boys with jugs and coats hung over their shoulders, and young girls with garlands of hops twisted about their hats, and all were as merry as if they had been on a picnic."[4]

Just as I am despairing of ever seeing a hop garden in Kent, I spot one: rows of hop vines twining around tall poles erected in long avenues, arranged like the columns of a Greek temple. It is the green flower of the hop vine, harvested in late summer, which gives beer its distinctive flavour. Inexpensive hops from America, New Zealand and Germany killed the English hops industry in the twentieth century. Of the 46,600 acres of hops that flourished in Kent when Elizabeth Robins Pennell cycled past, only about a thousand survive today.[5] But there is an active movement to revive the growing of English hops, including an annual hops festival in Faversham; so these fields may return to life yet, but never with the armies of agricultural labourers that Pennell saw, for the hops industry, like so many other things, has become mechanized. The small plantation I encounter is unusual. Hops are more commonly grown today in eight-foot hedges designed so that mechanical harvesters can straddle them, replacing hundreds of workers with a single operator.

After the apple orchards and the hop garden, I enter a steeply rolling forest. This is Bigbury Wood, and it was at Bigbury Hill in 54 BCE that Julius Caesar fought his first significant battle in his second invasion of Britain—the first attempt, a year before, had ended in failure. Anchoring his fleet on the coast of Kent, Caesar marched his legions inland. A brief but inconclusive skirmish was fought at a river crossing just south of Canterbury, and the British forces retreated to the top of Bigbury Hill. At the top of the hill stood an Iron Age hill fort, surrounded by a steep ditch and an earthen bank, with wooden palisades blocking the entrances. The Roman Seventh Legion stormed the hill, driving the Britons back into the fort, but they were unable to cross the deep ditch. Under the shelter of a *testudo*, a roof of shields (literally a "tortoise"), the Romans carried baskets of earth up the hill and slowly filled in the ditch until they had raised an earthen ramp to the height of the inner bank. Then the infantry advanced across the ramp behind their shields and took the fortress. The lightly armed British were no match for the well-trained and heavily armoured Roman legions, and those Britons who were not killed in the battle fled west into the forest. Caesar wrote that only a handful of his soldiers were wounded, none killed.[6] It was a decisive victory. The settlement at Bigbury was abandoned, and a new settlement under Roman leadership begun at Canterbury. Archeologists have shaved the forest off the face of Bigbury Hill above the trail. You can still see the ditch that the Roman legionaries had to cross, under a hail of stones and spears, to reach the summit.

From Bigbury Hill it isn't far to Harbledown. The village of Harbledown stretches along the top of an undulating ridge that drops down into the valley of the Stour and leads to the city of Canterbury. It is called "Bob-Up-and-Down" in *The Canterbury Tales*—in joking reference to the hilly terrain—and it is the last significant landmark before I reach the end of my pilgrimage. In the past, pilgrims caught their first glimpse of the golden towers of Canterbury Cathedral from this eminence, a reward for days of hard travel, but today modern construction and mature trees block the view. Harbledown is also famous for its leper colony, and it was here that Erasmus had his run-in with the importunate beggar who tried to charge him to kiss an old shoe. And it was on the long coast down to Canterbury from Harbledown that Elizabeth Robins Pennell met the cheerful hop pickers, her attitude toward them changed perhaps because of her sense of accomplishment and the imminent conclusion of her pilgrimage.

I enter Harbledown through the well-kept gardens of the old almshouses. The almshouses were constructed in 1840 on the grounds of the old leper hospital erected by Archbishop Lanfranc in 1084. Lanfranc was the first Norman Archbishop of Canterbury following the Conquest, his appointment supported by William the Conqueror for services rendered in smoothing William's marriage to Mathilda of Flanders. Lanfranc was born in Pavia in Italy, and studied law, but at some point, rejected that world and withdrew to the Abbey at Bec in France and joined the Benedictine order. The abbey was short of funds and the abbot, aware of Lanfranc's advanced education, convinced him to open a school, which, if judged by the later accomplishments of some of his pupils, was a great success—one pupil became Pope Alexander II and another Lanfranc's successor at Canterbury, St. Anselm. There was a move, after Lanfranc died, to nominate him for sainthood, but nothing came of it, for in truth Lanfranc never had the leisure to acquire the odour of sanctity. Instead, his life was caught up in religious and political controversies. Like Gundulf, whom we met at Rochester, Lanfranc proved a powerful support to his sovereign, and so his accomplishments were worldly rather than spiritual.

At the bottom of the garden, and after some searching, I locate the Black Prince's Well, a spring framed by a small masonry arch set into the side of the hill. It is overgrown and old, and the stone-work seems to have been scavenged from other monuments. Upon the keystone of the arch are carved three feathers, the symbol of the Prince of Wales. The story goes that, on his deathbed, the Black Prince, Edward of Woodstock, son of King Edward III, and perhaps the greatest soldier of his age (he defeated the French at Crécy and Poitiers) asked for water from this well. The water is supposed to possess special healing properties, especially for leprosy and diseases of the eye. Today, it makes a nice garden feature, but the pool of water looks a little green and scummy. I climb to the top of the hill, through the neatly manicured gardens, past the well-maintained almshouses, to the Church of St. Nicholas. I had read that this Norman church had special pews for the lepers, and that the stone-flagged floor was tilted, so that it could be sluiced down with water following each service to prevent infection. Alas, the church is locked, so I am unable to confirm this, but I rest for a few minutes in a shady arbour, catch my breath and rehydrate—though not with water from Edward's well.

Walking down the high road through Harbledown I pass a succession of lovely houses, each seemingly a conscious example of a different age of architecture. I saunter past another church, which is active though built less than a hundred years after the first. Then it is a quick downhill walk into Canterbury past modern suburban villas and ring roads.

The death of Thomas Becket haunted Henry II. He had not wanted it, and the murder of Becket had turned public opinion against him. In July 1174, four years after Becket's assassination, Henry made a very public penance. He sailed from France to Southampton, and then took the road to Canterbury, following more or less the same route as I have. He stopped at the outskirts of Canterbury, in the small parish church of St. Dunstan's, to change out of his royal robes and into a hair shirt, and then he walked barefoot to the Cathedral to undergo the public humiliation of seeking absolution for his sins. Before a throng of ordinary pilgrims, he lay face down before the tomb, confessed his sins, and received five lashes from each of the attending bishops. He then spent the entire night lying on the cold floor, fasting and praying before the tomb of Becket. Henry was not a particularly bad king, but much of his kingdom was in revolt at the time (and, by now, his kingdom included not just England and most of France, but parts of Ireland and Scotland as well). Henry publicly avowed that the revolt, which involved three of his sons, must be a punishment for his sins, so he needed to atone. It must have worked, for shortly after his pilgrimage, the Great Revolt, as it became known to history, collapsed.

When I arrive at St. Dunstan's the mood is much less sombre, for there is a floral show in progress. For the price of a ticket, I tour the church and examine the elaborate floral arrangements on display, some quite bizarre, each vying for a prize. The place is crowded with gardening enthusiasts and judges. It's very hard to picture a remorseful king in this setting, and that's perhaps just as well. After a quick look around, I head back out onto the main street, now called St. Dunstan's, and continue marking Henry's footsteps all the way to the Cathedral of Canterbury.

I pass an old timbered house whose facade is so crooked it looks like a reflection in a funhouse mirror. This is the House of Agnes, or at least that is what it is called today, for it is rumoured that this was the dwelling Dickens used as a model for the home of Agnes Wickfield, his heroine in *David Copperfield*. Across the street is an equally old coaching inn called the Falstaff, and it will be my home for the evening. I dodge across the street, enter the air-conditioned lobby through the mullioned doors and check my rucksack at the desk. I don't linger though, for I still hope to make the Evensong service at the cathedral. Exiting the Falstaff, I carry on down St. Dunstan's and enter the old city through the arch of the surviving medieval west gate. In no time at all, I have threaded the crooked lanes of old Canterbury and arrive at the cathedral.

I am glad my journey is over for the day. For the past two days, the little toe on my right foot has been killing me—swollen, bruised, and blistered with the nail turning purple. I'm not sure I could have walked on it for another day. I enter the cathedral, tell the volunteer guide I wish to attend the Evensong service, and she directs me toward the choir in the centre of the vast space. Four rows of tiered seats with red cushions face each other across a central aisle that leads to the altar. It is subdued and solemn and strangely intimate. The seats slowly fill up with visitors, many like me wearing walking attire. I take a seat in the middle of the back row. Each seat is like an oaken throne, heavily carved, creating a sense of spiritual privacy. A nun takes the seat beside me. She is tall, gaunt, and severe. Her costume—a brown habit belted with a simple white cord, a black veil, and simple leather sandals—identifies her as a Poor Clare, one of the Franciscan orders. In her chanted responses, I detect a vaguely Scandinavian or perhaps German accent. She frowns at my nodded greeting and wrinkles her nose. I wonder just how bad I must smell. Later, in the privacy of my hotel room, when I remove my T-shirt, I note that there are salt stains on the back in the form of a "Y" where my rucksack has rested all day long. Nevertheless, the service is beautiful, and I am glad I made the effort. Afterwards, I limp back to the Falstaff and have a long luxurious soak in the enormous enamelled bathtub in my room, something with clawed feet and big enough to bathe a hippopotamus. After drying off and doctoring my feet, I put on my last clean T-shirt and decide to explore the city.

It is early evening and the throngs of tourists that cluttered Canterbury earlier in the day have departed. The shadows grow long as, once more, I thread the narrow stone passage beneath the old west gate. I am transported back in time. Canterbury is a congested city of cobblestones, dark passages, projecting gables, hidden water channels and odd angles. It is an ancient city of brick and flint, tile and old timber. In the Second World War about thirty percent of the old city was destroyed by the Luftwaffe, so here and there the gaps between old buildings have been filled in with nondescript postwar rectangles of ugly red brick. But on the whole, it is a pleasing mélange of styles and crooked lanes. A city only looks like this when it has been allowed a long, uninterrupted history of organic growth. Fortunately, the cathedral and its precincts were spared the conflagration of the Second World War. They still look much as Chaucer might have seen them. Wartime Canterbury is best captured in the 1944 Powell and Pressburger film *A Canterbury Tale*, a decidedly odd film about four wartime pilgrims to Canterbury. I remember a scene where there are sheep grazing amid the rubble of the bombed-out city, making the whole place look extremely pastoral.

As I cross a reach of the river Stour on the King's Bridge, I notice some timber-framed houses bending over the water. These were once the homes of Huguenot weavers who had sought sanctuary in Canterbury from persecution in France and Spain. I wind my way down St. Peters Street, past numerous crooked old shop fronts spanning many centuries. I pass the Hospital of St. Thomas the Martyr upon Eastbridge, an ancient hospice for poor pilgrims, the sort of place Chaucer's clerk or parson might have stayed, and turn down Stour Street. I stumble upon a modern shop front whose window display features child-size models of the beloved characters from the Rupert the Bear cartoons found in the English *Daily Express*. As a young child, I remember receiving the book-length Rupert annuals from my English maternal grandfather at Christmas. Reading the caption on the display, I am surprised to discover that the creator of the comic strip, Mary Tourtel, was a Canterbury native. I have no real itinerary. I walk past the Poor Priest's Hospital and the entrance to the Grey Friars, a Franciscan establishment, the oldest in England, built upon an island in the Stour. I pass narrow passages with names like Water Lane, Beer Cart Lane, Hospital Lane, each hinting at a former use in earlier times. I reach the ruins of Canterbury Castle, where groups of scruffy youngsters lurk in the shrubbery, drinking beer from cans.

Beyond the castle I am able to ascend to the ramparts of the medieval city wall. The surviving wall sweeps around the eastern half of the city, from the south gate (where I now stand) to the old north gate. Canterbury was originally a Roman town called Durovernum, but nothing of the old Roman town remains, save the outline of the old Roman walls. The gates, though rebuilt in medieval times, stand where the Roman ones once stood. Outside the wall, a modern ring road separates the old city from the more recent suburbs. Cars and buses whiz by below me. Looking inward, there are older alleys of row housing, reminding me of *Coronation Street*, and probably still holding working-class families. These car-crowded lanes show that parking is at a premium, but the streets are eerily deserted. In contrast, the walkway along the top of the wall is full of Canterburians performing the evening's *passeggiata*. Couples amble by, attempting to catch a breath of wind and escape the day's heat. Everyone is outrageously underdressed, pierced and tattooed. Soon the wall overlooks a broad green park, called Dane John Garden, full of families enjoying the cooler evening air. Young men punt a soccer...sorry, football back and forth, and clutches of mothers push strollers along the winding garden paths. I climb Dane John Mound, the site of the original Norman motte-and-bailey castle in Canterbury, to get a bird's eye view of the city. ("Dane John" is thought to be a corruption of the French "donjon," the origin of our word "dungeon.") Then I carry on to the east gate, descend from the wall and cross the four-lane road to visit the ruins of the Augustinian priory.

When Ethelbert, an early King of Kent, married the Frankish Princess Bertha, their marriage settlement allowed Bertha to continue to practise her adopted religion, Christianity. Ethelbert, though a Saxon and a pagan, rebuilt an old Roman chapel for Bertha's use, and she dedicated it to St. Martin of Tours, a fellow Frank. As an aside, St. Martin's, which is still in use today, remains the oldest parish church in continuous use in the English-speaking world. In 597, Pope Gregory the Great, hearing that a Christian queen now sat on the throne of Kent, decided that the time was ripe for missionary work among the heathen Britons. He sent a Roman priest named Augustine with forty assistants to the Isle of Thanet, off the coast of Kent. Ethelbert, though initially suspicious of these interlopers, agreed to meet the missionaries. He insisted on meeting them in the open air, however, for he believed they could not practise their witchcraft upon him under the open sky. Reassured they meant him no harm, Ethelbert invited the missionaries to settle in Canterbury and granted them land where Augustine established his cathedral and his priory. Augustine must have been a persuasive preacher, for the following year Ethelbert was baptized in St. Martin's Church and became the first Christian king in England.

When I arrive at the ruins of Augustine's priory, the grounds are closed for the day. But leaning over the gate I can see the ruined walls of a once sizable monastic establishment surrounded by neatly trimmed green lawns, which the setting sun has cast into soft relief, the shadows and hollows revealing where vanished features survive as undulating mounds and ditches. A young couple is walking their standard poodle on the grounds in clear violation of the "closed" sign. I briefly debate hopping over the gate and joining them but think better of it and turn back toward the city centre. While passing through Lady Wootton's Green, I meet Queen Bertha—or at least a life-size bronze representation of her—striding purposefully down the middle of the boulevard in all of her stern glory, with the Good Book clasped firmly in her left hand. The sculptor has portrayed her as a rather forbidding woman. I would not want to argue with her, and, I suspect, neither did her husband. I cross the traffic circle again and pass through the city wall at Burgate.

Walking down winding Burgate Street, I soon come to a busy pub called the Thomas Ingoldsby. "Thomas Ingoldsby of Tapenham Manor" was the penname for the Reverend Richard Harris Barham, whom I briefly introduced you to back in Westwell in an earlier chapter. Barham wrote a series of faux medieval ballads that were first published in a magazine called *Bentley's Miscellany* (edited by the young Charles Dickens), and later gathered together into a bestselling book called *The Ingoldsby Legends*. These darkly humorous folk tales proved enormously popular in their day, though they are little read today. Barham was another Canterbury native. He was born at No. 61 Burgate, just close by, though the home of his birth no longer exists. It took a direct hit during the Blitz. Several of Barham's eerie tales were set in this city, in particular, the story of Nell Cook and the Dark Entry.

The Dark Entry is a real place, a gloomy narrow stone-flagged tunnel which runs under the Prior's Lodging and connects the cathedral with an ancient public school called the King's School. Barham may have passed through this passage as a lad and remembered the fear it generated in a young boy's heart. According to the tale, Nell Cook was the servant of a cathedral canon. She was a pious and modest woman with great skill in the kitchen. The Canon, by contrast, was a bit of a degenerate, a man of vast appetites, who was entertaining a "niece" whose father was away at sea. Observing the canon and his niece together, Nell began to suspect that the pretty young woman was not all that she pretended:

> *"Now, welcome! welcome; dearest Niece; come lay thy mantle by!"*
> *The Canon kiss'd her ruby lip—he had a merry eye, —*
> *But Nelly Cook askew did look, —it came into her mind*
> *They were a little less than 'kin,' and rather more than 'kind.'[7]*

When Nell discovered that the two were, in fact, illicit lovers, she was outraged and poisoned them in their bed. When the crime was discovered, the cathedral monks buried Nell alive in a cell beneath the flagstones of the Dark Entry. Her ghost is said to haunt the passage every Friday night. If you should meet with Nell, beware:

> *But one thing's clear—that all the year on every Friday night,*
> *Throughout that Entry dark doth roam Nell Cook's unquiet*
> *Sprite...*

And whoso in that Entry dark doth feel that fatal breath,
He ever dies within the year, some dire, untimely death.[8]

It's a great story, but, alas, as far as anyone can tell, it's all humbug. It's probable that Barham made the whole thing up.

Continuing along Burgate Street, I pass the isolated tower of St. Mary Magdalene Church. The church, which had fallen into ruin, was torn down in the nineteenth century, but the tower itself was restored, and the baroque confection in marble found in the interior of the tower, a memorial to the Whitfield family dated 1680, was preserved, creating a unique form of sidewalk art. Behind the tower is the newer church of St. Thomas of Canterbury. It was here in August 1924 that the funeral for novelist Joseph Conrad was held. Unfortunately, the funeral coincided with the annual cricket festival, and the cortege had to cope with crowds of rowdy cricket fans who blocked the streets and cared little for English literature or the man who had given us *Lord Jim* and *Heart of Darkness*.

There is another ruined tower found not far away on High Street, a lonely church spire—all that is left of St. George's Church following the Blitz. This part of town was obliterated during the war. Everything around the orphaned spire is new and commercial, from the busy bus station to the shining shopping precincts. This was the parish where Christopher Marlowe grew up, and it was in this church that he was baptized. Marlowe—poet, playwright, and quite possibly Elizabethan spy—met his sticky end in a brawl in Deptford, a rough borough of London near the dockyards, in 1593, aged just 29. He was the foremost tragedian of his age and a contemporary of Shakespeare. Marlowe's short life has created an enormous amount of controversy—how he died, why he died, or even if he died at all. One theory is that he faked his own death and then fled to northern Italy where he wrote a few plays set in places like Padua, Verona and Venice, which Shakespeare passed off as his own. I find this hard to credit. But conspiracy theorists exist, I believe, to keep the rest of us entertained. I don't know if the final word on Kit Marlowe will ever be written, and I really don't care as long as his plays continue to be performed.

I continue along Burgate, back to the Cathedral, and find the great wooden doors of the Butter Gate now closed. Christ leans down sadly from above, regarding passing pilgrims from his throne upon the lavishly ensculptured and escutcheoned tower. Across the square, the Sun Hotel leans drunkenly over the street. Here it was that Mr. and Mrs. Micawber prodigally and improvidently entertained young David Copperfield to "a beautiful little dinner. Quite an elegant dish of fish; the kidney end of a loin of veal roasted; fried sausage-meat; a partridge and a pudding." I dodge around the Cathedral precincts to try and see the older part of the King's School and catch a glimpse of the Dark Entry where Nell Cook's ghost is said to lurk. Like Winchester College, which we visited earlier, the King's School has a long and distinguished history, graduating many famous scholars, like the artist Edmund de Waal; writers like W. Somerset Maugham, Michael Morpurgo, Hugh Walpole, and Christopher Marlowe; critics like Walter Pater; soldiers like Field Marshal Montgomery of Alamein; and film types like Carol Reed and Orlando Bloom.

But my favourite King's scholar never graduated at all. He was given the boot. The travel writer Patrick Leigh Fermor was reportedly kicked out of King's for consorting with the grocer's daughter. Never mind. He went on to serve with great distinction in the Second World War, masterminding the daring kidnap of German General Kreipe on occupied Crete, and to write some of my favourite books, including an enchanting account of his walk from Holland to Constantinople in the years leading up to war, which begins in *A Time of Gifts*, continues in *Through the Woods and the Water*, and ends with *The Broken Road*. Fermor's lyrical, youthful escapade captures a gentler Europe, one which the war and the Iron Curtain would erase, and it directly inspired my own wanderlust.

The evening sun is now low in the sky. The walls and towers of Canterbury Cathedral glow with a honey-coloured warmth. I wander the old lanes back to my bed for the night, stopping on my way to pick up takeout to eat in my room, and am soon fast asleep.

16

Canterbury

And the end of all our exploring
Will be to arrive where we started
And know the place for the first time.
—T.S. ELIOT, "Little Gidding"

WAKING EARLY, I decide to finish _Pilgrim's Progress_. When I last
left Christian, he had escaped Doubting Castle in the company of
Hopeful. In the final stretch, Christian and Hopeful meet Atheist
who tells them to abandon their quest and be content with what
they have. "I have been seeking this [Celestial] City these twenty
years," he tells them. "But find no more of it, than I did the first day
I set out."[1] Persuaded that faith is a trap, Atheist decides it is pref-
erable to live in the world as he finds it, and to count his blessings,
than to hope for a better world in the hereafter. But Christian and
Hopeful persevere. They then bump into youthful Ignorance who
prattles on self-importantly about his beliefs, beliefs which appall
Christian for they seem to be entirely invented, a patchwork of

comfortable assertions conforming to no recognizable doctrine or creed. He accuses Ignorance of heresy and offers to instruct him in the true faith, but the cocky young lad blows him off and refuses their company, saying that he "takes his pleasure in walking alone."[2] This portrait of Ignorance strikes uncomfortably close to home. Christian and Hopeful enter the Celestial City together, while Ignorance is turned back at the pearly gates. He lacks the proper credentials.

I have a few hours before I have to catch my train to Heathrow Airport, so I pack my bags and leave them with the concierge. I decide to visit the Cathedral one more time, since my flying visit the day before hadn't allowed for a proper look around. I do the usual tourist things. I visit the chapter house, once the centre of the cathedral's monastic life, and hunt for the carved "Green Men" in the cloisters (I find six). I stand in awe in the vast empty nave, eyes drawn aloft, and move to the foot of the quire steps in the great crossing and gape up at the exquisite fan vaulting.

I visit the tomb of Edward, Prince of Wales, hero of Crécy and Poitiers, in the Trinity Chapel, whose spring I did not drink from in Harbledown. Why he is known to history as the Black Prince is subject to some debate. Some say it was because of the cruelty he showed to his enemies, others for the black shield he carried into battle. Certainly no one called him "the Black Prince" to his face. The life-size bronze effigy adorning his tomb is justifiably famous. It depicts the prince in full armour, lying on his back, with a dog at his heels, and his hands clasped in prayer upon his breast. It is the picture of a chivalric knight that most of us carry in our heads. (Edward was, in fact, one of the founding members of the Most Noble Order of the Garter, and the first person to be vested with that emblem of chivalry). The epitaph, written in French and engraved around the tomb, follows the traditional theme of the transience of earthly fame and power, and begins:

Such as thou art, so once was I.
As I am now, so shalt thou be.[3]

The shrine of St. Thomas would have once stood in the Trinity Chapel as well, the destination for thousands of pilgrims, but it was demolished in 1538 at the orders of King Henry VIII; so instead of the tomb, I visit the place of Becket's martyrdom, now marked by a simple stone altar and a triptych of iron swords, one broken, that form a kind of Golgotha on the wall above the place where he died. It is surprisingly moving.

I end my tour in the eleventh-century crypt, the oldest part of the cathedral, and pause in St. Gabriel's Chapel, which houses some of the oldest wall paintings to survive in England. There is no one around, so I take a seat. My eye is drawn to a twelfth-century depiction of the scene where the infant John the Baptist is given his name. In the picture, the baby is lying in the arms of his mother, Elizabeth, while his father, Zachariah, struck dumb in wonder— both parents were very old when John was born, so his birth was viewed as a miracle—writes the name of his infant son on a piece of parchment. It is a moment that makes me think again of my own father. Fatherhood, and the feelings of wonder and joy that come with being a parent, are something we both share with Zachariah. My greatest happiness in life is in my children. I hope my father felt the same.

So I have come to the end of my pilgrimage. What am I supposed to feel? I had hoped for some kind of spiritual renewal, but that hasn't happened. If I were a less honest writer, I would have engineered something, knowing my publisher would be expecting a big finish. I can honestly say I feel spiritually refreshed, but there has been no hand of God reaching down to touch me on the forehead, no Vision on the Road to Damascus. Instead, what I found was happiness. I loved the journey. As the days progressed I became more relaxed. At first, I worried that I was too old for this sort of thing. I worried about losing my way or taking too long to reach my destination. But gradually, as each day bled into the next, I lost track of time, and I put my watch away. It didn't matter. If I felt like stopping, I would stop. If I fell into conversation with someone like Peter at Eastwell, I would take the time to listen. And at each encounter I couldn't help thinking how much my father would have enjoyed this adventure.

There is a wonderful simplicity about a pilgrimage. Each morning, you rise and put on the same clothes you were wearing the day before. You break your fast, hoist your pack onto your shoulders, and hit the road. As the miles crunch beneath your boots, you are free to admire the wildflowers, listen to the birds, or talk to Brother Fox if he pauses in your path. And with each footstep, you grow closer to your goal, which, hopefully, is enlightenment. This is not possible in our daily lives, for we are too mired in striving. Ambition, greed, fear, jealousy, enmity—all of these weigh us down, and our lives are frittered away in worry. But simplicity, as Thoreau understood it, is liberating. "Simplify, simplify," was his motto.[4]

St. Francis also understood this. It was not until he embraced radical poverty that Francis was truly free, truly happy. A recent study at the University of Zurich showed that people who gave money away were happier than those who hoarded it.[5] Why this should have been a surprise to anyone is a mystery to me. For there is a levity of spirit in having little, in simplifying your life. "It is easier for a camel to go through the eye of a needle," said Jesus, "than for a rich man to enter the kingdom of God."[6] Curiously too, when Jesus sent his disciples off into the world to preach the Gospel, he instructed them to "take nothing for their journey except a staff: no bread, no bag, no money in their purse," to wear sandals but not an extra tunic.[7] It could be the advice one gives to a pilgrim. "If you are ready to leave father and mother, and brother and sister, and wife and child and friends, and never see them again—if you have paid your debts, and made your will, and settled all your affairs, and are a free man," wrote Thoreau, "then you are ready for a walk."[8]

People say that happiness is an act of will, but I'm not so sure. Happiness is a by-product of something else, like being with someone you love or doing an activity you enjoy. You can't pursue happiness; it finds you. It found me on the road to Canterbury.

And so when I finally did approach Canterbury and saw Bell Harry Tower looming over the crooked roofs and chimney pots of the city, it was not with a sense of accomplishment, but with a sense of regret, for I knew that my journey was coming to an end. I'd set out two weeks before intending to honour my father, and, deep down, hoping that the journey would do me some good as well. I'd hoped for something extraordinary. Instead, as I sit here in the undercroft of the great cathedral, at the end of all my striving, I feel a measure of peace and dream of further journeys.

The last stage in Phil Cousineau's *The Art of Pilgrimage*, the one that comes after you arrive at your destination, is called "bringing back the boon"—a phrase he borrows from the American mythologist Joseph Campbell.[9] In other words, the pilgrimage is pointless unless we bring back some lesson to share with others. So here is what I learned, none of it very profound, but I offer these personal insights in the spirit of fellowship, for you have been patient with me on my journey thus far.

Walking is good, especially for people suffering from depression. A pilot study published in the British Journal of Sports Medicine showed that just thirty minutes of walking on a treadmill each day can produce substantial improvement in mood in patients with major depressive disorders.[10] We should all walk more. I had hoped to walk myself into a better frame of mind, and it worked. Walking releases endorphins, and endorphins encourage happiness. And walking is easy and it doesn't cost a thing. Walking with a purpose is even better. Walk to work. Walk to the store.

I learned that going on a pilgrimage is more about the intention than the destination, that the journey itself is important, and that life is too short to sleepwalk through. In future, I will try to create an opening in my life for spiritual practice. I will remain open to the possibility of the divine, even if in my gut I suspect it is all hogwash, and I will listen to those people whose sincerity and goodness I respect. But I won't worry overmuch. After all, as Epicurus pointed out, we don't worry about what happened to us before we were born, so why should we worry about what happens to us after we die? Live the life you are given. Don't worry too much about money, position or reputation. None of these things will matter after you are dead, and they are traps for the living anyway. For what is the cause of unhappiness, concluded the Buddha, but desire?

And finally, I will try to be kind. Kindness it turns out is the greatest virtue of all. And it takes so little effort to be kind, much more to be cruel.

On a personal level I learned that I needed to change my life, and the first step will be to work my way out of my current job. Of course, I need to do this in a responsible manner. People depend on me. I can't copy Bunyan's Christian. I need to make a succession plan, put my house in order, and ensure that things are in good kip before I say goodbye. The trick will be to not succumb to my old life and not fall back into old habits of quiet desperation, but to keep moving forward. And who knows? Once that is done, perhaps I will go on another pilgrimage, a longer one. For what is life, if not a pilgrimage?

Courage, Paul Tillich teaches us, is an affirmation of one's life despite the fact that it will soon end and has no discernible purpose. The faithful man, therefore, embraces life despite its apparent aimlessness. Faith is a belief based on conviction rather than proof.

As I sit quietly in the empty chapel, prayer, bottled up for so long, overflows. "Help me to be a better man," I pray, "a better husband and father. Help me to find my path in life, or if not my path, help me to be content with the life I have. Thank you. Thank you. *Thank you.*" Then I say a prayer for my father, gather my things, and depart.

There are different kinds of pilgrimages, just as there are different kinds of pilgrims. Some go to expiate sin, some to pray for a miracle. For others, it is simply a holiday. For me, it was an opportunity to reset my priorities, and what I discovered was simple (and I wondered that I needed to leave home to learn this): stop and be in the moment. You will never come this way again. This book of pilgrimage is my boon to you. Make of it what you will, but I hope it inspires you to take journeys of your own.

Acknowledgements

NO BOOK IS WRITTEN WITHOUT ASSISTANCE, and I certainly had a lot of help with this one. Thank you, first of all, to the members of the Collingwood Writers Collective, who critiqued the manuscript, chapter by chapter, in installments, in our twice-monthly meetings. Thank you to my friends and fellow writers—Arlene F. Marks, Andy Potter, and Walter Weckers—who read and commented on later drafts of this book. It was extremely helpful to have such well-meaning yet honest criticism.

Once again, it has been a pleasure to work with the staff at the University of Alberta Press. Without their help and professionalism, this book would not look as good as it does. Thank you, Cathie Crooks, Alan Brownoff and Duncan Turner, for your patience with my queries. I would particularly like to single out Mat Buntin, who championed my book at press meetings and who, I suspect, rescued my manuscript from oblivion.

Sometimes, when you have been working on a manuscript for many years, you stop seeing its faults and need a fresh perspective. Lauren Carter, my editor, suggested some important changes when I could no longer see the wood for the trees. Thank you also to my copy editor, Maya Fowler Sutherland, who detected the errors I'd stopped seeing. If errors of fact or phrasing remain, they are entirely mine.

Derek Bright of Walk Awhile made my journey to Canterbury possible and worry-free, and I am very grateful for his care and concern.

Thank you to Gail Pirkis and Hazel Wood, editors of *Slightly Foxed: The Real Reader's Quarterly*, who published excerpts from this manuscript while it was still in progress. This was great encouragement to carry on and complete the project. A portion of chapter 2 was published as "'Study to be quiet'," (No. 54, Summer 2017, 65–70). A portion of chapter 13 was published as "Mr Polly Walks to Freedom," (No. 59, Autumn 2018, 43–46).

Thank you to my wonderful family, who have always been very supportive of my writing efforts, even if they don't always understand why I pursue them. Especially, to my wife, Nancy, who has always been my first and best reader and who has somehow always managed to balance being kind with being critical. And finally, thank you to my father, who is my hero and who always followed a manner of living I still strive to emulate. Thanks Dad.

Acknowledgements

Photographs

All photographs are by Ken Haigh.

Prelude
Pilgrims' Way.

1 | Winchester
Keats' Walk.

2 | Winchester to Alresford
Winchester Cathedral, west front.

3 | New Alresford to Alton
Jane Austen's house, Chawton.

4 | Alton to Farnham
William Cobbett's birthplace, Farnham.

5 | Farnham to Newlands Corner
Watts Mortuary Chapel (interior), Compton.

6 | Newlands Corner to Dorking
Box Hill in the distance, with the River Mole at its foot.

7 | Dorking to Reigate

Stepping stones across the River Mole.

8 | Reigate to Godstone

The Church of St. Peter and St. Paul, Chaldon.

9 | Godstone to Otford

St. Botolph's Church, Chevening.

10 | Otford to Addington

Coldrum Stones with a view of the Medway Valley.

11 | Addington to Rochester

Wheel of Fortune, Rochester Cathedral.

12 | Rochester to Thurnham

Kit's Coty House.

13 | Thurnham to Lenham

Medway Valley with Leeds Castle in the middle distance.

14 | Lenham to Wye

Chalk memorial cross above Lenham.

15 | Wye to Canterbury

First view of Canterbury.

16 | Canterbury

Canterbury Cathedral.

Photographs

Notes

Prelude

1.   Julian Barnes, *Nothing to be Frightened of* (Toronto: Vintage Canada, 2009), 1.

1 | Winchester

1.   John Aubrey, "Sir Walter Raleigh," in *Brief Lives, 1669–1696*, ed. Clark (1898) 2:177–94. http://spenserians.cath.vt.edu/BiographyRecord. php?action=GET&bioid=4375.

2.   "The Trial of Sir Walter Ralegh: a transcript," ed. Mathew Lyons, accessed April 16, 2021, https://mathewlyons.co.uk/2011/11/18/the-trial-of-sir-walter-ralegh-a-transcript/. Lyons also has a useful summary of the trial here: https://mathewlyons.co.uk/2019/01/31/bbc-history-the-1603-trial-of-walter-ralegh/

3.   Ibid.

4.   William Stebbing, *Sir Walter Ralegh: A Biography* (Oxford: The Clarendon Press, 1891), 378, https://www.gutenberg.org/files/25029/25029-h/25029-h.htm

5.   Ibid., 379.

6.   *The Oxford Book of English Verse, 1250–1918*, chosen and edited by Sir Arthur Quiller-Couch (Oxford: The Clarendon Press, 1939), 110.

7.   Ibid., 110.

8.   Julia Cartwright, *The Pilgrims' Way from Winchester to Canterbury* (New York: E.P. Dutton and Company, 1911), 6.

9.   Derek Bright, *The Pilgrims' Way: Fact and Fiction of an Ancient Trackway* (Stroud: The History Press, 2011), 56.

10. Ibid., 129

2 | Winchester to New Alresford

1. Johann Wolfgang von Goethe, "Of German Architecture (1772)," in *Art History and Its Methods: A Critical Review,* selection and commentary by Eric Fernie (London: Phaidon Press Limited, 1995), 82.

2. John Ruskin, "The Stones of Venice," in *Prose of the Victorian Period*, ed. William E. Buckler (Boston: Houghton Mifflin Company, 1958), 388.

3. Erwin Panofsky, *Abbot Suger: On the Abbey Church of St. Denis and its Art Treasures,* 2nd ed. (Princeton: Princeton University Press, 1979), 47–49.

4. Izaak Walton, *The Compleat Angler* (London: J.M. Dent & Co., 1906), 13.

5. "St. Swithin's Day," accessed April 16, 2021, http://projectbritain.com/stswithun.html

6. "The Changing Story of Cnut and the Waves," accessed April 16, 2021, https://www.medievalists.net/2015/05/the-changing-story-of-cnut-and-the-waves/

7. William Hazlitt, "On Going A Journey," in *New Monthly Magazine*, January 1822, accessed April 16, 2021, https://sites.ualberta.ca/~dmiall/Travel/hazlitt.htm.

8. Charles Kingsley and Frances Eliza Grenfell Kingsley, *Charles Kingsley: His Letters and Memories of his Life in Two Volumes, Vol. II, edited by his wife* (London: Macmillan and Co., 1894), 126–27, https://archive.org/details/charleskingsleyho2king.

9. Charles Kingsley, *The Water Babies: A Fairy Tale for a Land-Baby* (London: Macmillan and Co., Limited, 1922), 61, https://www.gutenberg.org/files/25564/25564-h/25564-h.htm.

3 | New Alresford to Alton

1. Robert Louis Stevenson, *Travels with a Donkey in the Cevennes* (London: The Folio Society, 1967), 50–51.

2. Dhruti Shah, "Antarctic Mission: Who was Captain Lawrence Oates?" accessed April 16, 2021, https://www.bbc.com/news/uk-17269397.

4 | Alton to Farnham

1. William Cobbett, *Rural Rides* (London: Folio Society, 2010), 106–07.

2. Ibid., 107.

5 | Farnham to Newlands Corner

1. George A. Aitken, introduction to *The Journal to Stella*, by Jonathan Swift (London: Methuen & Co., 1901), xxviii. https://www.gutenberg.org/files/4208/4208-h/4208-h.htm.

2. John Donne, "Holy Sonnet XVII," in *John Donne's Poetry*, selected and edited by A.L. Clements (New York: W.W. Norton & Company, 1966), 89.

3. Hilaire Belloc, *The Old Road* (London: Constable and Company Limited, 1910), 166–67.

6 | Newlands Corner to Dorking

1. Christopher Hitchens, *God is Not Great: How Religion Poisons Everything* (Toronto: McClelland & Stewart Ltd., 2007), 8.

2. Bstan-'dzin-rgya-mtsho, Dalai Lama XIV, *Freedom in Exile: The Autobiography of the Dalai Lama* (New York: HarperCollins Publishers, 1990), 98–99.

3. Gavin Maxwell, *The House of Elrig* (London: Longmans Green & Co., Ltd., 1965), 166.

4. "Christine Carpenter: The Anchoress of Shere" (Shere: St. James' Church, 1986), [2].

5. Ibid. [4].

6. Fosco Maraini, *Secret Tibet*, trans. Eric Mosbacher and Guido Waldman (London: The Harvill Press, 2000), 263–65.

7. Geoffrey Hindley, *A Brief History of the Crusades* (London: Constable & Robinson Ltd., 2003), 19.

8. Charles Dickens, The Posthumous Papers of the Pickwick Club, Vol. 1 (New York: Hurd and Houghton, 1868), 245, https://archive.org/details/pickwickpapers02dickgoog/page/n10/mode/2up.

9. Alison Flood, "Britain has closed almost 800 libraries since 2010, figures show," *The Guardian*, December 6, 2019, https://www.theguardian.com/books/2019/dec/06/britain-has-closed-almost-800-libraries-since-2010-figures-show.

10. Sian Cain, "Nearly 130 public libraries closed across Britain last year," *The Guardian*, December 7, 2018, https://www.theguardian.com/books/2018/dec/07/nearly-130-public-libraries-closed-across-britain-in-the-last-year.

11. John Bunyan, *The Pilgrim's Progress*, edited and with an introduction by N.H. Keeble (Oxford: Oxford University Press, 1984), 35.

7 | Dorking to Reigate

1. John Keats, *The Letters of John Keats*, ed. Maurice Buxton Forman (London: Reeves & Turner, 1895), 55, https://babel.hathitrust.org/cgi/pt?id=nyp.33433043972813&view=1up&seq=11.

2. Ibid., 49.

3. Edmund Spenser, *Spenser's Faerie Queene: A Poem in Six Books; with the Fragment Mutabilitie*, ed. by Thomas J. Wise, pictured by Walter Crane, Book IV, Canto

XI (London: G. Allen, 1895–97), 1023, https://archive.org/details/
spensersfaeriequo4spenuoft/mode/2up.

4. Henri Nouwen, *The Way of the Heart: The Spirituality of the Desert Fathers and Mothers* (New York: HarperCollins, 1991), 50.

5. Jane Austen, *Emma* (London: Macmillan and Co., Limited, 1896), 334, https://archive.org/details/EmmaJaneAusten_753/mode/2up.

6. Ibid., 338.

8 | Reigate to Godstone

1. *Cobbett's Weekly Political Register, Vol. XV, from January to June, 1809,* ed. William Cobbett (London: T.C. Hansard, 1809), 971.

2. Ibid.

3. Christopher John Wright, *A Guide to the Pilgrims' Way and the North Downs Way, third ed.* (London: Constable & Company Ltd., 1981), 134.

4. Jean-Jacques Rousseau, *The Social Contract and Discourses* (London: J.M. Dent & Sons Ltd., 1911), 5.

5. William Cobbett, *Rural Rides, Vol. I* (London: J.M. Dent & Sons Ltd, 1832), 66, https://archive.org/details/ruralrideso1cobb/mode/2up.

6. Psalm 23:4 in John Bunyan, *The Pilgrim's Progress,* edited and with an introduction by N.H. Keeble (Oxford: Oxford University Press, 1984), 53.

7. 1 Corinthians 13:1–3, ibid., 66.

9 | Godstone to Otford

1. Steven Pinker, *The Blank Slate: The Modern Denial of Human Nature* (New York: Viking, 2002), 224.

2. Ibid., 240.

3. Ibid., 42–43.

4. Ibid., 240.

5. Friedrich Nietzsche, quoted in Phil Cousineau, *The Art of Pilgrimage: The Seeker's Guide to Making Travel Sacred* (Berkeley: Conari Press, 1998), 25.

6. Soren Kierkegaard, "Letter to Henrietta Lund," 1847 (trans. Henrik Rosenmeier, 1978), accessed on April 16, 2021, https://www.nottinghilleditions.com/i-walk-for-health-and-salvation-by-soren-aaby-kierkegaard/.

7. Bruce Chatwin, "It's a Nomad Nomad World," in *The Anatomy of Restlessness: Selected Writings, 1969–1989* (New York: Viking, 1996), 103.

10 | Otford to Addington

1. Jonathan Sumption, *The Age of Pilgrimage: The Medieval Journey to God* (Mahwah, N.J.: HiddenSpring, 2003), 162; Dee Dyas, *Pilgrimage in Medieval English Literature, 700–1500* (Cambridge: D.S. Brewer, 2001), 179.

2. Frank Barlow, *Thomas Becket* (London: The Folio Society, 2002), 295.

3. Ibid., 307–08.

4. Ibid., 310.

5. Ibid., 311.

6. Christopher John Wright, *A Guide to the Pilgrims' Way and the North Downs Way, third ed.* (London: Constable, 1981), 166.

7. Arthur Paul Boers, *The Way is Made by Walking: A Pilgrimage Along the Camino de Santiago* (Downers Grove, Illinois: IVP Books, 2007), 48.

8. C.G. Jung, *Memories, Dreams, Reflections*, rev. ed., recorded and edited by Aniela Jaffe, translated by Richard and Clara Winston (New York: Vintage Books, 1989), x.

9. Michael Wysocki et al., "Dates, Diet and Dismemberment: Evidence from the Coldrum Megalith Monument, Kent," in *Proceedings of the Prehistoric Society* 79, accessed September 14, 2017, http://clok.uclan.ac.uk/10742/.

10. John Bunyan, *The Pilgrim's Progress*, edited and with an introduction by N.H. Keeble (Oxford: Oxford University Press, 1984), 73.

11 | Addington to Rochester

1. Charles Dickens, *The Mystery of Edwin Drood*, completed by Thomas Power James (Brattleboro, Vermont: Published by T.P. James, 1874), 5, https://archive.org/details/mysteryedwindrooojamegoog/page/n6/mode/2up.

2. "Dunstan," Wikipedia, accessed April 20, 2021, https://en.wikipedia.org/wiki/Dunstan.

3. "Anselm: Ontological Argument for God's Existence," Internet Encyclopedia of Philosophy, accessed April 20, 2021, https://iep.utm.edu/ont-arg/.

4. Matthew Arnold, "Dover Beach," in *Victorian Poetry and Poetics*, second ed., edited by Walter E. Houghton and G. Robert Stange (Boston: Houghton Mifflin Company, 1968), 484-85.

5. Bruce Cockburn, "The Trouble with Normal," Track 1 on *The Trouble with Normal* LP, True North, 1983.

6. Charles Dickens, *David Copperfield* (London: Penguin Books, 1966), 238.

12 | Rochester to Thurnham

1. Wallace Stegner, "The Sense of Place," in *Where the Bluebird Sings to the Lemonade Springs: Living and Writing in the West* (Toronto: Penguin, 1992), 202, 205.

2. The theory of ley lines was only invented in 1921 by a British amateur archeologist named Alfred Watkins, who believed that there had once been straight trackways connecting many of Britain's ancient monuments. But

Watkins, it should be noted, hadn't invested these trackways with any mystical significance. They were just roads. The mystical stuff would come later when his theories were resurrected by a writer called John Michell in his bestselling *The View over Atlantis* (1969). Michell's book connected Watkins' ley lines with Chinese *feng shui* and posited a magical network of magnetic fields veining the planet.

13 | Thurnham to Lenham

1. Karen Armstrong, *The Spiral Staircase: My Climb out of Darkness* (New York: Alfred A. Knopf, 2004), 292.
2. H.G. Wells, *The History of Mr. Polly* (London: W. Collins Sons & Co Ltd, 1920), 214–15, https://archive.org/details/in.ernet.dli.2015.93688/page/n5/mode/2up.
3. Ibid., 28.
4. Ibid., 28–29.
5. Ibid., 217.
6. Richard Jefferies, "Red Roofs of London" in *The Open Air* (London: Chatto & Windus, 1893), 263, https://books.google.ca/books?id=lXmLAAAAIAAJ&pg=PP7 #v=onepage&q&f=false.

14 | Lenham to Wye

1. E. Nesbit, *The Wouldbegoods*, illustrated by Reginald B. Birch (New York: Harper & Brothers Publishers, 1901), 251, https://www.gutenberg.org/ files/32466/32466-h/32466-h.htm.
2. Ibid., 255–56.
3. Ibid., 258.
4. Ibid., 261.
5. Ibid., 262.

15 | Wye to Canterbury

1. Quoted in Nigel Nicolson, *The World of Jane Austen* (London: Phoenix Illustrated, 1998), 67.
2. Ibid., 69.
3. Ibid., 72.
4. Elizabeth Robins Pennell and Joseph Pennell. *A Canterbury Pilgrimage/An Italian Pilgrimage* (Edmonton: The University of Alberta Press, 2015), 31.
5. Elizabeth Grice, "Hop Growing in the Garden of England," *The Telegraph*, September 2, 2011. http://www.telegraph.co.uk/news/earth/ countryside/8734914/Hop-growing-in-the-Garden-of-England.html.

6.   C. Julius Caesar, *Caesar's Gallic War*, Book V, Chapters 8–9, trans. W.A. McDevitte and W.S. Bohn (New York: Harper & Brothers, 1869), accessed September 14, 2017, http://www.perseus.tufts.edu/hopper/text?doc=urn:cts:lati nLit:phi0448.phi001.perseus-eng1:5.9

7.   Thomas Ingoldby, esq. [pseud. for Rev. Richard Harris Barham], "Nell Cook: A Legend of the 'Dark Entry'" in *The Ingoldsby Legends, or Mirth and Marvels* (London: Frederick Warne and Co., 1889), 301, http://www.gutenberg.org/ files/59236/59236-h/59236-h.htm#NELL_COOK

8.   Ibid., 304.

16 | Canterbury

1.   John Bunyan, *The Pilgrim's Progress*, edited and with an introduction by N.H. Keeble (Oxford: Oxford University Press, 1984), 110.

2.   Ibid., 118.

3.   Barbara W. Tuchman, *A Distant Mirror: The Calamitous 14th Century* (New York: Alfred A. Knopf, 1979), 295.

4.   Henry David Thoreau, "Where I lived, and What I Lived For" in *Walden* in *The Portable Thoreau*, edited, and with an introduction, by Carl Bode (New York: The Viking Press, 1947), 344.

5.   Soyoung Q. Park et al., "A Neural Link between Generosity and Happiness," *Nature Communications* 8, 15964 (2017), https://www.nature.com/articles/ ncomms15964.

6.   Mark 10:25, King James Version.

7.   Mark 6:8–9, Modern English Version.

8.   Thoreau, "Walking" in *The Portable Thoreau*, 593.

9.   Phil Cousineau, *The Art of Pilgrimage: The Seeker's Guide to Making Travel Sacred* (Berkeley: Conari Press, 1998), 217.

10. Dimeo, F. et al. "Benefits from aerobic exercise in patients with major depression: a pilot study." *British Journal of Sports Medicine* vol. 35, 2 (2001): 114–17. https://ncbi.nlm.nih.gov/pmc/articles/PMC1724301/.

Suggested Reading

On the History of the Pilgrims' Way

Belloc, Hilaire. *The Old Road*. London: Constable and Company Limited, 1910.

Bright, Derek. *The Pilgrims' Way: Fact and Fiction of an Ancient Trackway*. Stroud: The
    History Press, 2011.

Cartwright, Julia. *The Pilgrims' Way from Winchester to Canterbury*. New York: E.P.
    Dutton and Company, 1911.

Guidebooks

Curtis, Neil and Jim Walker. *North Downs Way*. London: Aurum Press, 2005.

Hatts, Leigh. *Walking The Pilgrims' Way: To Canterbury from Winchester and London*.
    Kendal, Cumbria: Cicerone, 2017.

Wright, Christopher John. *A Guide to the Pilgrims' Way and the North Downs Way*,
    fourth rev. ed. London: Constable, 1993.

On Pilgrimage

Cousineau, Phil. *The Art of Pilgrimage: The Seeker's Guide to Making Travel Sacred*.
    Berkeley: Conari Press, 1998.

Sumption, Jonathan. *The Age of Pilgrimage: The Medieval Journey to God*. Mahwah,
    New Jersey: HiddenSpring, 2003.

Ure, John. *Pilgrimages: The Great Adventure of the Middle Ages.* New York: Carroll & Graf Publishers, 2006.

History

Barlow, Frank. *Thomas Becket.* London: Orion Books Ltd., 1997.

Literary Companions for the Journey

Austen, Jane. *Pride and Prejudice.*

Austen, Jane. *Emma.*

Bunyan, John. *Pilgrim's Progress.*

Chaucer, Geoffrey. *The Canterbury Tales.*

Cobbett, William. *Rural Rides.*

Dickens, Charles. *David Copperfield.*

Dickens, Charles. *The Mystery of Edwin Drood.*

Dickens, Charles. *The Pickwick Papers.*

Eliot, T.S. *Murder in the Cathedral.*

Keats, John. "To Autumn"

Kingsley, Charles. *The Water Babies.*

Nesbit, E. *The Wouldbegoods.*

Trollope, Anthony. *The Warden.*

Walton, Izaac. *The Compleat Angler.*

Wells, H.G. *The History of Mr. Polly*

White, Gilbert. *The Natural History of Selborne.*

Other Titles from University of Alberta Press

Under the Holy Lake

A Memoir of Eastern Bhutan

KEN HAIGH

Experience a Canadian teacher's transformative years
teaching in the remote Himalayan village of Khaling,
Bhutan.

Wayfarer Series

A Canterbury Pilgrimage/An Italian Pilgrimage

ELIZABETH ROBINS PENNELL &
JOSEPH PENNELL

Edited by DAVE BUCHANAN

This sprightly American couple pioneered leisure cycle
tourism in Europe via illustrated travel memoirs
in the 1880s.

Wayfarer Series

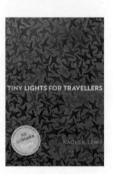

Tiny Lights for Travellers

NAOMI K. LEWIS

Vulnerable and funny, this memoir explores Jewish
identity, family, the Holocaust, and belonging.

Wayfarer Series

More information at uap.ualberta.ca